THE ESSENTIALS OF JAVA

Arunesh Goyal

Topper, B.Sc. (H) Mathematics
Hitherto, Hon. Director, Institute for Studies in Mathematics
and Related Sciences in Computers (ISMRSC), Delhi
M.C.A., University of Delhi, Delhi-110 007
Formerly, Computer Analyst/Consultant, St. Stephen's Hospital, Delhi

KHANNA BOOK PUBLISHING CO. (P) LTD.

Publisher of Engineering and Computer Books

4C/4344, Ansari Road, Darya Ganj, New Delhi-110002
Phone : 011-23244447-48 **Mobile:** +91-9910909320
E-mail : contact@khannabooks.com
Website : www.khannabooks.com

Dear Readers,

To prevent the piracy, this book is secured with HIGH SECURITY HOLOGRAM on the front title cover. In case you don't find the hologram on the front cover title, please write us to at contact@khannabooks.com or whatsapp us at +91-99109 09320 and avail special gift voucher for yourself.

Specimen of Hologram on front Cover title:

Moreover, there is a SPECIAL DISCOUNT COUPON for you with EVERY HOLOGRAM.
How to avail this SPECIAL DISCOUNT:
Step 1: Scratch the hologram
Step 2: Under the scratch area, your "coupon code" is available
Step 3: Logon to www.khannabooks.com
Step 4: Use your "coupon code" in the shopping cart and get your copy at a special discount
Step 5: Enjoy your reading!

ISBN: 978-93-8106-863-2

THE ESSENTIALS OF JAVA
by **Arunesh Goyal**

Edition: 2017
Reprint: 2026

Published by:

CIN: U22110DL1998PTC095547
Khanna Book Publishing Co. (P) Ltd.

Visit us at: **www.khannabooks.com**
Write us at: **contact@khannabooks.com**

To view complete list of books, Please scan the QR Code:

KPH

Printed in India.

To

Goddess Durga

&

Lord Shiva

The Real Father & MOTHER of All!

PREFACE

As is clear from the title, this book intends to make you learn practically the essentials of the Java programming language. I shall briefly describe the structure and composition of the book in the following paragraphs.

This books deals exclusively and intensively with the Java language. The book follows a step-by-step approach towards 'JAVA' learning. It deals with both the theoretical and practical aspects of the language.

The first chapter includes all that you need to get started with Java. It introduces the portability and cross-platform feature of Java via bytecodes through the use of JVM besides the object-oriented paradigm consisting of encapsulation, inheritance, and polymorphism. It also discusses the evolution of Java and as to how it differs from C/C++. It introduces the various syntax rules, data types, and decision control constructs in addition to arrays and the basic gist of strings. The concept of classes, objects, command-line arguments and mathematical functions/methods is also described in short.

The second chapter is of vital significance as it forms the backbone of object-oriented languages like Java. It elaborates classes, objects, and methods. It introduces the concepts of constructors, finalize() method, garbage collection, "this", access control, call by value/reference, recursion, and static besides the use of final named constants and variable number of arguments, i.e., varargs..

The third chapter discusses inheritance, method overriding, abstract methods/classes, dynamic method dispatch, use of the 'super' keyword as well as the use of the 'final' keyword in relation to inheritance besides the Object class, which is the superclass of all classes in Java,vividly.

Packages and interfaces form part of the next chapter. Herein, explicit interface implementations, standard packages as supported by the Java library, creating and importing packages, nesting and inheritance in interfaces, and the use of the access mode - 'protected' are brought out succinctly.

Exception handling has become, of late, one of the most important aspects of modern object-oriented languages. This is what is precisely discussed in the fifth chapter of the book. It teaches the art of handling run-time errors gracefully, built-in exceptions of Java as well as creating your own customized exception subclasses.

The sixth chapter of the book is on Input/Output (without which no language can survive in the world of computers). It also describes NIO (New I/O, which is a relatively new addition to Java based on the concept of channels and buffers) and the Formatter class (by means of which one can make the output look more nice akin to the printf() function in C/C++).

String handling, which was introduced in the first chapter, is discussed in more depth in the next chapter including the StringBuffer and StringBuilder classes while the final chapter of the book is on type wrappers, auto-boxing/unboxing, enumerations, and annotations. Of these, the first two are closely related to the value/reference types, enumerations provide a convenient means to assign integer values to named constants while annotations, to put it simply, is just metadata.

There are eight case studies in all which are discussed in the foregoing chapters pertaining to wide ranging topics. We hope these will help you to see the practical side of applying JAVA in the real world and understand the theoretical subject matter of the text much better. Besides, there are one hundred eleven odd solved examples to help you out.

There is a specially designed set of one hundred solved Java Interview Questions. Besides, there is a set of fifteen miscellaneous problems which you will do well to try your hand at in your own interest besides taking up the practical sessions affixed at the end of each chapter. In all, these amount to one hundred thirty odd practical problems and exercises. We are confident that if you can solve all these problems on your own, you will be on your way to understanding and gaining self-confidence in JAVA.

The appendix contains the essence of the JAVAAPI package which includes fifty-nine libraries in all. The acronyms, the glossary and the index section are for your ready reference. The acronyms and the glossary, in particular, have been so designed that you are able to understand much of the computer jargon associated with JAVA environment in a big way.

I must also mention the "Winding It Up!" sessions at the end of each chapter. They not only discuss and elucidate a potential problem area but also throw open a wide quizzical region which arouse the readers' interest in the subject matter to a large extent. We hope these will be of vital help to each one of you in your own way.

Before finishing off, I must say that:

"There are no shortcuts in life; if you want to go to heaven, you have to die yourself; you can't ask someone else to die for you!"

I am confident that you would be able to learn "The Essentials of JAVA" after having thoroughly studied this book!!

Arunesh Goyal

ACKNOWLEDGEMENTS

I would, in particular, like to acknowledge the spirited role played by my parents, Smt. Sita & Shri Rabinder Nath Goyal, in the face of adverse onslaught, tricky circumstances and situations.

I would also like to laud the role played by each and every one who came into interaction with me during the course of writing this book, nay the whole cosmos, as otherwise this work may perhaps would not have been possible.

I also take this opportunity to thank, laud and acknowledge the role played by M/s Khanna Publishing Co. (P) Ltd., especially Mr. Mukul Seth, its Executive Director, in making this work finally possible.

But, above all, I would like to put on record and acknowledge my Sad_Guru_Dev, Shri Siddheshwar Baba (Formerly, Sh. B.S. Goel, M.A., Ph.D.; founder of Third Eye Foundation of India) for constantly encouraging me whenever my spirits were down and out. It is, indeed, rightly said:

"Gurura Brahma, Gurura Vishnu, Gurura Devo Maheshwara,
Gurura Sakshat Para_Brahma, Tasmai Shri Guruvey Namah:"!

Arunesh Goyal

AN ANECDOTE

"Success is not being intelligent; it's about how you apply your intelligence!"

A little anecdote shall prove the above point.

There were two friends, one from a rich family and the other one from a poor background. Both of them were intelligent and smart in their own ways. But each of them claimed to be more intelligent than the other guy. Soon, a quarrel ensued between them and they decided to approach a wise old man to decide the issue. Upon listening to their story, the wise man explained to them a technique for making a special recipe and asked both of them to cook it for him next day. "The one who shall prepare a tastier and better meal would be the winner!", he frowned.

Next day, the poor young man came with his cooked recipe at the appointed hour but there was no trace of the rich chap even after five hours. The young fella along with the old wise man then went to the rich friend's house only to find him in the kitchen pacing up and down. "What's the problem?", the wise person enquired. "Oh! You have not taught me properly. See, I have everything ready as told by you for more than eight hours now but the recipe is still not cooked", answered the flabbergasted rich young man.

"I see, why? Have you bothered to use your common sense and light the hearth?", the wise old man remarked. The rich man came to his senses immediately, understanding the cause of his predicament for so long. But, the battle had been lost by now.

Moral of the story: Use your intelligence to earn money by all means but not at the cost of your name!

CONTENTS

Chapter 1

GETTING STARTED WITH JAVA

1.0 INTRODUCTION

Java is one of the most popular computer languages in the world today. It enjoys an eminent position in the cyberspace contributing to its popularity on the Internet as well. Even the new C# language has derived many of its features from Java. In fact, Java and C# are close cousins. Both derive their syntax from C and the object-oriented paradigm from C++.

1.1 EVOLUTION OF JAVA

A research team at Sun Microsystems was working on the development of home automation applications that could be integrated into cellular telephones and real-time portable systems all of which were developed using C++. This type of development imposed certain restrictions due to the differing hardware architectures, interconnection problems between different machines etc. C++ was not particularly suitable for this kind of development as it is greedy on memory, lacks portability across processes, and pointer management risks the deletion of data vital to the operation of the application.

Given such problems, one of the team members, namely James Gosling endeavoured to write a new programming language. Given its application domain, this language needed to be object-oriented, high performance oriented, fast and such as to ensure portability between different types of hardware. At first, it was called C++--, then Oak, and finally Java - a slang term for "coffee" - due to the amount of coffee consumed by the developers.

In 1994, to demonstrate the possibilities of Java, two Sun programmers, Patrick Naughton and Jonathan Peayne, created a Web browser called HotJava fully programmmed in Java. HotJava enabled the running of Java programs called applets (different from stand alone applications) in web pages. Subsequently, Java applets became implementable in other Web browsers such as Netscape Navigator.

Java not only opened the door to immense possibilities on the Internet, but is inherently suitable for administrative data processing (via database processing), for development using client/server architectures as well as for something it was tailor-made: industrial and loaded data processing.

Without any doubt, we can say that Java shall remain a popular programming language for many many future years to come.

1.2 HOW JAVA DIFFERS FROM C & C++?

We have aready stated that Java is closely related to both C and C++, deriving its syntax from C and the object-oriented features from C++. In the next two subsections, we shall see in what ways it differs from them. You need not to worry about any new terms you encounter in these sections. We shall be discussing them in due course.

1.2.1 Java & C

- Java does not have the C keywords: *sizeof, typedef, auto, extern, register, signed, unsigned.*
- Java adds new operators such as *instanceof* and >>> (unsigned right shift).
- Java adds labelled break and continue statements.
- Java does not support the data types *struct* and *union.*
- Java does not have an explicit *pointer* type.
- Java does not have a *preprocessor* and thus, does not support any preprocessor directive such as *#define, #include, #ifdef* etc.

1.2.2 Java & C++

- Java does not support *operator overloading.*
- Java does not allow *default arguments.*
- Java does not support *multiple inheritance.*
- Although Java supports constructors, it does not have *destructors*. Instead, it has a *finalize()* function.
- Java does not allow the *goto.*
- Java does not have the *delete* operator.
- Java does not support *global variables/functions* as all the code in a Java program is encapsulated within one or more classes.
- The << and >> in Java are not overloaded for I/O operations.
- In Java, objects are passed by *reference* only. In C++, they could be pased by reference as well as by value.
- Java adds *multithreading, packages, interfaces*, a third comment type: the *documentation comment* that begins with /** and ends with */, and a built-in string type called *String.*
- Java does not have C++ type libraries but has its own set of *API* (Application Program Interface) classes.
- While both Java and C++ support a boolean data type, their implementation is different.

In C++, a nonzero value is true while zero value is false. But, in Java, true and false are treated as *predefined literals*.

- In a C++ class, the access operators apply to a group of statements while in Java, they apply only to the *declarations* they immediately precede.
- Both Java and C++ support exception handling. But, in C++, there is no particular requirement that a thrown exception be *necessarily caught* as is the case in Java.

1.3 WHY JAVA?

Java serves both as a programming language as well as a platform. As a programming language, Java is simple, object-oriented, distributed, interpreted, robust, secure, architecture-neutral, portable, high performance based, multithreaded and dynamic. By definition, a platform is a hardware/software environment in which a program can be run. The majority of present day platforms are a combination of hardware (the machine) and software (the operating system). The Java platform is quite different in the sense that it consists only of of a software component that can be run on varying hardware. It consists of the Java Virtual Machine(JVM) and the Java Application Programming Interface (JAVAAPI).

Java is simple with a syntax similar to that of C and C++ but without their semantic complexity that make them confusing and insecure. Thus, there is no need for pointer management etc. In the following section, we shall be discussing as to how Java is object-oriented. Java is distributed in the sense that network access protocols like TCP/IP, UDP, HTTP, and FTP are supplied with it that allows for the development of client/server model in order to access data on a distant/remote machine. Once again, a Java program does not operate in the normal way. Rather, it is interpreted by the JVM. Java achieves robustness by strict program checking during compilation as well as execution. The Java code is verified both during compilation and run-time by the interpreter making it free drom errors and ensuring security. Java is inherently architecture-neutral as the Java compiler produces Java bytecodes independent of any specific environment. The primary data in Java is primarily of the same size (generally IEEE754) ensuring portability across varying platforms. Although the Java program is interpreted resulting in it being slow to a degree but, still, Java uses JIT (Just In Time), a code interpretation optimizing technique resulting in almost the same performance as C++. Java introduces multithreading, a concept that allows for many things/applications being run simultaneously and increases response time. Finally, in Java, one doesn't have to edit links (mandatory in C++) resulting in executables having a lower memory size. Thus, Java is dynamic as well!

The Java Virtual Machine (JVM) is the base of the Java platform and is essential for running the Java programs. It is compatible with any type of computer machine. The JVM undertakes the loading of Java bytecodes, classes, memory management, security management and, if necessary, interfacing with native code such as C. JAVAAPI (for a complete description of the JAVAAPI package, consult Appendix 'C') contains a collection of prefabricated software components that supply a number of functions like the management of graphical interface etc. The Java Application Interface is organized as a collection of packages just as libraries in C/C++. Each package has Java classes that are predefined language objects directly reusable. The

Java platform consisting of the JVM and the JAVAAPI is the link between the hardware and the Java program. To compile Java source code, we need to use the compiler dedicated to our machine. After compilation, the file remains independent of the hardware platform and the operating system. The interpreter runs Java programs. To run Java applets, the interpreter is incorporated into Java compatible Web browsers such as HotJava, Netscape Navigator etc. To run independent stand alone Java applications, we need to run the virtual machine (JVM) supplied with the Java development Kit (JDK) or the Java runtime Environment (JRE).

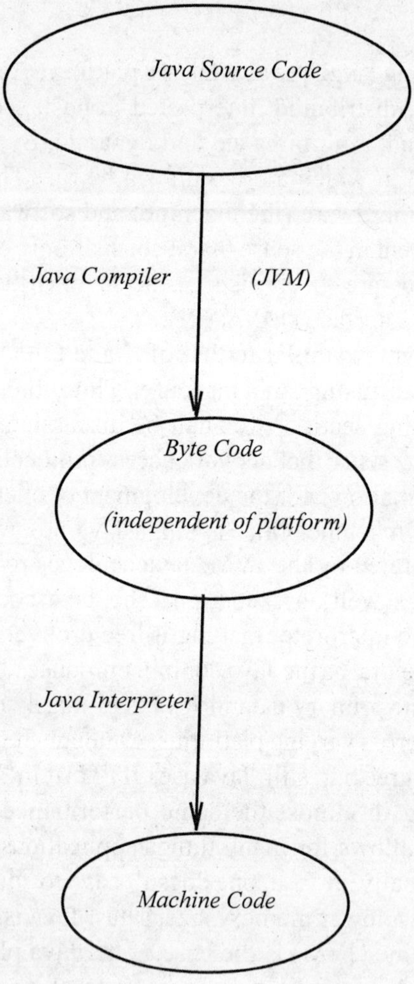

Figure 1.1 Running a Java Program on any Platform

As discussed above, a Java program is independent of the operating system/platform on which it is run. This is achieved by means of the Java Virtual Machine (JVM) that converts the original source code into bytecodes (which is platform independent). Finally, the Java interpreter on the concerned operating system converts these bytecodes into machine code which can be run on that particular machine. All this is illustrated in Figure 1.1 above.

1.4 THE OBJECT-ORIENTED PARADIGM UNFOLDED

Java' s object-oriented framework and for that matter any object-based programming language is based on three basic buzzwords viz., encapsulation, inheritance, and polymorphism. In this context, it would be relevant and useful to define two terms: a class and an object.

Class: A class is a group of data and methods that share some common properties and relationships.

Object: An object is an instance of a class. Thus, it is an identifiable entity with certain characteristics and behaviour.

1.4.1 Encapsulation

In order to use an object, it is not mandatory to have access to all of its attributes and methods or to know the details of its internal functions. What is more important is to know how to use the object, howsoever complex, without having to bother about the details of its production. This concept is called encapsulation meaning that attributes and methods declared as private and thus inaccessible from outside are encapsulated in the object.

1.4.2 Inheritance

Inheritance is a vital aspect of object-oriented programming. In fact, it allows the creation of object hierarchies influencing the way we organize our Java program. It enables a class to inherit all the methods and attributes of another class making it redundant to rewrite that class's code. A class that is inherited is referred to as a superclass and the one that inherits is referred to as a subclass. This concept of inheritance makes the code reusable.

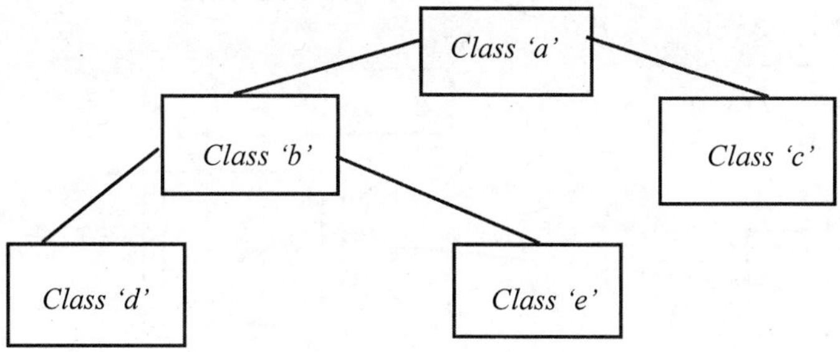

Figure 1.2 Simple Inheritance

In the above diagram (Figure 1.2), Class 'a' is a superclass of Classes 'b' & 'c' while Class 'b' is a superclass of Classes 'd' & 'e' respectively. In other words, Classes 'b' and 'c' are subclasses of Class 'a' while Classes 'd' & 'e' are subclasses of Class 'b' respectively.

In Java programming, there is one class of the top of the hierarchy of every Java program, the Object class. Thus, all Java classes inherit attributes and methods from the Object class (to know more about the Object class, refer section 3.8). Unlike C++, Java does not support multiple inheritance. However, it does have a mechanism called the interface enabling the concept of multiple inheritance.

1.4.3 Polymorphism

Polymorphism is a combination of the concept of inheritance and the redefinition of a method/variable. Thus, two objects may have the same method signature but the implementation of each method is different.

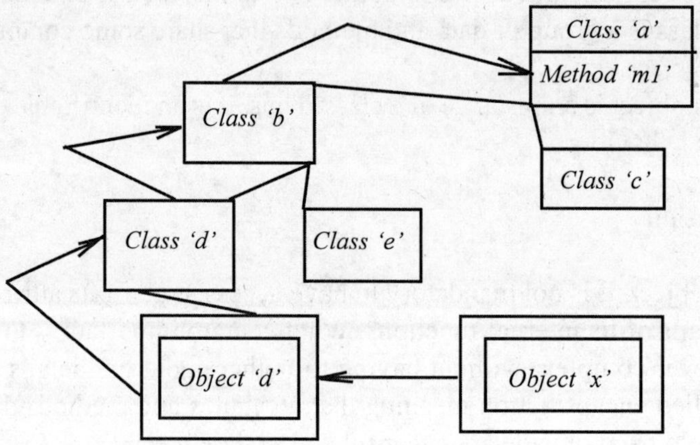

Figure 1.3 Search for a Method

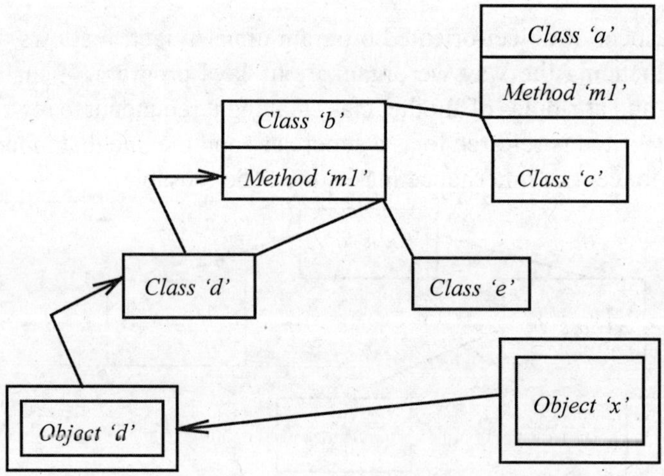

Figure 1.4 Polymorphic Search for a Method

We now take up an example of the polymorph method inside a class hierarchy by means of two diagrams (Figures 1.3 & 1.4). In Figure 1.3, for instance, when Object'x' calls the instance method 'm1' of Object 'd', Java looks for the definition of the method in the class of the object, viz. Class 'd'. When it is not found, Java searches further up the class hierarchy until the method definition is found in Class 'a'. But, in Figure 1.4, a subclass of Class A, i.e. Class B has the same method 'm1' redefined with the same signature but a different implementation. Object 'x' calls the instance method 'm1' of Object 'd'. Java looks for the definition of the method in Class 'd' as before. When it is not found, Java searches further up the class hierarchy until it is found this time in Class 'b'. The redefinition of the method 'm1' masks the original method 'm1' that was inherited from the superclass Class 'a'. Thus, when 'm1' is called, Java runs the code as redefined in Class 'b'.

1.5 OUR FIRST JAVA PROGRAM

Now that we have discussed Java' s basic object-oriented nature, it's time to write our first Java program as given below:

```
// Our First Java Program
/* We can call this: "First.java";
Author: Arunesh; Date: 01/03/2011 */
class First
{
        /** Our program begins with a call to main() as shown below. */
        public static void main(String args[ ])
        {
                System.out.println("This is our First Java Program!");
        }
}
```

The above program, although quite short, deserves a closer look at some of the key features of any Java program. Let's take a brief look:

i. There are three types of comments allowed in Java as exemplified by:
   (a) The single line comment beginning with //:
   // Our First Java Program
   (b) The multi-line comment begining with /* and ending with */:
   / We can call this: "First.java".*
   *Author: Arunesh; Date: 01/03/2011 */*
   (c) The documentation comment beginning with /** and ending with */:
   */** Our program begins with a call to main() as shown below. */*

ii. Look at the declaration:

```
class First
{
............................................
............................................
............................................
............................................
............................................
}
```

This code creates a new class First with the help of the keyword *class* and the identifier *First* with the entire class definition being enclosed within the opening brace {" and the closing brace "}".

iii. Now, look at the declaration:

```
public static void main(String args[ ])
{
    ..............................................
}
```

This code begins the method *main()*. The *public* keyword is an access specifier that controls the visibility (for a detailed account of visibility control, refer sectin 3.7) of the class members (the exact opposite of public is private, as we shall learn later on). Note that *main()* must be declared *public* as it has to be called by code outside of its class when the program begins. The keyword *static* allows *main()* to be called without having to instantiate a particular instance of the class. This is essential as the Java interpreter calls *main()* before any objects are made (to know more about static, refer section 2.5.6). The keyword *void* indicates that *main()* does not return any value. *String args[ ]* declares a parameter *args[ ]* that is an array (arrays are discussed in section 1.8) of instances of the class String (String is briefly introduced in section 1.9) and this parameter receives any command-line arguments (in this case, none; by the way, command-line arguments are discussed in section 1.12). The body of *main()* is enclosed within the opening brace "{" and the closing brace "}". One final point: in case we are using Java applets, we won't need *main()* at all as the Web browsers have a different way to begin the execution of applets.

iv. Finally, have a look at the code inside *main()*:

```
System.out.println("This is our First Java Program!");
```

This line results in the output:

This is our First Java Program!

followed by a new line.

Note that the above statement ends with a semicolon as do all statements in Java.

1.6 HOW TO COMPILE & RUN A JAVA PROGRAM

In most of the programming languages, the name of the file containing the source code is arbitrary. But, in Java, this is not the case. That's why, in our first Java program (refer Section 1.5), we called our program:First.java and thus, the source file name is First.java. This is so as the method *main()* belongs to the class First. To compile this program, we can use the compiler *javac* as shown below:

```
C:\> javac First.java
```

This would create the file *First.class* containing the bytecodes of the program. Now, to run the program, we must use the Java interpreter called *java* as shown below:

```
C:\> java First
```

This would result in the output as desired:

This is our First Java Program!

1.7 SYNTAX RULES

1.7.1 Instructions, Blocks & Expressions

An instruction is a command of any nature ending with a semi-colon (;), e.g.

System.out.println("This is our First Java Program!");

A group of instructions within the opening brace "{" and the closing brace "}" is called a block, e.g.

```
{
        System.out.print("This is our First Java Program!");
        System.out.println;
}
```

// Note that output in both the cases above remains the same.

Some instructions have the effect of producing a value. Such instructions are referred to as expressions while the value returned is called the return value of the expression, e.g.

```
int i = (j - k) / (l + m);
int i = 100;
obj.i = 100;
```

1.7.2 Identifiers

An identifier is the name by which a variable, method, a class, an interface or a package is referenced. There are certain rules for creating identifier names:

- √ The first character must be a letter, an underscore _, or the dollar sign $. If we want to use C/C++ libraries, we must not use _ or $.
- √ After this, the rest of the identifier can be built up of characters, letters, or any Unicode character greater than 0X00C0.
- √ The identifier can not contain any blanks, tabs, line or paragraph breaks.
- √ Reserved keywords cannot be used as identifiers.
- √ Finally, remember that Java is case-sensitive. Thus, main() and Main() are different.

Also, there are some conventional rules as well:

- √ The identifier should generally reflect that to which it refers.
- √ For class/interface name, first letter of each word of the identifier should be uppercase.
- √ For variable/method name, the identifier should begin with a lowercase letter. If the variable name consists of more than one word, then, the first word should begin with a lowercase letter while rest of the words should begin with uppercase ones.
- √ For a constant name, all letters should be uppercase and in case of more than one word, the words should be separated by the underscore _.

Now we take up some examples of identifiers:

```
Num, num, $Num, _Num          // Correct
Complex theComplex;           // Correct
int number_Of_Oranges;        // Correct

3Three     // Incorrect: 3 as first character
if         // Incorrect: reserved word
num#       // Incorrect: # not greater than 0X00C0
```

1.7.3 Comments

We have already discussed the three type of comments allowed in Java (refer Section 1.5).

1.7.4 Literals

A constant repersenting a constant value (that cannot be modified) is referred to as a literal. A literal can be a number (integer or float), a character, a character string or a boolean.
Integer literals can be decimal (base 10), octal (base 8) or hexadecimal (base 16). To represent an integer as a literal using octal notation, 0 must precede the number but in the case of literals using hexadecimal notation, 0X or 0x must precede the number. A decimal literal is stored in the normal way without any 0 preceding the number, e.g.,

the decimal number 14 is written as 16 in octal notation and 0XE or 0xE in hexadecimal notation.

An integer can be a byte (8 bits), short (16 bits), int (32 bits) or long (64 bits). By default, Java stores integer literals as int except in cases when the literal is bigger than the value field for int data (in such cases, the literal is stored as long data). We can also store integer literals stored as long data by affixing "l" or L" at the end of the literal value, e.g.,

```
long i = 8;     // 8 may be stored as an int type.
                // Java stores the value of i in 32 bits.
long i = 8l;    // note the suffix l.
                //  program code forces i to be stored as a long type.
                // Java stores the value of i in 64 bits.
```

A floating point value can be stored as float (32 bits) or double (64 bits): the default. We can force a literal to be stored as float by adding the suffix "f" or "F", e.g.,

```
float i = 7.8;     // stored as a double
float i = 7.8F;  // stored as a float
```

We can also use notations with exponents in the case of floating point literals by adding "e" or "E', followed by an exponent represented by an integer at the end of the literal, e.g.,

```
double i = 7.8E7;
double i = 7.8e-8;
```

Boolean literals can take the values true or false (no 0 or 1 as in C/C++), e.g.,

boolean GOD = true;
boolean MATTER = false;

Character literals are represented by a single character between single quotation marks, e.g., *a', 'B'* etc.

Such characters are stored as 16-bit data [65536 characters: ASCII(256) & the rest:Unicode].

Java, like other languages, uses character literals called escape sequences (Table 1.1) that enable the use of special characters.

Table 1.1 Escape Sequences

Escape Sequence / Control Character	Meaning
\\	*Backslash*
\	*Continuation*
\'	*Single Quotation Mark*
\"	*Double Quotation Mark*
\b	*Backspace*
\r	*Carriage return*
\t	*Tab*
\f	*Form Feed*
\n	*New Line*
\\<*octal value*>	*Octal Character*
\\<*hexadecimal value*>	*Hexadecimal Character*
\\<*unicode value*>	*Unicode Character*

Finally, character string literals are a series of characters placed between double quotation marks, e.g.,

String colour = "blue";

/* In Java, there is no database for character strings but, as already mentioned, there is a *String* class. Thus, in Java, a string is an object. This has some advantages such as the object attributes can be used to edit character strings, e.g. *comparison, concatenation, substrings* etc. */

1.7.5 Keywords

A keyword is a *reserved word* that is used for a specific purpose. There are 49 keywords in Java as enumerated below in alphabetical order:

abstract	Used to declare a class and when certain methods of that class are declared.
assert	Used to create an assertion.
boolean	A variable/function identifier may be declared to be of type *boolean.*
break	Used to exit a loop early.
byte	A variable/function identifier may be declared to be of type *byte.*
case	Used to test a condition in the switch construct.
catch	Used in exception handling along with *try*.
char	A variable/function identifier may be declared to be of type *char.*
class	Used to declare a *class.*
continue	Used to prohibit a loop from running when a condition is fulfilled.
default	Used in the *switch... case* construct as the *default case.*
do	Used in a *do .... while* loop.
double	A variable/function identifier may be declared to be of type *double.*
else	Used with *if* statement.
extends	Used to *extend* a class in order to inherit attributes and methods of the superclass.
false	One of the values for *boolean* type.
final	Used to indicate that a class cannot be subclassed.
finally	Used with *try ... catch* block.
float	A variable/function identifier may be declared to be of type *float.*
for	Used in the *for* loop to repeat a set of instructions.
if	Used to test whether a condition is fulfilled.
implements	Used to indicate that a class *implements* an interface.
import	Used at the beginning of an application to call Java packages not in the application.
instanceof	Used to find out the type of an object.
int	A variable/function identifier may be declared to be of type *int.*
interface	Used when an *interface class* is declared.
long	A variable/function identifier may be declared to be of type *long.*
native	Used to call the structure of an external program written in *native* code such as C.
new	Used to instantiate a class.
null	Used to indicate a value that does not exist.
package	Used to declare a Java *package.*
private	Used to define a class, a variable or a *private* method.
protected	Used to define a class, a variable or a *protected* method.
public	Used to define a class, a variable or a *public* method.
return	Used to *return* a value or transfer control.
short	A variable/function identifier may be declared to be of type *short.*
static	Used to define a class, a variable or a *static* method.
super	Used to refer to the superclass of the current class.
switch	Used in the *switch ... case* contruct.
synchronized	Used to *synchronize* the multiple threads in a Java program.
this	Refers to the current object.
throw	Used in exception handling.
throws	Used in exception handling.
transient	Used to enable an object to be persistent.
true	One of the values for boolean type.
try	Used in the *try... catch* block for exception handling.

void	Used to indicate no return value.
volatile	Modifier to authorize an attribute of an object to be modified independently of a Java program.
while	Used in the *do ... while* loop and the *while...* loop.

1.7.6 Operators

Operators can either be unary (Tables 1.2) requiring a single operand or binary requiring two operands.

Table 1.2 Unary Operators

Unary Operator	Result
+	*Positive Value*
-	*Negation*
~	*Complement*
++	*Increment*
--	*Decrement*
!	*Opposite*

The increment and decrement operators can either be prefixed or postfixed, e.g.

```
x --;     // Subtract 1 fro the value of x after evaluating x
-- x;     // Subtract 1 from the value of x before evaluating x
```

Binary operators can be arithmetic, relational, logical, or bitwise (Tables 1.3 - 1.6).

Table 1.3 Arithmetic Operators

Arithmetic Operator	Result
+	*Addition*
-	*Subtraction*
*	*Multiplication*
/	*Division*
%	*Modulus (remainder of division)*

Note1: The operator '+' is also used for concatenating character strings.

Note2: Division by 0 and the modulus of a division by 0 generate a run-time exception error.

Table 1.4 Relational Operators

<table>
<tr><th>Relational Operator</th><th>Result</th></tr>
<tr><td>==</td><td>Equal to</td></tr>
<tr><td>!=</td><td>Not Equal to</td></tr>
<tr><td>></td><td>Greater than</td></tr>
<tr><td>>=</td><td>Greater or Equal than</td></tr>
<tr><td><</td><td>Less than</td></tr>
<tr><td><=</td><td>Less or Equal than</td></tr>
</table>

Table 1.5 Logical Operators

<table>
<tr><th>Logical Operator</th><th>Result</th></tr>
<tr><td>!</td><td>Logical NOT</td></tr>
<tr><td>&</td><td>Logical AND</td></tr>
<tr><td>|</td><td>Logical OR</td></tr>
<tr><td>^</td><td>Exclusive OR</td></tr>
<tr><td>&&</td><td>Short-Circuit Logical AND</td></tr>
<tr><td>||</td><td>Short-Circuit Logical OR</td></tr>
</table>

Table 1.6 Bitwise Operators

<table>
<tr><th>Bitwise Operator</th><th>Result</th></tr>
<tr><td>~</td><td>Bitwise Unary NOT</td></tr>
<tr><td>&</td><td>Bitwise AND</td></tr>
<tr><td>|</td><td>Bitwise OR</td></tr>
<tr><td>^</td><td>Bitwise Exclusive OR</td></tr>
<tr><td>>></td><td>Shift Right</td></tr>
<tr><td>>>></td><td>Shift Right Zero Fill</td></tr>
<tr><td><<</td><td>Shift Left</td></tr>
</table>

In Table 1.5, we have two types of logical AND operators: & and the Short-Circuit &&. When the operator & is used, Java evaluates the value of the expressions on either side of the operator. But, if && is used, Java evaluates the value of the expression on the left hand side(LHS) of the operator. If it is false, the right hand side (RHS) expression is not evaluated and the result of the operation is false. Similar is the case with | and | | operators. If the expression on the LHS of | | is true, the RHS is not evaluated and the result of the operation is true.

Besies these operators, Java also has assignment operators as enumerated in Table 1.7.

Table 1.7 Assignment Operators

Assignment Operator	Result
=	*Assignment*
+=	*Addition Assignment*
-=	*Subtraction Assignment*
*=	*Multiplication Assignment*
/=	*Division Assignment*
%=	*Modulus Assignment*
&=	*AND Assignment*
|=	*OR Assignment*
^=	*Exclusive OR Assignment*
>>=	*Shift Right Assignment*
>>>=	*Shift Right Zero Fill Assignment*
<<=	*Shift Left Assignment*

Java includes a special *ternary* (three-way) operator that can replace certain types of if-then-else statements (refer section 1.10 for such statements as also for this operator). This is denoted by ?: and has the general form:

expression1 ? expression2 : expression3;

where, expression1 is any expression evaluating to a boolean value. If expression1 is true, expression2 is evaluated; otherwise expression3 is evaluated. The result of the operator is the final expression evaluated, e.g.,

result = denominator == 0 ? denominator : numerator / denominator;

Thus, if the denominator happens to be 0, the result of the division is 0; otherwise the result is the dividend of the division operation.

We also have the parantheses ( ) that can alter the precedence of the operations, the square brackets [ ] for array indexing, and the dot operator . to dereference objects.

Table 1.8 details the complete precedence of Java operators from the highest to the lowest. Note that op is any operator that can be used along with the assignment operator = as shown in Table 1.7.

Table 1.8 Operator Precedence

From Highest			
()	[]	.	
++	--	~	!
*	/	%	
+	-		
>>	>>>	<<	
>	>=	<	<=
==	!=		
&			
^			
|			
&&			
||			
?:			
=	*op*=		
To Lowest			

From the above table (Table 1.8), it is obvious that Java follows the following precedence of operators:

- brackets
- incrementation & decrementation operators
- arithmetic operators
- relational operators
- logical operators
- assignment operators

1.7.7 Data Types

There are two types of Java data types: simple and complex or compound. The simple types are integers, floating point, characters, and boolean. The group of integers includes *byte, short, int* and *long* that are whole-valued signed numbers. The group of floating point numbers includes *float* and *double* that represent single and double precision fractional real numbers. Characters are represented by *char* that include symbols in a character set (letters and digits). Boolean is represented by *boolean* that is a special type for *true/false* values.

All these simple types are directly comprehensible by the compiler and don't require the use of specific Java libraries. The compound types are *tables, character strings, and class/ interface names* and the use of these complex/compound data types can require the use of specific classes from the Java library.

Note that Java is a very strongly typed language. Thus, for instance, you cannot assign floating point values to integers as in C/C++.

Next, we take up a *case study* to illustrate the various Java data types.

Java Data Types - A *CASE STUDY*

In this *case study*, we shall take up four examples (Example 1 - Example 4) to practically demonstrate the different data types in Java.

Example 1

```
// Byte_Short_Int_Long_Example.java
/* Number of seconds in a year;
Author: Arunesh; Date: 01/03/2011 */
class Byte_Short_Int_Long_Example
{
        public static void main (String args[ ])
        {
                long year_seconds;
                int days_year = 365;
                short hours_day = 24;
                byte seconds_hour = 3600;

                year_seconds = days_year * hours_day * seconds_hour;
                System.out.println("There are " + year_seconds +
                                                        " seconds in a year.");
        }
}
```

Output:

There are 31536000 seconds in a year.

Example 2

```
// Float_Double_Example.java
/* Compute the area of a circle with a given radius;
Author: Arunesh; Date: 01/03/2011 */
class Float_Double_Example
{
        public static void main (String args[ ])
        {
                float r, pi = 3.14;
                double a;
                r = 5.25;
                a = pi * r * r;
                System.out.println("Area of circle with radius " + r + " units is"
                                                                + a + " sq. units.);
        }
}
```

Output:

Area of circle with radius 5.25 units is 86.54625 sq. units.

Example 3

```
// Char_Example.java
/* Character variables can be incremented/decremented;
Author: Arunesh; Date: 01/03/2011 */
class Char_Example
{
        public static void main (String args[ ])
        {

                char c = 'I';

                System.out.println("Value of c is" + c);
                c++;
                System.out.println("Value of c is now " + c);
                c --;
                System.out.println("Value of c is now" + c);
        }
}
```

Output:

Value of c is I
Value of c is now J
Value of c is now I

Example 4

```
// Boolean_Example.java
/* Demonstration of Boolean Variables;
Author: Arunesh; Date: 01/03/2011 */
class Boolean_Example
{
	public static void main (String args[ ])
	{
		boolean bool = true;

		if (bool)
			System.out.println("Value of bool is" + bool);
		bool = ( 1 > 2);
		if (bool = false)
			System.out.println("Value of c is now " + bool);
	}
}
```

Output:

Value of bool is true
Value of bool is now false

In this *case study*, we have considered the simple Java data types only. We shall be taking up the complex ones in subsequent text and the chapters to follow.

1.7.8 Variables (their Scope and Lifetime)

The basic unit of storage in a Java program is the variable. It is a combination of an identifier, a data type and an optional initializer with the most general form:

<data type> identifier [= value][, identifier [= value ....];

All the variable that have been used so far were declared at the beginning of the *main()* method. But, variables can be declared within any block in Java (a block begins with an opening curly brace '{' and ends with a closing curly brace '}'). Each time a new block is created, a new scope is also created. A scope determines what variables are visible to other parts of the concerned program. It also determines the lifetime of those variables. In general, variables declared within a scope are not accessible to code outside that scope. In fact, the variables within a scope are local to that scope and whence, protected from unauthorized access/modification. These scope rules form the very basis for encapsulation.

Further, scopes may be nested with the outer scope enclosing the inner scope. This implies that variables/objects declared in the outer scope shall remain visible/accessible to code within the inner scope. However, the reverse is false, that is to say, variables/objects declared in the inner scope shall remain hidden to code outside it.

We now take up an example (Example 5) to see the effect of nested scopes.

Example 5

```
// Variable_Scope.java
/* Nested Variable Scope;
Author: Arunesh; Date: 01/03/2011 */
class Variable_Scope
{
        public static void main (String args[ ])
        {
                int i;
                // known to all code within main()

                i = 1;
                if (i == 1)
                {
                        int j = 2;
                        // known only to this block
                        System.out.println(" i = " + i + " j = " + j);
                        /* i & j are both known here */
                        i = j /2;
                }
                j = 3;
                // Error! j not known here
                System.out.println(" i = " + i);
                // i is still known here
        }
}
```

As we shall learn in the following chapter, the lifetime of a variable/object is confined to its scope. This, in fact, implies that a variable shall not hold its value once it goes out of scope. In other words, variables/objects are created when they enter their scope, and destroyed when they leave their scope. Thus, if a variable declaration includes an initializer, then that variable shall be reinitialized each time it enters its block. As a case in point, take the following example (Example 6).

Example 6

```
// Variable_Lifetime.java
/* Lifetime of a vartiable;
Author: Arunesh; Date: 01/03/2011 */
class Variable_Lifetime
{
    public static void main (String args[ ])
    {
        int i;

        for (i = 0; i < 3; i++)
        // for loops are discussed later in this chapter
        {

            int j = 100;
            // j is initialized to 100 each time the for block is entered
            System.out.println("value of j = " + j);
            // always outputs j = 100
            j = -1;
            System.out.println("new value of j = " + j);
        }
    }
}
```

Output:

```
value of j = 100
new value of j = -1
value of j = 100
new value of j = -1
value of j = 100
new value of j = -1
```

/* As you can see, *j* is reinitialized to 100 each time the inner 'for' loop is entered; although it is subsequenly assined the value -1, this value is lost. */

One of Java's scope rules may surprise you, especially if you come from a C/C++ background. Even though blocks can be nested, variables in the inner scope cannot bear the same name as the ones in the enclosing scope. In C/C++, there is no such restriction. However, the designers of Java opined that such "name hiding" could well lead to programming errors and whence, disallowed it.As a case in point, take the following example (Example 7).

Example 7

```
// Variable_Error.java
/* Tries to give the same name to variables in inner and outer scopes;
Author: Arunesh; Date: 01/03/2011 */
class Variable_Error
{
        public static void main (String args[ ])
        {
                int i;

                for (i = 0; i < 3; i++)
                // for loops are discussed later in this chapter
                {
                        System.out.println("value of i = " + i);

                        int i = 0;
                        // Error! i is already declared in main()

                        System.out.println("new value of i = " + i);
                        // will not print
                }
        }
}
```

// The Java program in Example 7 above is illegal and shall result in compile-time error!

1.7.9 Type Conversion & Casting

In general, we can convert to and from types of the same size or from one type to a larger type. Table 1.9 shows the possible conversions. Note that in this table,' Y' stands for "Yes" and 'L' stands for "Loses".

Table 1.9 Possible Conversions

To/From	byte	short	int	long	float	double	char
byte	*Y*	*Y*	*Y*	*Y*	*Y*	*Y*	*Y*
short		*Y*	*Y*	*Y*	*Y*	*Y*	*Y*
int			*Y*	*Y*	*Y*	*Y*	
long				*Y*			
float			*L*	*L*	*Y*	*Y*	
double				*L*		*Y*	
char		*Y*	*Y*	*Y*	*Y*	*Y*	*Y*

Y - Yes; L - Loses

In case we want to convert between two incompatible types, we must use a cast. A cast is an explicit type conversion with the most general form:

(target-DataType) value;

where, target-DataType is the specified data type to which we wish to convert the specified value, e.g. the following code fragment casts an integer to a short:

```
int i;
short s;
............. /* some
.............          Java
.............                  Code */
s = (short) i;
```

1.8 ARRAYS

An array is a variable that contains a list of elements of the same type of simple or compound data such as a class. Each element is stored in its own cell that makes it easier to access the different elements of the array. An array variable can contain any sort of information: numeric (integers, floating-pont etc.), character strings (*String*), or any object. It is also possible to create a multi-dimensional array that is an array of arrays.

To use an array in Java, we declare the defined type of the variable, create the array object, and finally store the desired information iun the array. To declare an array variable, we use the following form:

```
<Type> <Name> [ ];
```

where, *<Type>* represents the data type to be stored in the array and *<Name>* is the name of the array variable, e.g.,

```
int i_arr[ ];       //array of integer called i_arr
float f_arr[5]; // array of five floating-point variables f_arr[0], f_arr[1], ......, f_arr[4]
String surname[ ];        // string array called surname
complex compp[ ];         // array of complex objects calleed compp
long l_arr[2][3];         /* 2 by 3 two-dimensional array with elements:
                                  l_arr[0][0], l_arr[0][1], ..........., l_arr[1][2] */
short s_arr[ ] [ ][ ];    // three-dimensional array of shorts called s_arr
```

Once an array variable is declared, we must fix its size and allocate it memory space. As arrays are Java objects, we should either use the *new* operator (we shall learn more about *new* in the next chapter) to create a new instance in an array or directly initialize the contents of the array using accolade operators, viz. { }. We can use either of the two methods given as follows:

```
<Type> <Name> = new  <Type> [nElements];or
<Type>  <Name> = {element1, element 2, ..............................., elementN};
```

where, *nElements* is the size of the array i.e., the number of cells and *N* is a whole number, e.g.,

```
int coordinates[ ] [ ] = new int [2] [3];
int coordinates [] [] = { {7, 8, 9}, {-1, -2, -3}};
```

Finally, we can store desired information in our array variable as shown below:

```
int coordinates [ ] [ ] = new int [2] [3];
coordinates[0][0] = 7;            //<Name> [<index>][<index>] = <value>;
coordinates[0][1] = 8;
................................
................................
................................
coordinates[1][2] = -3;
```

Note: If we try to access, say, the sixth element of a five-element array, the *ArrayIndexOutOfBoundsException* (exceptions are discussed separately in a later chapter) is raised during run-time (for one-dimensional array, we have *<Name>[<index>] = <value>;*) Moreover, arrays are implemented as objects (we shall learn about objects in the next chapter.).

To know the size of an array, we use the property *length,* e.g.,

```
int x, y = new int [5];
x = y.length;     //x = 5;
int y = new int [2][4];
x = y.length;     //x = 2 * 4 = 8;
```

Now, we take up a *case study* to practically demonstrate the use of arrays in different ways.

Arrays - A *CASE STUDY*

In this case study, we shall take up four examples (Example 8 - Example 11) pertaining to arrays.

Example 8

```
// D1Array.java
/* Initializing a one-dimensional array;
Author: Arunesh; Date: 01/03/201;
class D1Array
{
        public static void main(String args[])
        {
                int days_month [ ] = {31, 28, 31, 30, 31, 30, 31, 31, 30, 31, 30, 31};

                System.out.println("March has " + days_month[2] + "days.");
        }
}
```

Output:

March has 31 days.

/* Note that although March is the third month of the year, index two has been used corresponding to this month since array indexing in Java begins at zero. */

Example 9

```
// D2Array.java
/* Initializing a two-dimensional array;
Author: Arunesh; Date: 01/03/2011  */
class D2Array
{
        public static void main(String args[])
        {
                int d2_arr [ ] [ ] = new int [2][3];
                int i, j, k  = 0;

                for ( i = 0; i < 2; i++)
                /*  for loops are discussed later in in this chapter */
                {

                        for (j = 0; j < 3; j++)
                                {
                                        d2_arr[i][j] = k;
                                        System.out.print(d2_arr[i][j] + "    ");
                                        k = k + 1;
                                }
                }
                System.out.println();
        }
}
```

Output:

0 1 2 3 4 5

/* Note that two '*for*' loops, an outer and an inner respectively, have been used corresponding to the two dimensions of the two-dimensional (2 x 3) array used in the program example. */

Example 10

```
// Dm2Array.java
/* Manually allocating differing  second dimensions;
Author: Arunesh; Date: 01/03/2011  */
class Dm2Array
{
        public static void main(String args[])
        {
                int d2_arr [ ] [ ] = new int [3][ ];
                d2_arr[0] = new int [1];
                d2_arr[1] = new int [2];
                d2_arr[2] = new int [3];
                int i, j, k  = 0;

                for ( i = 0; i < 3; i++)
                /*  for loops are discussed later in in this chapter */
                {
                        for (j = 0; j < (i + 1); j++)
                        {
                                d2_arr[i][j] = k;
                                        k = k + 1;
                        }
                }

                for ( i = 0; i < 3; i++)
                /*  for loops are discussed later in in this chapter */
                {
                        for (j = 0; j < (i + 1); j++)
                                System.out.print(d2_arr[i][j] + "    ");
                }
                System.out.println();
        }
}
```

Output:

```
0
1   2
3   4   5
```

Example 11

```
// Dm3Array.java
/* Demonstration of a three-dimensional array and the property length;
Author: Arunesh; Date: 01/03/2011 */
class Dm3Array
{
        public static void main(String args[])
        {
                int d3_arr [ ] [ ] [ ] = new int [1][1][1];

                System.out.println("length of given array = " + d3arr.length);

                for (int i = 0; i < 1; i++)
                /* for loops are discussed later in this chapter */
                {
                        for (int j = 0; j < 1; j++)
                        {
                                for(int k = 0; k < 1; k++)
                                {
                                        d3_arr[i][j][k] = i + j + k;
                                        System.out.println("Contents: " +
                                                                d3_arr[i][j][k]);
                                }
                        }
                }
        }
}
```

Output:

length of given array = 1
Contents: 0

/* Note how three '*for*' loops have been used corresponding to the three dimensions of the three-dimensional (1 x 1 x 1) array used in the program example. Also, note how three different variables, *i*, *j*, and *k* have been employed for the three '*for*' loops, respectively.*/

1.9 STRINGS: A BRIEF INTRODUCTION

This section introduces strings succinctly. String handling is discussed in more detail in chapter 9. Java's string type called *String* is not a simple type nor it is a simple array of characters (as are strings in C/C++). Rather, *String* defines an object and we need to study objects first before discussing *String* in detail. However, we can use simple strings in our programs meanwhile.

The *String* type is used to declare string variables. We can also declare arrays of strings. A quoted string constant can be assigned to a *String* variable. A variable of type *String* may be assigned to another variable of type *String*. We can also use an object of type *String* as an argument to println(), e.g., consider the following code fragment:

String s = "Test string";
System.out.println(s);

In this case, *s* is an object of type *String*.
It is assigned the quoted sting constant *"Test string"*.
This string is, in turn, displayed by the *println()* statement.

Another thing to understand about strings is that objects of type *String* are immutable, i.e. once a *String* object is created, its contents cannot be altered. This may look like a serious drawback but it is not on two accounts. First, if we need to change a string, we can always create a new string with the desired modifications. Second, Java defines a peer class *StringBuffer* (we shall discuss this class later on in another chapter.) of the class *String*, which allows strings to be modified so that all the normal string manipulations are still available in Java.

For *String* objects, Java provides the operator '+' to concatenate two strings. The *String* class contains several methods (we shall be taking up methods in the next chapter.) we can use like:

```
boolean equals(String object)   // test two strings for equality
int length()                    // length of a string
char charAt(int index)          // get character at the specified index within a string
```

We can also have arrays of strings in a manner similar to that we can have arrays of any other type of objects.

We now take up a *case study* to practically demonstrate the concepts covered in this section.

Strings in Java - A *CASE STUDY*

In this *case study*, we shall consider two examples (Eample12, Example 13) pertaining to the various facets of strings in Java.

Example 12

```
// StringExample1.java
/* Demonstration of  String methods;
Author: Arunesh; Date: 01/03/2011  */
class StringExample1
{
        public static void main(String args[])
        {
                String sobj1 = "ONE 1";
                String sobj2 = "TWO 2";
                String sobj3 = sobj1 + " + " + sobj2;
                String sobj4 = sobj3;

                System.out.println(sobj1);
                System.out.println(sobj2);
                System.out.println(sobj3);

                if (sobj4 != sobj3)
                        System.out.println(" NOT Equal");
                else
                        System.out.println("Equal");

                System.out.print("Character at index 2 in sobj1: ");

                System.out.println(sobj1.charAt(2));
        }
}
```

Output:

ONE 1
TW0 2
ONE 1 + TWO 2
Equal
Character at index 2 in sobj1: *E*

Example 13

```
// StringExample2.java
/* Demonstration of  String arrays;
Author: Arunesh; Date: 01/03/2011  */
class StringExample2
{
        public static void main(String args[])
        {
                String sobj[]= { "ONE 1", "TWO  2", "THREE 3"};

                for (int k = 0; k < sobj.length; k++)
                // for loop taken up in the next section
                        System.out.println("sobj[ + k + "]: " + sobj[k]);
        }
}
```

Output:

```
sobj[0]:        ONE 1
sobj[1]:        TW0 2
sobj[2]:        THREE 3
```

1.10 DECISION CONTROL STRUCTURES

A programming language uses control structures to pave the way for the advancement and branching of the flow of execution based on changes to the state of the program. Java's program control statements can be put in three distinct categories: conditional/selection, repetitive/iterative, and jump. We shall discuss one by one all of these in the following subsections.

1.10.1 Conditional Statements

1.10.1.1 if

if puts a condition on the execution of an instruction. The test of the *<condition>* must return a boolean i.e. true/false value.

Syntax 1:

```
if (<condition>) <instruction>;
```

For example,

```
if (X > Y) System.out.println("X is Greater than Y");
```

Syntax 2:

```
if  (<condition>) <instruction 1>;
else
 <instruction 2>;
```

For example,

```
if (X > Y) System.out.println("X is Greater than Y");
else
system.out.println("X is Less than or Equal to Y");
```

Syntax 3:

```
if (<condition>)
{
        <instruction sequence>;
}
```

For example,

```
if (X > Y)
{
        System.out.println("X is Greater than Y");
        System.out.println("Y is Less than X");
}
```

Syntax 4:

```
if (<condition>)
{
        <instruction sequence 1>;
}
else
{
```

```
<instruction sequence 2>;
}
```

For example,

```
if (X > Y)
{
        System.out.println("X is Greater than Y");
        System.out.println("Y is Less than X");
}
else
{
        System.out.println("X is Less than or Equal to Y");
        System.out.println("Y is Greater than or Equal to X");
}
```

It is also possible to interlink the conditions by means of the *if-else if - else* ladder.

Syntax 5:

```
if (<condition 1>)
{
        <instruction sequence 1>;
}
else if (<condition 2>)
{
        <instruction sequence 2>;
}
else if (<condition 3>
{
        <instruction sequence 3>;
}
.............................................................. /* conditions 4,
..........................................................                  5,
..............................................................              6 etc. */
else            // none of the above conditions 1,2 3, 4, 5, 6 etc. is fulfilled
{
        <instruction sequence 7>;
}
```

For example,

```
if (X > Y)
{
        System.out.println("X is Greater than Y");
        System.out.println("Y is Less than X");
}
else if (X < Y)
{
```

```
        System.out.println("X is Less than Y");
        System.out.println("Y is Greater than X");
}
else
        System.out.println("X is Equal to Y");
```

1.10.1.2 exp_1 ? exp_2 : exp_3;

Java also has the above expression.

Here, if *exp_1* is true, *exp_2* is evaluated else *exp_3* is evaluated.

This is equivalent to:

```
if (exp_1) exp_2;
else
exp_3;
```

For instance, consider the following example:

```
if (ball == "red") ball = "blue";
else ball = "white";
```

This is equivalent to the expression:

```
ball = (ball == "red" ? "blue" : "white");
```

1.10.1.3 switch

Rather than stringing together a series of if-elseif-elseif .... -else tests and statements, it sometimes makes more sense to use the *switch* statement that enables the running of a specified sequence of instructions depending on the value of a specified expression.

Syntax:

```
switch (<test_expression>)
{
        case <value 1> : <instruction sequence 1>;
                         break;
        case <value 2> : <instruction sequence 2>;
                         break;
        case <value 3> : <instruction sequence 3>;
                         break;
        .......................................................................//     value 4,
        .................................................................                   5,
        ......................................................................              6 etc.

        default : <instruction sequence>;
}
```

The *break* statement is necessary to isolate each case(In the absence of the *break* statement, execution continues on into the next case.). If a case value matches the *test_expression*, its corresponding instructions are executed and the break provides an early exit from the *switch* construct and the following values are not checked. The *default* label can be used to execute an instruction sequence when there are no matches for the *test_expression*.

The *test_expression* must be of type *byte, short, int,* or *char* and each of the values specified in the case statements must be of a type compatible with the *test_expression*. Also, each case value must be a unique literal (i.e., it must be a constant, not a variable). Moreover, duplicate case values are not allowed.

Now, we take up an example (Example 14) to illustrate the 'switch' statement.

Example 14

```
// SwitchSeason.java
/* Demonstration of the switch statement;
Author: Arunesh; Date: 01/03/2011 */
class SwitchSeason
{
	public static void main(String args[ ])
	{
		int mon = 1;
		String sea;
		switch(mon)
		{
			case 12:
			case 1:
			case 2:
					sea = "Winter";
					break;
			case 3:
			case 4:
			case 5:
					sea = "Spring";
					break;
			case 6:
			case 7:
			case 8:
					sea = "Summer";
					break;
			case 9:
			case 10:
			case 11:
					sea = "Autmn";
					break;
			default:
					sea = "Invalid Month";
		}
		System.out.println("January is in the " + sea + " season.");
	}
}
```

Output:

January is in the Winter season.

1.10.2 Iterative Constructs

1.10.2.1 while

Runs an *instruction sequence* while the *condition* is verified. The *condition* is tested before the loop is run. If, in the first test itself, the *condition* happens to be false, the loop shall never be run.

Syntax:

```
while (<condition>)
{
        <instruction sequence>;
}
```

For example,

```
// a never ending infinite loop
while (true)
{
        System.out.println("Infinite Loop");
}
```

1.10.2.2 do...while

In this case, the *condition* is after the loop. Thus, the *instruction sequence* is executed at least once and then is repeated as long as the *condition* is fulfilled, i.e. true.

Syntax:

```
do
{
        <instruction sequence>;
}while (<condition>);
```

For example,

```
// the loop runs as long as the variable v is not equal to 5
int v = 0;
do
{
        v++;
        System.out.println("v:      ", + v);
}
while (v ! = 5);
```

Output:

```
v:      1
v:      2
v:      3
v:      4
v:      5
```

1.10.2.3 for

This loop enables the execution of an *instruction sequence* a certain number of times repetitively as long as a *condition* is fulfilled i.e. true.

Syntax:

for (<counter = start>; <test counter>; <increment/decrement counter>)
{
    <instruction sequence>;
}

where,

<counter = start>: local initialization of the variable counter

<test counter>: condition. If condition is true, the loop is executed.

<increment/decrement counter>: modifies counter in order to make the condition false after a certain number of passages throgh the loop. Otherwise, it becomes an infinite loop.

We now take up a *case study* pertaining to the *'for'* loop as well as its *for-each* version.

'for' Loop and its *for-each* Version - A *CASE STUDY*

In this *case study,* we shall first consider a practical program example (Example 15) as regards the 'for' loop before moving on to its for-each version, which we shall again be practically illustrating with the help of another program example (Example 16).

Example 15

```
// ForPrimes.java
/* Testing for Primes;
Author: Arunesh; Date: 01/03/2011  */
class ForPrimes
{
	public static void main(String args[ ])
	{
		int n;

		boolean b = true;
		n = 14;

		for (int i = 2; i <= n/2; i++)
		{
```

```
                if ((n % i )== 0)
                {
                        b = false;
                        break;
                        // break statement is discussed in the next subsection
                }
        }
        if (b)
                System.out.println(n + " is Prime.");
        else
                System.out.println("n + " is Not Prime.");
    }
}
```

Output:

14 is Not Prime.

Note that the *'for'* loop given as follows:

for(; ;);

is an *infinite* loop.

Also, <u>note</u> that like all other programming languages, Java allows <u>nested loops</u> (one loop inside another).Here, the loops could be any combination of *while, do ... while* or *for* loops.

<u>for-each Version of the for Loop</u>

JDK5 introduced the for-each style loop as an enhanced version of the *for* loop. Unlike languages like C#, that use the <u>foreach</u> keyword, Java adds the for-each style by simply enhancing its *for* loop. The major advantage of this fact is that no keyword is required and no pre-existing legacy code is broken. The most general form of for-each style loop is:

```
for (var_type var_name : coll)
{
        statement(s);
}
```

where, *var_type* and *var_name* specify the type and name of the iteration variable and the collection being cycled through is referred to by *coll.*

We elaborate the difference between the traditional *for* loop and the for-each style *for* loop with the help of the following code:

```
int arr[ ] = {1, 2, 3, 4, 5};
int total = 0;
for (int z = 0; z , 5; z++)
        total + = arr[z];
```

Thus, each element in the array *arr[ ]* is read in strictly sequential order from start to finish. This is achieved by manually indexing *arr[ ]* by *z*, the loop control variable.

But, the for-each version automates the loop as shown:

```
int arr[ ] = {1, 2, 3, 4, 5};
int total = 0;
for (int z : arr)
        total + = z;
```

Thus, the syntax is streamlined besides preventing any boundary errors. An important point to note about the for-each version is that its iteration variable is read-only, e.g.,

```
int arr[ ] = {1, 2, 3, 4, 5};
for (int z : arr)
        z *= -1;
        // no effect on arr[ ]
```

Thus, even after the execution of the for-each style loop, there is no change of sign in the members of *arr[ ]*, and they continue to retain their original values, viz., *1, 2, 3, 4, 5*.

The for-each vesion can also be used to iterate over multi-dimensional arrays. Remember that while using the for-each style to iterate over an array of *M* dimensions, the objects obtained will be arrays of *(M - 1)* dimensions. This shall become clear in the light of the following code, which used nested for-each style *for* loops to obtain the elements of a two-dimensional array in row order, from first to last:

```
int arr[ ] [ ]= { {1, 2, 3,}
                { 2, 4, 6},
                {3, 6, 9}
              };
int total = 0;
for (int z[ ] : arr)
        for (int x : z)
        {
                System.out.println(x);
                total + = x;
        }
System.out.println("Sum = " + total);
```

<u>Output</u>:

```
        1
        2
        3
        2
        4
        6
        3
        6
        9
        Sum = 38
```

In the aforesaid code, note how *z* is declared in the line:
for (int z[ ] : arr)
It's a reference to an one-dimensional array of integers.

Now, for the applications of the for-each style loop. It is an excellent choice for computing an average, finding the maximum/minimum of a set of values, looking for duplicates or searching an unsorted list for a specific value, and so on.

To just let you know how easy and efficient the code becomes by using the for-each version, we now take up Example 16 which computes the average of a given set of values.

Example 16

```
// Average.java
/* Using the for-each style for loop to compute the average of a given array of
integers;
Author: Arunesh; Date: 04/07/2011  */
class Average
{
        public static void main(String args[ ])
        {
                int arr[ ] = {6, 8, 5, 7, 3, 1, 6, 4);
                int total = 0;
                int n = 0;
                for (int z: arr)
                {
                        total + = z;
                        n++;
                }
                System.out.println("Sum of given " + n " values = " + total);
                System.out.println("Their average = " + (total/n));
}
```

Output:

Sum of given 8 values = 40
Thir average = 5

Remark: In this chapter, we have been using the for-each style for loop only on arrays. But, this style is extremely and especially useful when operating on collection defined by the Collections Framework.

1.10.3 Jump Statements

1.10.3.1 break

The *break* statement has three important uses. Firstly, we have already seen that it terminates a case statement in a *switch* construct. Second, it can be used to exit a loop (if a *break* statement is encountered inside a loop, the loop is terminated and program control resumes at the next statement following the loop) as we saw in the previous example (Example 15: *Testing for Primes*). Finally, it can be used as a "civilized" form of *goto*.

This can be achieved by means of the *labeled break* statement as given below:

break label;

where, *label* is a name that identifies a block of code. Once we have labeled a block, we can use this *label* as the target of a *break* statement. Doing so causes execution to resume at the end of the labeled block.

Now, we take up an example (Example 17) to illustrate the use of the 'break' statement.

Example 17

```
// BreakAsGoto.java
/* break as a convenient/civilized form of goto;
Author: Arunesh; Date: 01/03/2011 */
class BreakAsGoto
{
        public static void main(String args[])
        {
                boolean b = true;
                one:    {
                        two:    {
                                three:  {
                                                System.out.println("Before break.");
                                                if (b) break two;
                                                // break out of block two

                                                System.out.println("Shall not print.");
                                        }
                                System.out.println("Shall not print.");
                                }
                        System.out.println("After block two.");
                        }
        }
}
```

Output:

Before break.
After block two.

One of the most common uses of a *labeled break* statement is to exit from *nested loops*. We now take up an example (Example 18) to demonstrate this fact.

Example 18

```
// ExitNestedloops.java
/* break to exit from nested loops;
Author: Arunesh; Date: 01/03/2011 */
class ExitNestedLoops
{
    public static void main(String args[])
    {
        one:    for (int l = 0; l < 10; l++)
                {
                    System.out.print("Loop " + l + ":     ");

                    for (int m = 0; m < 50; m++)
                    {
                        if (m == 5) break one;
                        // exit both loops

                        System.out.print(m + "  ");
                    }

                    System.out.println("This shall NOT Execute!");
                }

                System.out.println("Block one COMPLETE!");
    }
}
```

Output:

```
    Loop 0:     0    1    2    3    4    Block one COMPLETE!
```

1.10.3.2 continue

Sometimes we may wish to force an early iteration of a loop. This, in effect, is a *goto* past the body of the loop to the end of the loop. In *while* and *do ... while* loops, a *continue* statement causes the control to be transferred to the *condition* of the loops but in a *for* loop, control first goes to the *iteration,* i.e. *increment/decrement* portion and then to the *condition/test* part of the loop. For all these three loops, any intermediate code is bypassed.

We now take up an example (Example 19) to illustrate the aforesaid use of the 'continue' statement.

Example 19

```
// Cont.java
/* Demonstration of the continue statement;
Author: Arunesh; Date: 01/03/2011  */
class Cont
{
        public static void main(String args[])
        {
                i = 0;

                while (i <= 5)
                {
                        System.out.print(i + "   ");

                        i = i + 1;

                        if ((i % 2) == 0) continue;
                        /* if i is even, go to beginning condition of loop */

                        System.out.println();
                }
        }
}
```

Output:

```
        0       1
        2       3
        4       5
```

As with the *labeled break* statement, we may have a *labeled continue* statement to tell which enclosing loop/(block of code) to *continue*.

This use of the 'continue' statement is illustrated next in Example 20.

Example 20

```
// LabelContinue.java
/* Demonstration of the labeled continue statement;
Author: Arunesh; Date: 01/03/2011 */
class LabelContinue
{
	public static void main(String args[])
	{
		one:	for (int l = 0; l < 4; l++)
			{
				for (int m = 0; m < 4; m++)
				{
					if (m > l)
					{
						System.out.println();

						continue one;
						// multiplication table of l over
					}

				System.out.print((l * m) + "      ");

				}
			}

			System.out.println();
	}
}
```

Output:

```
0
0	1
0	2	4
0	3	6	9
```

1.10.3.3 return

A complete discussion of this statement cannot be taken up until we have discussed the concept of methods in the next chapter. For now, we take a preliminary look at it.

At any time in a method, the *return* statement might be used to cause execution to branch back to the caller of the method. In other words, the *return* statement terminates the method in which it is executed immediately.

We illustrate the 'return' statement next in Example 21.

Example 21

```
// DemonstrateReturn.java
/* Using the return statement;
Author: Arunesh; Date: 01/03/2011 */
class DemonstrateReturn
{
        public static void main(String args[])
        {
                boolean b = true;

                System.out.println("Before Returning!");

                if (b) return;
                // back to caller

                System.out.println("This shall NOT print!");
        }
}
```

Output:

Before Returning!

Note that the *if(b)* statement is necessary because if it is not there, the Java compiler would flash an "unreachable code" error as it would know that the last *println()* statement would never be executed, in effect, and is thus unreachable.

The *if* statement has been used as a way to to eliminate this compiler error (it is a sort of a trick employed, of course!) and demonstrate the *return* statement here.

1.10.3.4 exception handling

In addition to the *jump* statements discussed above, Java has another way by means of which the flow of execution of the program can be altered, viz. by means of *exception handling*.

It is the means by which run-time errors can be trapped and handled. It is implemented by means of the keywords: *try, catch, throw, throws,* and *finally*.

This *exception handling* mechanism allows the program to make a nonlocal branch, in effect. We shall take up this topic in detail in a separate chapter later on.

1.11 AN APPLICATION WITH MULTIPLE (TWO) CLASSES

The following example (Example 22) is an application with two classes, namely, Circle and CircleArea.

Example 22

```
// CircleArea.java
/* An application with two classes;
Author: Arunesh; Date: 01/03/2011 */
class Circle
{
        float radius;
        void get(float x)
        {
                radius = x;
        }
}
class CircleArea
{
        public static void main(String args[])
        {
                float area;

                Circle Circle1 = new Circle();
                /* we shall take up 'new' in a later chapter;
                for now, understand that it creates an object Circle1 */

                Circle1.get(5);
                // assigns value to radius

                area = 3.14 * Circle1.radius * Circle1.radius;
                System.out.println("area of Circle = " + area + " sq. units.");
        }
}
```

Output:

```
        area of circle = 78.5 sq. units.
```

In this case, *Circle1* is, in fact, an object of type class *Circle* while *new* is an operator that helps to create it dynamically at run-time.

We shall be discussing more of this in the next chapter on Classes, Objects, and Methods.

1.12 USE OF COMMAND LINE ARGUMENTS

We already know that all Java applications execute beginning with the static *main()* (we shall be learning more about static in the next chapter) method. The *main()* method takes one argument that is an array of *String* objects, which, in turn, represents any arguments thay may have been entered by the user on the command line. The number of arguments is determined through the expression *args.length*. The individual arguments themselves are accessed via *args[0], args[1], args[2],* and so on.

The following example (Example 23) makes use of the command line arguments.

Example 23

```
// CommandLineArguments.java
/* Demonstration of Command LineArguments;
Author: Arunesh; Date: 01/03/2011 */
class CommandLineArguments
{
        public static void main(String args[])
        {
                int ctr, k = 0;
                String str;
                ctr = args.length;

                if (ctr == 0)
                        break;

                System.out.println(Java is”)

                while (k < ctr)
                {
                        str = args[k];
                        System.out.println(“args[“ + k + “]:   “ + str + “.” );
                }

                System.out.println(“No. of Command Line Arguments:   “ + ctr);
        }
}
```

A sample run:

```
java CommandLineArguments portable multithreaded dynamic
Java is
args[0]:      portable.
args[1]:      multithreaded.
args[2]:      dynamic.
No. of Command Line arguments:      3
```

Note:All command line arguments are passed as strings only.

1.13 USE OF MATHEMATICAL FUNCTIONS

Real-life problems frequently employ and use mathematical functions such as *sin, cos, sqrt, log* etc. Java supports all these functions through the *Math Class* defined in the *java.lang package* (a package is essentially a grouping or set of classes; we shall learn more about packages in a subsequent chapter separately).

These functions can be used as shown in Example 24.

Example 24

```
// MathFunctions.java
/* Using Mathematical Functions;
Author: Arunesh; Date: 01/03/2011 */
import java.lang.*;
// for including the Math class in the standard Java Library
class MathFunctions
{
        public static void main(String args[])
        {
                double d1, d2 = 6.25;

                d1 = Math.sqrt(d2);

                System.out.println("Square root of " d2 + " is " + d1 + "." );
        }
}
```

Output:

Square root of 6.25 is 2.5.

1.14 WINDING IT UP!

In this chapter, we have introduced you to the basic tenets of Java. Now, a word about pointers. Java does not support or allow pointers. The reason for that is simple. Java cannot allow pointers as by doing so, Java applets would be able to breach the firewall between the Java Runtime Environment and the host computer (this is because pointers can be assigned any address in memory - even those outside the Java runtime system.).

C/C++ programmers make extensive use of pointers and they might be inclined to think that their loss puts Java at a significant disadvantage. But, this is false. Java is designed in such a manner that as long as one stays within the boundaries of its execution environment, he will never feel the need to use a pointer. Moreover, he would not get any additional benefit by doing that either. We must also add here that C/C++ code making use of pointers can be converted conveniently to Java code that makes no use of such pointers.

PRACTICAL SESSION

1. (a) Briefly explain the object-oriented paradigm.
   (b) Distinguish between inheritance and polymorphism.

2. (a) List five major differences between C and Java.
   (b) List five major differences between C++ and Java.

3. (a) Is Java a platform-independent language? Support your answer with appropriate reason(s).
   (b) Is Java strongly associated with the Internet? Support your answer with appropriate reason(s).

4. What makes Java such a popular language with the programmers today? Elucidate.

5. (a) Can we use a keyword in Java as a variable name? Why or why not? Elaborate.
   (b) Describe the rules and conventions followed to create an identifier in Java.

6. (a) How do we compile and run a stand-alone Java program/application?
   (b) Can we use command line arguments in Java? If yes, give a suitable example.

7. What is a literal? Elucidate.

8. What basic data types are used in Java? List with suitable examples.

9. (a) What is an array?
   (b) Why are arrays easier to use rather than a bunch of related variables?
   (c) How can we initialize arrays? Explain giving examples of both one-dimensional and two-dimensional arrays.

10. Suppose there are 50 students in a class and five subjects for each students. How can we make use of the concept of arrays to assign marks to all the students in all the subjects?

11. Given two one-dimensional arrays X and Y sorted in ascending order, write a program to merge them into a single sorted array Z containing every element from X and Y, in:
    i. ascending order.
    ii. descending order.

12. (a) How do we type cast a data type in Java?
    (b) What kind of type conversion is supported by Java?

13. Indicate the valid and invalid variable names amongst the following giving reason(s) for your answer:

int *second.first* *$v* *i+j* *2var* *marks total* *total-salary*

14. Write a program to convert a given temperature in degrees celsius to fahrenheit. { Tip: Use the formula F = 1.8 C + 32.}

15. Point out the errors, if any, in the following Java statements:

i. *Double d;*
ii. *int TALL, length;*
iii. *final double sum;*
iv. *character c;*
v. *int short si;*

16. Point out the errors, if any, in the following codes:

i.
```
Class main
{
        public static void main(String args[])
        {
                int i = 5;
        }
}
```

ii.
```
class Scope
{
        public static void main(String args[])
        {
                int i = 5;
        }
        int i = 10;
}
```

17. Point out the errors, if any, in each of the following Java statements:

i. *x = ++y * 10;*
ii. *b = sqrt(25);*
iii. *a/ = b*c;*
iv. *u = /t;*
v. *a = b = 6.9, -8.7;*

18. Distinguish between:

i. A *while* loop and a *do...while* loop.
ii. *break* and *continue*.

19. Determine the value of each of the following logical expressions given that:
x = 6; y = -9; z = 9;
   - i *x = = y && z > x*
   - ii. *x > z | | x < y*
   - iii. *x < z && z > x*
   - iv. *y > 0 | | y < 0*
   - v. *x > 5 && z < 10 && y > -10*

20. In a right angled triangle with sides a and b, the hypotenuse h is given by:
h = sqrt(a^2 + b^2);
Write a complete Java program to calculate the values of h for five given sets of values of a and b.

21. State True(T) or False(F):
   - i. One *if* can have more than one *else* clause.
   - ii. When we use nested *if's*, the last *else* gets associated with the nearest *if* without an *else*.
   - iii. A series of *if...else* statements can always be replaced by the *switch* construct.
   - iv. We can have duplicate case values in a *switch* statement.
   - v. On encountering a *break* statement, the program execution is terminated.

22. Consider the following code fragment:

```
a = 2;
b = 2;
if (k > 0)
        a = a + 1;
        b = b - 1;
```

What shall be the values of *a* and *b* if:
   - i. *n = 2;*
   - ii. *n = 0;*

23. Write a complete Java program to find the sum of all integers greater than 1000 and less than 2000 that are divisible by 3.

24. Using *if* statements and a given list of marks(between 0 and 100) of students, find the number of students who have got distinction and those who have failed using the criteria:
marks between 75 - 100: distinction;
marks between 0 - 35: fail.

25. Given a certain value of *x*, write a program that will evaluate the value of *y* as:
y = greatest integer not greater than *x*.

26. Write a program to print the following pattern:

```
1
2   3
4   5   6
7   8   9   10
```

27. Point out the errors, if any, in the following code fragment:

```
sum = 0;
do
{
        sum++;
        System.out.println("sum is = \t" + sum + "\n");
}
while (sum = 1);
```

28. Given any whole number, write a program that computes and prints its factorial. { *Tip*: For a whole number *n, factorial n = n! = n * (n-1) * (n-2) * .... * 1.* }

29. Using *for* loops, write a program to print the following pattern:

```
1   2   3   4   5
    2   3   4   5
        3   4   5
            4   5
                5
```

30. Check the following code for errors, if any, and rectify them:

```
class Chk
{
        public static void main(String args[])
        {
                int k = 100;
                if (k = 100)
                        System.out.println("Check is Right.");
                else    System.out.println("Check is Wrong.");
        }
}
```

31. Can parts of the *for* loop be left empty? If yes, cite appropriate circumstances/situations under which this can be done and considered suitable as well!

32. Write a program to <u>output</u> the question: "<u>Can you elaborate on how Java evolved?</u>".

33. Check the following code for compilation errors, if any, and rectify them:

```
class Val
{
        public static void main(String args[])
        {
                int val = 4;
                switch(val)
                {
                        case 0:
                                System.out.println("Val = " + 0 + ".");
                                break;
                        case 1:
                                System.out.println("Val = " + 1 + ".");
                                break;
                        case 2:
                                System.out.println("Val = " + 2 + ".");
                                break;
                        case 3:
                                System.out.println("Val = " + 3 + ".");
                                break;
                        case 4:
                        case 4:
                                System.out.println("Val = " + 4 + ".");
                                break;
                        case 5:
                                System.out.println("Val = " + 5 + ".");
                                break;
                        default:
                                System.out.println("Val < 0 || > 5.");
                }
        }
}
```

34. Three candidates contest a election for an assembly constituency. The candidates are numbered 1 to 3. The electorate votes by marking the candidate number on the ballot paper. Write a program to count the votes polled for each candidate. In case, a vote is marked outside the range 1 - 3, the vote should be considered as a "Bogus Vote". The program should also count the number of bogus votes as well as announce the winner based on this counting of votes.
{*Tip*: Try to use the concept of *arrays* and the *switch* statement. }

35. Pick out the errors, if any, in the following code fragment:

```
int x;
int m[ ] = int[5];
int[ ]n = int[6];
for (x = 1; x <= 5; ++x)
        m[x] = n[x] = x;
m = n = new int[10];
for (x = 0; x < 5; ++x)
        System.out.println(m[x]);
```

36. Debug the following programs:

(a)

```
class I_Array
{
        public static void main(String args[])
        {
                int a_Arr [];
                for (int x = 0; x < a_Arr.length; x++)
                {
                        a_Arr[x] = x;
                        System.out.print(a_Arr[x] + "  ");
                }
                System.out.println();
        }
}
```

(b)

```
class II_Array
{
        public static void main(String args[])
        {
                String s_Arr [] =
                        { "Simple", "Secure", "Robust", "Distributed" } ;
                for (int x = 0; x < s_Arr.length(); x++)
                        System.out.print(s_Arr[x] + "...          ");
                System.out.println();
        }
}
```

37. Write a program with multiple (two) classes to calculate the area of a rectangle with length 7 units and breadth 5 units.

38. Explain giving suitable examples the concept of:
    i. break and labeled break statements respectively;
    ii. continue and labeled continue statements respectively; and
    iii. return statement.

39. Getting a call for an interview is subject to the following criteria:
    i. Marks in Mathematics >= 60
    ii. Marks in Computer Science >= 50
    iii. Total Marks in the two subjects >= 140

    Given the marks in the two subjects, write a Java program to determine the eligiblity of the candidates for the interview.

40. Write a complete program using command line arguments rendering the following output:

    Delhi is the capital of India!
    Mumbai is the capital of Maharashtra!
    Chennai is the capital of Tamil Nadu!
    Bangalore is the capital of Karnataka!
    Hydrebad is the capital of Andhra Pradesh!

Chapter 2

CLASSES, OBJECTS, AND METHODS

2.0 INTRODUCTION

We have been using the most elementary form of a class in the first chapter mainly to encapsulate the *main()* method. A class is the basis for object-oriented programming in Java (indeed, for that matter, for any computer language that uses object-oriented programming such as C++, C# etc.) because we need to encapsulate within the class any concept that we may wish to implement. The concept of encapsulation has already been dealt with adequately in the first chapter and need not be repeated here.

2.1 DEFINING A CLASS

To define a class, we need to declare its exact form, nature, and contents by specifying the data it contains along with the code that operates on this data. Later on, we shall come to know that the code within a class is the interface to its data.

We define a class using the keyword (a keyword, as we have learnt in the previous chapter, is a reserved word) 'class' in the following manner:

```
class class_name
{
        data_type(s) instance variable(s);
        data_type(s) method_name(s) (parameter_list(s))
        {
                // body of method(s)
        }
}
```

We need to tell you here that data/variables declared inside a class are known as *instance variables* while the code is written in the form of *methods* (similar to *functions* in C/C++). Thus, instance variables, or simply variables, and methods are the members of a class. Although all methods have the same general form as *main()*, every method may not be *static* and/or *public* (we shall be discussing static methods and the access specifier, public, in more detail in sections 2.5.6 & 2.5.5, respectively). We also need to point out here that it is not mandatory for Java classes to have the *main()* method. In fact, it is required only in case it is the starting point/ beginning of program execution. Moreover, Java applets, in general, are devoid of the *main()* method at all! You may note that we are not going to discuss applets and graphics programming (including AWT - the Abstract Window Toolkit) in this book.

2.1.1 Simple Demonstration of the Concept of Classes

Let us now consider a simple example (Example 25) to illustrate and further understand the concept of classes.

Example 25

```
// RoomDemo.java
/* Simple Demonstration of a class;
Author: Arunesh; Date: 02/03/2011  */
class Room
{
        double length;
        double width;
        double height;
}
class RoomDemo
{
        public static void main (String args[ ])
        {
                Room room1 = new Room();
                Room room2 = new Room();
                        // the dynamic object creating new operator is discussed in section 2.2
                double volume;

                /* assigning values/dimensions to the two rooms */
                room1.length = 20;
                room1.width = 10;
                room1.height = 15;

                room2.length = 15;
                room2.width = 20;
                room2.height = 5;

                /* computing and printing/outputting the volumes of the two rooms */
                volume = room1.length * room1.width * room1.height;
                System.out.println("Volume of room1 = " + volume);

                System.out.println("Volume of room2 = " +
                                        room2.length * room2.width * room2.height);
        }
}
```

Output:

```
        Volume of room1 = 3000.0
        Volume of room2 = 1500.0
```

Note: It is not mandatory to declare the two objects, viz. *room1* and *room2*, as in Example 24. We can define one or any number of objects with the same declaration also:

```
Room room1, room2;
        // room1and room2 declared with a single statement

room1 = new Room();   // needed when we actually wish to allocate memory to room1
room2 = new Room();   // needed when we actually wish to allocate memory to room2
```

You are also advised to consult section 2.2 to know more in this regard.

2.1.2 Nested & Inner Classes

What is meant by a nested class? As the name suggests, a class defined within another class! If class Y is nested within class X, then Y is known to X, but not outside of X, i.e., the scope of a nested class is bounded by the scope of its enclosing class. We would like to mention one more point in this context. Class Y has access to all the members of X (including *private* members; for a detailed discussion of the access modifier, private, see section 2.5.5), but X has no access to the members of Y.

The most important type of a nested class is the non-static, or inner nested class (as previously also mentioned, a detailed account of 'static' is presented in section 2.5.6) .

Let us now consider the following example (Example 26) of a non-static nested or inner class..

Example 26

```
// InnerClass.java
/* Demonstration of non-static nested, i.e. inner class;
Author: Arunesh; Date: 02/03/2011  */
class Out
{
        int out_o = 5;
        void testing()
        {
                In in = new In();
                in.disp();
        }
        class In
        {
                void disp()
                {
                        System.out.println("out_o = " + out_o); /* okay; out_o, an instance
                                        variable of enclosing class Out is known to inner class In */
                }
        }
}
```

```
class InnerClass
{
        public static void main (String args[ ])
        {
                Out out = new Out();
                out.testing();
        }
}
```

Output:

```
        out_o = 5
```

/* Example 26 amply demonstrates the fact which we have already stated, viz. an inner class has access to all the members of its enclosing class. However, the reverse does not hold good, that is, an enclosing class Y has no access to the members of its inner class Y. This shall become more clear in the light of Example 27 as given below. */

Example 27

```
// XY.java
/* Further demonstration of the concept of inner class;
Author: Arunesh; Date: 02/03/2011  */
class X          // enclosing outer class
{
        int o = 5;
        void testing()
        {
                Y y = new Y();
                y.disp();
        }
        class Y // inner class
        {
                int i = 100;
                void disp()
                {
                        System.out.println("o = " + o);
                                /* okay; o, an instance variable of enclosing class X
                                        is known to inner class Y */
                }
        }
        void disp_i()
        {
                System.out.println(" i = " + i);
                                /* not  okay; i, an instance variable of  inner class Y
                                        is local to Y and unknown to enclosing class X;
                                        shall give a compile-time error! */
```

```
        }
}
class XY
{
        public static void main(String args[])
        {
                X x = new X();
                x.testing();
        }
}
```

/* In the preceding example (Example 26), *i* is an instance variable of the inner class Y and is unknown to its enclosing class X. Whence, it cannot be used by *disp_i()* which happens to be a member methid of X. */

2.2 DECLARATION OF OBJECTS

In section 2.1.1, we had used a declaration of the type:

```
Room room = new Room();
```

We can also split this up into two parts as:

```
Room room;           // declaring a reference to an object
room = new Room();   // allocating a Room object
```

The first part declares *room* as a reference to an object of type *Room*. When, this gets executed, *room* has the value 'null' indicative of the fact that it does not point to an actual object as yet. If we try to use *room* at this time, we shall get a compilation error.

The second part allocates an actual object and causes a reference to it to *room*. When this gets executed, we can use *room* as an actual *Room* object. In real terms, however, *room* has simply the naming address of the actual *Room* object.

The following figure (Figure 2.1) is illustrative of whatever we have stated in this section so far.

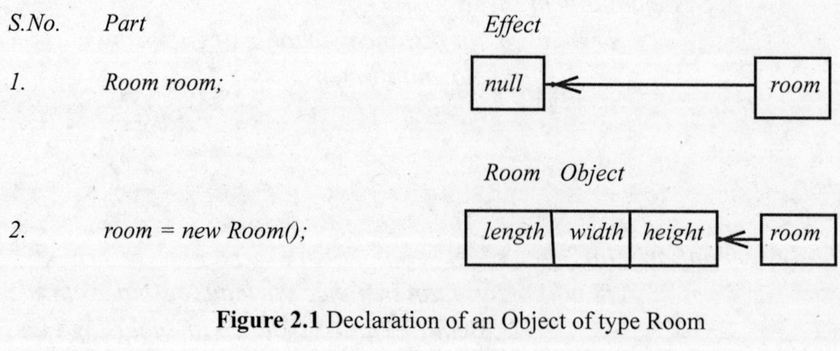

Figure 2.1 Declaration of an Object of type Room

A word about the *new* operator. The *new* operator dynamically allocates memory for an object. Its most general form is:

class_var = new class_name();

where, *class_var* is the variable of the class type being created while *class_name* is the name of the instance of the class being created. What is important to understand is that *new* allocates memory for an object during run-time. If it is unable to allocate memory due to some reson such as insufficient memory space etc., a run-time exception occurs (incidentally, exception handling is being dealt with in a later chapter separately).

The *class_name* followed by parentheses introduces the constructors for that class. We shall be learning about constructors in detail in section 2.4. For now, it is sufficient to say that a constructor specifies what occurs when an object of a class is created. Constructors have many uses and form an important part of all classes. In the real world, most classes explicitly define their own constructors. If no constructor is defined, Java, by itself, supplies a default constructor, as was the case with *Room*.

Now, consider the following code fragment:

Room room1 = new Room();
Room room2 = room1;

We might be tempted to think that *room1* and *room2* are two separate and distinct objects. We might also imagine that *room2* is being assigned to a copy of the object being referred to by *room1*.

Far from it! Both *room1* and *room2*, instead, refer to the same object so that any change to the object through *room2* shall affect the object to which *room1* is referring. This is illustrated in the form of the following diagram (Figure 2.2):

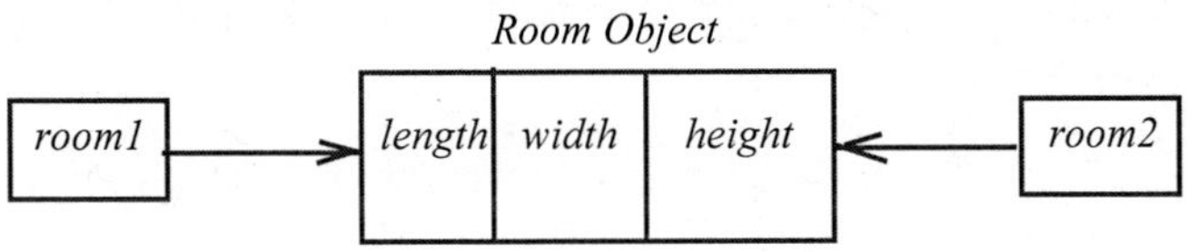

Figure 2.2 Both room1 & room2 Refer to the Room object

We would like to mention one more point here. Both *room1* and *room2* refer to the same object but have no other link to each other, e.g. consider the following code fragment:

Room room1 = new Room();
Room room2 = room1;
//......some..................................
//......other..................................
//......code..................................
room1 = null;

Thus, *room1* has been unhooked from the original object and set to '*null*' without affecting the original object or *room2*. In other words, *room2* still points to the original object *Room*.

2.3 CREATING/ADDING METHODS

In section 2.1, we had briefly mentioned that classes consist of data / instance variables and the methods that operate on this data. The most general form of a method is:

```
data_type method_name(partameter_list)
{
        // body of method
}
```

where, *data_type* is the type of the data returned by the method (incase, no *data_type* is returned, *void* must be mentioned instead), *method_name* is the name of the method while *parameter_list* is the list of parameters / arguments separated by commas. In case a method has no parameters, the *parameter_list* shall be empty. Methods having a return *data_type* other than *void* return a value to the calling routine in the following way:

```
return value;
```

where, *value* is the value that is returned by the method.

We shall now add a method to Example 25 (*RoomDemo.java*) discussed earlier in this chapter (section 2.l.1 to be precise) to come up with the following example (Example 28).

<u>Example 28</u>

```
// RoomMethod.java
/* Simple Demonstration of a method;
Author: Arunesh; Date: 03/03/2011  */
class Room
{
        double length;
        double width;
        double height;

        double Volume()
        {
                System.out.println("Volume of room = ");
                return length * width * height;
        }
}
class RoomMethod
{
        public static void main (String args[ ])
        {
                double v;

                Room room = new Room();
```

```
        /* assigning values/dimensions to the room */
        room.length = 100;
        room.width = 50;
        room.height = 10;

        /* computing and printing/outputting the volume of the room */
        v = room.Volume();
        System.out.println(v);
    }
}
```

Output:

Volume of room = 50000.0

/* In the preceding example (Example 28), we introduced the method *Volume()* that computes the volume of the Room as a product of its length, width, and height. */

2.3.1 Parametrized Methods

Incidentally, the aforesaid method *Volume()* has no parameter_list, that is to say, it is without any parameters. We shall next be considering methods parameter_list, viz., parameterized methods as in the following example (Example 29).

Example 29

```
// RoomParameters.java
/* Simple Demonstration of a Parameterized method;
Author: Arunesh; Date: 03/03/2011 */
class Room
{
    double length;
    double width;
    double height;

    double Volume()
    {
        return length * width * height;
    }
    /* Room Dimensions */
    void Dim(double l, double w, double h)
    {
        length = l;
        width = w;
        height = h;
    }
}
```

```
class RoomParameters
{
        public static void main (String args[ ])
        {
                double v;

                Room room = new Room();
                /* assigning values/dimensions to the room */
                room.Dim(100, 50, 10);

                /* computing and printing/outputting the volume of the room */
                v = room.Volume();
                System.out.println("Volume of room = " + v);
        }
}
```

Output:

```
        Volume of room = 50000.0
```

/* In the preceding example (Example 28), the parametrized *Dim()* method is very useful. In the statement: *room Dim(100, 50, 10);*

100 is copied into parameter l, 50 into w, and 10 into h. These values of l, w, and h are subsequently passed on to length, width, and height, respectively. */

2.3.2 Overloading Methods

We are permitted in Java to use two or more methods (in the same class) sharing a common name but different parameter_lists / return types. This phenomenon is referred to as method overloading. We take up Example 30 to understand this phenomenon further.

Example 30

```
// Meth_Overload.java
/* Simple Demonstration of the concept of Method Overloading;
Author: Arunesh; Date: 03/03/2011 */
class Over
{
        void secure()
        {
                System.out.println("Without Parameters");
        }
        void secure (int x)
        {
                System.out.println("With one Parameter:\t" + x);
        }
```

```
        void secure(int x, int y)
        {
                System.out.println("With two Parameters:\t" + x + "\t" + y + "\tSum:\t" +
                                                                                (x + y));
        }
        void secure (double d)
        {
                System.out.println("With Parameter of type double:\t" + d + "\tCube\t: "
                                                                                (d * d * d));
        }
}
class Meth_Overload
{
        public static void main (String args[])
        {
                Over over = new Over();

                over.secure();          // form 1: without parameters

                over.secure(5);         // form2: with one parameter

                over.secure(3, 10);     // form3: with two parameters

                over.secure(1.5);       // form4: with parameter of type double
        }
}
```

Output:

```
        Without Parameters
        With one Parameter:     5
        With two Parameters:    3       10      Sum:    13
        With Parameter of type double: 1.5      Cube:   3.375
```

/* In the preceding example (Example 30), the four overloaded forms/versions of the method *secure()* were used. The results are based on the particular form of these four versions. */

2.3.3 Passing Objects as Parameters

As seen earlier, we have passed simple data types as parameters to methods. However, it is possible to pass even objects as parameters to methods as seen in Example 31.

Example 31

```
// Object_Pass.java
/* Simple Demonstration of the concept of passing objects as parameters;
Author: Arunesh; Date: 03/03/2011 */
class secure
{
        double a, b;

        secure(double x, double y)          /* this is a user-defined constructor; you may refer to
                                            the next section for more information about
                                            constructors.*/
        {
                a = x;
                b = y;
        }

        int equality(secure s)
        {
                if (s.a == a && s.b == b)
                        return 1;
                else
                        return 0;
        }
}
class Object_Pass
{
        public static void main (String args[])
        {
                secure s1 = new secure(10.5, -10.5);
                secure s2 = new secure(-10.5, 10.5);
                secure s3 = new secure(10.5, -10.5);

                System.out.println("s1 equals s2:\t" + s1.equality(s2);
                System.out.println("s1 equals s3:\t" + s1.equality(s3);
                System.out.println("s2 equals s3:\t" + s2.equality(s3);
        }
}
```

Output:

```
s1 equals s2:   0
s1 equals s3:   1
s2 equals s3:   0
```

/* Here, we are treating 1 as boolean value "True" and 0 as boolean value "False" The *equality()* method inside the class secure compares two objects and returns the result. One of the most common uses of object parameters involves constructors. For an example in this regard, refer section 2.4.3. */

2.4 CONSTRUCTORS

In order that all the variables in a class are initialized each time an instance is created, we need constructors. Constructors have the same name as the class and their syntax is similar to that of a method. In the following example program (Example 32), we shall make use of and add a constructor to the code of Example 29 discussed earlier (section 2.3.1 to be precise).

Example 32

```
// Constr.java
/* Simple Demonstration of the concept of Constructors;
Author: Arunesh; Date: 03/03/2011 */
class Room
{
        double length;
        double width;
        double height;

        /* Constructing a Room */
        Room()
        {
                System.out.println("Construction of room");
                length = 100;
                width = 50;
                height = 10;
        }

        void Volume()
        {
                double v;
                v = length * width * height;
                System.out.println("Volume of room = " + v);
        }
}

class Constr
{
        public static void main (String args[ ])
        {
                Room room1, room2;
```

```
        room1 = new Room();
        room2 = new Room();

        room1.Volume();
        room2.Volume();
    }
}
```

Output:

```
    Construction of room
    Construction of room
    Volume of room = 50000.0
    Volume of room = 50000.0
```

2.4.1 Parametrized Constructors

In Example 32 discussed in the preceding section, the constructor *Room()* is quite handy to have but it fails on one account. All the rooms are set with the same dimensions. Solution to this problem is the use of parametrized constructors as seen in Example 33.

Example 33

```
// Param_Constr.java
/* Simple Demonstration of the concept of Parametrized Constructors;
Author: Arunesh; Date: 03/03/2011 */
class Room
{
    double length;
    double width;
    double height;

    /* Parametrized Constructor */
    Room(double l, double w, double h)
    {
        length = l;
        width = w;
        height = h;
    }

    double Volume()
    {
        double v;
        v = length * width * height;
        return v;
    }
}
```

```
class Param_Constr
{
        public static void main (String args[ ])
        {
                Room room1, room2;

                room1 = new Room(20, 10, 5);
                room2 = new Room(10, 5, 3);

                System.out.println("Volume of room1 = " + room1.Volume());
                System.out.println("Volume of room2 = " + room2.Volume());
        }
}
```

Output:

```
        Volume of room1 = 1000.0
        Volume of room2 = 150.0
```

2.4.2 Overloading Constructors

Overloading constructors is akin to method overloading. But, the question arises as to why should we overload constructors?

The reason is simple. In Example 33 (refer preceding section), we used a parametrized constructor. in fact, we provided for three parameters pertaining to the three dimensions of a room, namely, length, width, and height, respectively. Now, suppose that the room has the same length, width, and height. In that case, there is no need for to pass three parameters. One is enough.

Moreover, suppose we do not know the three parameters but still want to use default initial values. In other words, we want to use a constructor without any parameters.

All this is possible by overloading the *Room()* constructor as seen in Example 34.

Example 34

```
// Constr_Overload.java
/* Simple Demonstration of the concept of Constructor Overloading;
Author: Arunesh; Date: 03/03/2011  */
class Room
{
        double length;
        double width;
        double height;

        /* Constructor with three parameters*/
        Room(double l, double w, double h)
        {
                length = l;
```

```
                width = w;
                height = h;
        }

        /* Constructor with a single parameter*/
        Room(double lwh)
        {
                length = lwh;
                width = lwh;
                height = lwh;
        }

        /* Constructor with NO parameters*/
        Room()
        {
                // using -1 to indicate uninitialized room
                length = -1;
                width = -1;
                height = -1;
        }

        /* compute and return Volume */
        double Volume()
        {
                double v;
                v = length * width * height;
                return v;
        }
}
class Constr_Overload
{
        public static void main (String args[ ])
        {
                Room room1, room2, room3;
                /* create rooms using the various constructors */
                room1 = new Room(20, 10, 5);
                room2 = new Room(4);
                room3 = new Room();
                /* output the volumes of the three rooms */
                System.out.println("Volume of room1 = " + room1.Volume());
                System.out.println("Volume of room2 = " + room2.Volume());
                System.out.println("Volume of room3 = " + room3.Volume());
        }
}
```

Output:

Volume of room1 = 1000.0
Volume of room2 = 64.0
Volume of room3 = -1.0

/* As the output confirms, the appropriate constructor is called for each of the three rooms according to the number of parameters when there is a call to the dynamic operator *new*.
*/

2.4.3 Object Parameters involving Constructors

As already mentioned in section 2.3.3, a most common use of object parameters involves constructors. In this regard, it is pertinent to point out that we may need to construct a new object such that it is initially the same as some existing object, that is to say, we may need to construct a clone of an object. For this, we must define a constructor which takes an object of its class as a parameter. As a case in point, consider Example 35.

Example 35

```
// Constr_Overload2.java
/* Simple Demonstration of the concept of Constructor Overloading;
Author: Arunesh; Date: 03/03/2011  */
class Room
{
	double length;
	double width;
	double height;

	/* Constructor with three parameters*/
	Room(double l, double w, double h)
	{
		length = l;
		width = w;
		height = h;
	}

	/* Constructor with a single parameter*/
	Room(double lwh)
	{
		length = lwh;
		width = lwh;
		height = lwh;
	}
```

```
        /* Constructor with NO parameters*/
        Room()
        {
                // using -1 to indicate uninitialized room
                length = -1;
                width = -1;
                height = -1;
        }

        /* Construct clone of an object */
        Room (Room r)           // pass Room object as parameter to constructor
        {
                length = r.length;
                width = r.width;
                height = r.height;
        }

        /* compute and return Volume */
        double Volume()
        {
                double v;
                v = length * width * height;
                return v;
        }
}
class Constr_Overload2
{
        public static void main (String args[ ])
        {
                Room room1, room2, room3, roomclone;
                /* create rooms using the various constructors */
                room1 = new Room(20, 10, 5);
                room2 = new Room(4);
                room3 = new Room();

                roomclone = new Room(room1);

                /* output the volumes of the four rooms */
                System.out.println("Volume of room1 = " + room1.Volume());
                System.out.println("Volume of room2 = " + room2.Volume());
                System.out.println("Volume of room3 = " + room3.Volume());
                System.out.println("Volume of roomclone = " + roomclone.Volume());
        }
}
```

Output:

Volume of room1 = 1000.0
Volume of room2 = 64.0
Volume of room3 = -1.0
Volume of roomclone = 1000.0

2.5 OTHER MISCELLANEOUS TOPICS

In this section, we shall take up six different topics, each under a different subsection. First, we shall consider the 'this' keyword. Then, we shall take up the concept of "garbage collection". In the thid subsection, we shall consider the 'finalize()' method as well as the 'final' keyword. Calling by value/reference shall be our fourth topic of discussion. After this, we shall take a close look at "Access Control". Finally, we shall try to understand as to what is meant by 'static'?

2.5.1 'this' Keyword

When a method is called, it is, implicitly passed an argument which is a reference to the calling object, that is to say, the object on which the method is called. This reference is referred to as *this*. We shall try to understand *this* with the help of the following *case study*.

this Keyword - A *CASE STUDY*

In this *case study*, we first take up an example program (Example 36) as a simple practical use of the 'this' keyword. Then, based on this example, we will take our study of 'this' further.

Example 36

```
// this_Demo.java
/* Simple Demonstration of 'this' Keyword;
Author: Arunesh; Date: 15/03/2011 */
class Power
{
        double base;
        int exp;
        double value;

        Power(double b, int e)
        {
```

```
                this.base = b;
                this.exp = e;
                this.value = 1;

                if (e == 0)
                        return;
                for ( ; e > 0; e--)
                        this.value = this.value * b;
        }

        double Get_Power()
        {
                return this.value;
        }
}
class this_Demo
{
        public static void main(String args[])
        {
                Power i = new Power(3.3, 0);
                Power j = new Power(4.9, 1);
                Power k = new Power(6.0, 2);

                System.out.println(i.base + " to the power " + i.exp + " = " +
                                                                i.Get_Power());
                System.out.println(j.base + " to the power " + j.exp + " = " +
                                                                j.Get_Power());
                System.out.println(k.base + " to the power " + k.exp + " = " +
                                                                k.Get_Power());

        }
}
```

Output:

3.3 to the power 0 = 1.0
4.9 to the power 1 = 4.9
6.0 to the power 2 = 36.0

/* Inside *Get_Power()*, in the statement:

return this.value;

this refers to the object on which *Get_Power()* was invoked so that *this.value* refers to that object's copy of *value*, e.g., when *Get_Power()* is invoked on k, then this in the preceding statement refers to k. Writing the statement without *this* is just a shorthand, so to say. We can rewrite the entire Power class without using *this* reference as follows:

```
class Power
{
    double base;
    int exp;
    double value;

    Power(double b, int e)
    {
        b = base;
        e = exp;
        value = 1;
        if (e == 0)
            return;

    for ( ; e > 0; e--)
            value = value * b;
    }
    double Get_Power()
    {
        return value;
    }
}
```

Although we gain nothing significant in the above case (Example 36) by using *this*, there are certain situations that warrant the use of *this*.

Sometimes, it may happen that we wish to use the same name for instance variables as well as the parameters or the local variables (and, in Java, such use is syntactically absolutely valid). In such a situation, the local name hides or covers the inbstance variable name. However, we can have access to the hidden instance variable by referring to it by *this*. For example, cosider the *Power()* constructor written in the following way:

```
Power(double base, int exp)
{
    this.base = base;
    this.exp = exp;
    /* note that this.base and this.exp refer to the instance variables
    here and not to the local parameters */
    value = 1;
```

```
        if (exp == 0)
                return;
        for ( ; exp > 0; exp--)
                value = value * base;
    }
```

Thus, we can see that *this* is used to uncover or make the hidden instance variables visible (parameter names being the same as instance variable names has hidden them).
*/

2.5.2 Garbage Collection

We already know how to create an object and reference it from a variable with the help of *new* operator. When an object has no variable references left to it, it becomes eligible for "Garbage Collection". This is a very significant feature of the Java language that reclaims the memory used by an object automatically.

In some languages such as C++, one has to manually release and delete a dynamically allocated object. If this is not performed correctly, objects might be deleted accidentally even though some variables still hold references to them or we may soon run out of memory if a program happens to run for a long duration.

For such reasons, explicit deletion of objects is not allowed in Java. It is a major benefit of the Java language as it eliminates one of the common and potential sources of programming errors and mistakes.

However, we need to tell you here that an object may not be immediately garbage-collected even though it has no references by variables. Indeed, the task of *garbage collection* is remote-controlled by the JVM, which actually determines how to schedule and execute *garbage collection* (you may recall that the concept of JVM was introduced in chapter 1).

Moreover, different vendors employ different strategies and algorithms to implement *garbage collection*, the actual selection being made by the JVM developer. Thus, different run-time Java implementations may adopt varied approaches towards *garbage collection*, but, in general, you need not worry about it while programming in Java.

We now take up Example 37 to illustrate the concept of *garbage collection* further.

Example 37

```
// Demo_Garbage_Collection.java
/* Simple Demonstration of Garbage Collection;
Author: Arunesh; Date: 15/03/2011  */
class Demo_Garbage_Collection
{
        public static void main(String args[])
        {
                Double d = new  Double(4. 0);  // Double is a wrapper for
                                                // floatuing point values of type double
                System.out.println(d);
                d = new Double(3.0);
                System.out.println("Double(4.0) can be recycled, that is, garbage-collected!");
                System.out.println(d);
        }
}
```

Output:

```
        4.0
        Double(4.0) can be recycled, that is, garbage-collected!
        3.0
```

/* The output is quite self-explanatory. It suggests the fact that once *d* has been assigned a reference to the object created by *Double(3.0)*, the *Double(4.0)* object can be recycled or garbage-collected!
*/

2.5.3 'finalize()' Method / 'final' Keyword

This section has two subsections. In the first one, we are going to discuss the '*finalize()*' method while in the second, we shall try to understand the '*final*' keyword.

2.5.3.1 'finailize()' Method

Java provides for a process referred to as *finalization*. This mechanism allows us to define certain actions that shall take place just when an object is going to be recycled by the garbage collector. The mechanism is perfomed by means of the *finalize()* method. Whenever an object of the corresponding class is about to be reclaimed by the garbage collector, the Java run-time calls this method. The most general form of the method is as follows:

```
protected void finalize()
{
        // finalization actions/code goes here, if any
}
```

You will be wondering about the use of the keyword *protected*. The *protected* specifier has been used to prevent access to the *finalize()* method by any code defined outside the corresponding class. We shall learn in more detail about this access specifier in the section on "Access Control" (section 2.5.5 to be precise).

We must sound a word of caution here. The *finalize()* method is invoked just prior to garbage collection and, in general, is not called when an object goes out of scope. So, we can never know when or if at all, *finalize()* will get executed.

For the aforesaid reason, you must not solely rely on *finalize()* under normal circumstances but provide for other channels of releasing system resources used by any object.

Next, we take up Example 38 to illustrate *finalize()* further.

Example 38

```
// Finalize.java
/* Simple Demonstration of finalize() method;
Author: Arunesh; Date: 15/03/2011 */
class Demo_finalize
{
        int i;

        Demo_finalize(int z)
        {
                i = z;
        }
        protected void finalize()          // called when an object is recycled
        {
                System.out.println(i + " Finalized");
        }
        void generate(int z)               // generates an object which gets destroyed
                                           // immediately
        {
                Demo_finalize obj = new Demo_finalize(z);
        }
}
class Finalize
{
        public static void main(String args[])
        {
                int ctr;
                Demo_finalize o = new Demo_finalize(o);
                /* Generate a high population of objects;
                at some point, garbage collection shall take place. */
                for (ctr = 1; ctr < 1000000; ctr++)
                        o.generate(ctr);
        }
}
```

/* Note that the number of objects that are generated might have to be increased further in order that garbage collection is forced to occur!
*/

2.5.3.2 *'final' Keyword*

The 'final' keyword can be used in three different ways:

(a) To create named constants;
(b) To prevent method overriding; and,
(c) To prevent inheritance.

We discuss each of these one by one.

(a) Creating named constants: The keyword *final* can be applied to variables in order to create what are known as named constants. This is done by preceding the variable name with *final*. In such cases, the value of the variable cannnot be changed throughout the lifetime of the program. Variables declared as *final* do not occupy space on a per-instance basis. Thus, they are essentially constants (similar to *const* in C, C++, C#) and must be initialized at the time of declaration.

In Java, a common coding convention being followed is to use all uppercase identifiers for such *final* variables.

Next, we take up a practical *case study* to illustrate the use of such *final* named constants.

final named constants - A *CASE STUDY*

In this *case study*, we shall take up a practical case example program (Example 39), which shall serve to demonstrate the use of creating named constants using the keyword - *final*.

Example 39

```
// Demo_Final.java
/* Simple Demonstration of 'final' keyword;
Author: Arunesh; Date: 15/03/2011 */
class Error_Message
{
        // declaring final variables or named constants
        final int OUTERR = 0;
        final int INERR = 1;
        final int DISKERR = 2;
        final int INDEXERR = 3;
```

```
        String messages[ ] = {
                                        "Output error",
                                        "Input error",
                                        "Disk full",
                                        "Index out-of-bounds"
                              };

        String Get_Error_Message(int z)
        // return appropriate Error message
        {
                if (z >= 0 & z < messages.Length)
                        return messages[z];
                else
                        return "Invalid Error CODE";
        }
}
class Demo_Final
{
        public static void main(String args[])
        {
                Error_Message error = new Error_Message();

                /* using final variables or named constants */
                System.out.println(error.Get_Error_Message(error.INERR));
                System.out.println(error.Get_Error_Message(error.INDEXERR));
                System.out.println(error.Get_Error_Message(error.DISKERR));
                System.out.println(error.Get_Error_Message(error.OUTERR));

                System.out.println();
                System.out.println(error.Get_Error_Message(error.4));
        }
}
```

Output:

Input error
Index out-of-bounds
Disk full
Output error

Invalid Error CODE

/* You can see for yourself how the *final* constants have been used in *main()*. Since they happen to be members of the *Error_Message* class, they have been accessed through an object of this class.
*/

(b) Preventing method overriding: We can use *final* as a modifier at the beginning of a method declaration to prevent it from being overridden. (For more details, refer next chapter)

(c) Preventing inheritance: We can precede the declaration of a class with the keyword *final* to prevent it from being inherited. (For more details, refer next chapter)

2.5.4 "Call by Value" / "Call by Reference"

Essentially, there are two ways that an argument can be passed to a subroutine/function/method in any computer language. The first one copies the *value* of the argument into the formal parameter of the subroutine, and whence, changes made to the formal parameter of the subroutine have no effect on the original argument. This technique of passing an argument is referred to as "call by value".

In the second approach, instead of the value of the argument, a reference to the argument is passed to the formal parameter of the subroutine. The subroutine uses this reference to access the actual argument specified in the call, and whence, changes made to the formal parameter of the subroutine will affect the original argument used to call the subroutine. Quite appropriately, this technique of passing an argument is termed as "call by reference".

In Java, when a simple type is passed to a method, it is done using "call by value". On the other hand, objects are passed using "call by reference". We shall take up suitable examples illustrating both these techniques in the following two subsections.

2.5.4.1 "Call by Value"

Simple types are passed by value. Example 40 is a case in point.

Example 40

```
// Call by Value.java
/* Simple Demonstration of "call by value" technique of passing arguments;
Author: Arunesh; Date: 15/03/2011 */
class A
{
        void m(int y, int z)
        {
                y /= 4;
                z *= 4;
        }
}
```

```
class Call_by_Value
{
        public static void main(string args[])
        {
                A a = new A();

                int i = 20;
                int j = 5;

                System.out.println("Before calling:");
                System.out.println("i = " + i);
                System.out.println("j = " + j);

                System.out.println();

                a.m(i, j);
                // method m() called by value;
                // note that i, j are simple int type

                System.out.println("After calling:");
                System.out.println("i = " + i);
                System.out.println("j = " + j);
        }
}
```

Output:

```
        Before calling:
        i = 20
        j = 5

        After calling:
        i = 20
        j = 5
```

/* You can see for yourself how the operations occurring inside method *m()* have had no effect on the values of i and j used in the call, that is to say, their values did not change to 5 and 20, respectively, after the call.
*/

2.5.4.2 *"Call by Reference"*

Objects are passed by reference. Example 41 is a case in point.

<u>Example 41</u>

```
// Call_by_Reference.java
/* Simple Demonstration of "call by reference" technique of passing arguments;
Author: Arunesh; Date: 15/03/2011 */
class A
{
        int i;
        int j;

        A(int i, int j)
        {
                this.i = i;
                this.j = j;
                // note the use of the 'this' keyword to uncover the instance variables i and j
        }

        void m(A aa)
        {
                aa.i /= 4;

                aa.j *= 4;
        }
}
class Call_by_Reference
{
        public static void main(String args[])
        {
                A a = new A(20, 5);

                System.out.println("Before calling:");
                System.out.println("a.i = " + a.i);
                System.out.println("a.j = " + a.j);
                System.out.println();

                a.m(a);
                // method m() called by reference;
                // note that a is an object

                System.out.println("After calling:");
                System.out.println("a.i = " + a.i);
                System.out.println("a.j = " + a.j);
        }
}
```

Output:

Before calling:
a.i = 20
a.j = 5

After calling:
a.i = 5
a.j = 20

/* You can see for yourself how the operations occurring inside method *m()* have had an effect/impact on the object a used in the call as the argument.
*/

2.5.5 A Look at "Access Control"

We have already learnt that by means of encapsulation, data is linked to the code which operates upon it. Another important feature provided by encapsulation is "access control". By means of encapsulation, we can control what parts of a program are to be allowed access to the members of a class. Now, you might be wondering - "What is the use of access control?". Well, the simple answer is preventing misuse. For instance, we can prevent misuse of data by allowing access to it only via a well-defined collection/set of methods. The classes described so far do not meet this objective completely. We think, now, it's time to introduce you to the technique by means of which you can precisely, exactly, and accurately control access to the different members of a class.

It is the *access specifier* that determines how a member can be accessed. Java has three access specifiers - *public, protected,* and *private*. It also specifies a default access level. We shall be discussing *protected* in the next chapter on inheritance *(since protected comes into play only when inheritance is involved).*

When a member of a class is specified as *public*, it can be accessed by any other code. However, when a member of a class is modified by the *private* specifier, it can only be accessed by other members within its class.

In case no access specifier is provided, then the default access level is used, that is to say, the member is treated as *public* within its own package but cannot be accessed outside this package (packages have been discussed in a separate chapter along with interfaces; here, suffice it to say that a package is, in general, a grouping of classes).

You must have understood by now why *main()* has always been specified as *public*. It is called by the Java run-time system - a code outside the program. *Whence, the public specifier.*

An access specifier must come before rest of a member's type declaration/specification.

For example:

```
public double d;
private int i;
private double method_1(char c)
{
        // code for method_1
}
```

Now, we pick up an example (Example 42) to demonstrate the effects of *public* and *private* access.

Example 42

```
// Demo_Access_Control.java
/* Simple Demonstration of "access control";
Author: Arunesh; Date: 16/03/2011  */
class A
{
	int i;			// default access
	public int j;		// public access
	private int k;		// private access

	/* methods to access k */
	void set_k(int z)
	{
		k = z;
		// set value of k
	}

	int get_k()
	{
		return k;
		// get value of k
	}
}
class Demo_Access_Control
{
	public static void main(String args[])
	{
		A a = new A();

		a.i = 100;
		a.j = 50;
		// i and j having default and public access, respectively, can be accessed directly

		// a.k = 20;
		// Error! Therefore, commented out!!
		// k is private and can be accessed only through the methods of its class!!!

		a.set_k(20);
		// now, fine
```

```
            System.out.println("i = " + a.i);
            System.out.println("j = " + a.j);
            System.out.println("k = " + a.get_k());
      }
}
```

Output:

```
      i = 100
      j = 50
      k = 20
```

/* Inside class *A*, *i* uses default access, which for this case is the same as declaring it *public*; *j* is explicitly declared to be *public*; however, *k* has *private* access and whence, cannot be accessed by any code outside of its class. It is, for this reason, that inside the *Demo_Access_Control* class, *k* cannot be used directly but has to be accessed through its public methods, *set_k()* and *get_k()*, instead. Whence, the need for commenting out the line:

a.k = 20;

which would otherwise cause an access violation and conseqently lead to a compile-time error.

*/

2.5.6 What is 'static'?

Suppose, we want to define a class member that is to be used independently og any object of the class. We know that, in general, a class member has to be accessed through an object of its class. However, *static* allows us to create a member that can be used by itself, without any reference to a specific instance. Such a member can be created by preceding its declaration with the keyword *static*.

When a member is declared to be *static*, it can be accessed before any objects of its class are created, and without reference to any object. Both methods and variables can be declared *static*.

The most common and significant instance of a *static* member is *main()*; it is declared as *static* since it must be called before any objects exist. In fact, it is called by the operating system even before the program begins.

Outside the class, to use a *static* member, we need vonly specify the name of the class followed by the dot (.) operator. No objects need to be created. For instance, if we want to assign the value *60* to a *static* variable called *timer*, which is part of the *clock* class, we can do so by simply stating: *clock.timer = 60;*

This format is the same as the one we use to access normal instance variables via an object except that the class name is used. A *static* method can be called/invoked in the same way: *class_name.method_name()*, where *class_name* is the name of the class in which the *static* method called *method_name()* is declared.

Variables declared to be *static* are global in nature, essentially. When an object is created, no copy of the *static* variable is made; in fact, all instances of the class share the same *static* variable. We shall now take up an example (Example 43) to differentiate between a *static* variable and an instance variable.

Example 43

```
// Demo_Static1.java
/* Simple Demonstration of a static variable;
Author: Arunesh; Date: 16/03/2011 */
class Stat_Var
{
        int i;              // instance variable

        static int j;       // static variable; only one copy of j for all objects of Stat_Var to share
}

class Demo_Static1
{
        public static void main(String args[])
        {
                Stat_Var obj1 = new Stat_Var();
                Stat_Var obj2 = new Stat_Var();

                obj1.i = 50;
                obj2.i = 30;
                // obj1 and obj2 have their own copies of instance variable i

                System.out.println("obj1.i and obj2.i are independent");
                System.out.println("obj1.i = " + obj1.i);
                System.out.println("obj2.i = " + obj2.i);

                obj1.j = 20;

                System.out.println("Static Variable j is shared by obj1 and obj2);
                System.out.println("obj1.j = " + obj1.j);
                System.out.println("obj2.j = " + obj2.j);

                Stat_Var.j = 10;

                System.out.println("Static Variable j can be accessed through its class
                                                                        Stat_Var");
                System.out.println("Stat_Var.j = " + Stat_Var.j);
                System.out.println("obj1.j = " + obj1.j);
                System.out.println("obj2.j = " + obj2.j);
        }
}
```

Output:

```
obj1.i and obj2.i are independent
obj1.i = 50
obj2.i = 30
Static Variable j is shared by obj1 and obj2
obj1.j = 20
obj2.j = 20
Static Variable j can be accessed through its class Stat_Var
Stat_Var.j = 10
obj1.j = 10
obj2.j = 10
```

/* In this case (Example 42), you can see that the *static* variable *j* is shared by both the objects *obj1* and *obj2*. Changing it through one instance changes it for all instances. Moreover, *j* can be accessed either through an object name, as in *obj1.j*, or through its class name, as in *Stat_Var.j*.
*/

Now, we come to the difference between a *static* method and a normal method. The obvious difference is that the *static* method can be called through its class name, without any object of that class having been created. The *sqrt()* method is a *static* method in Java's standard *Math* class (we have already used the *sqrt()* method in Example 24 of chapter 1).

Next, we take up an example (Example 44), which creates a *static* method.

Example 44

```
// Demo_Static2.java
/* Simple Demonstration of a static method;
Author: Arunesh; Date: 16/03/2011 */
class Stat_Method
{
	static int value = 1000; // a static variable

	static int val_mult2()	// a static method
	{
		return value * 2;
	}
}

class Demo_Static2
{
	public static void main(String args[])
	{
```

```
        System.out.println("Value = " + Stat_Method.value);
        System.out.println("Stat_Method.val_mult2() = " + Stat_Method.val_mult2());

        Stat_Method.value = 2;

        System.out.println("Value = " + Stat_Method.value);
        System.out.println("Stat_Method.val_mult2() = " + Stat_Method.val_mult2());
    }
}
```

Output:

```
Value = 1000
Stat_Method.val_mult2() = 2000
Value = 2
Stat_Method.val_mult2() = 4
```

There are several restrictions imposed on methods declared as *static*:

(i) they can call only other *static* methods;
(ii) they must access only *static* data; and,
(iii) they cannot refer to *this* or *super* in any way.
(the keyword *super* is related to inheritance and is discussed in the next chapter)

Consider the following class where the *static* method *num_div_value()* is illegal:

```
class Stat_Error
{
        int num = 3000;                    // normal instance variable
        static int value = 3;      // static variable

        /* error in the following static method */
        static num_div_value()
        {
                return (num / value);      // compile-time error!
        }
}
```

In this case (*Stat_Error* class), *num* is a normal instance variable that cannot be accessed within the *static* method *num_div_value()*.

Now, we shall take up *static* blocks.

It may happen that a class requires some kind of initialization before getting ready to create objects. For instance, it might have to connect to a remote site or it might need to initialize certain *static* variables before any of its *static* methods comes into play. Such situations are handled by means of a *static* block. A *static* block is executed as soon as the class is first loaded. Example 45 illustrates the concept of *static* blocks in ample measure.

Example 45

```
// Demo_Static3.java
/* Simple Demonstration of a static block;
Author: Arunesh; Date: 16/03/2011  */
class Stat_Block
{
	static int sq_rootof4;
	static int sq_rootof9;

	static		// static block; this is executed first when the class is loaded
	{
		System.out.println("Static Block Executed");
		sq_rootof4 = Math.sqrt(4.0);
		sq_rootof9 = Math.sqrt(9.0);
		// Math.sqrt() takes a double argument and returns a double but it will be
		// truncated to int as both the static variables are int type
	}

	Stat_Block(String message)
	{
		System.out.println(message);
	}
}
class Demo_Static3
{
	public static void main(String args[])
	{
		Stat_Block sb = new Stat_Block("Constructor Executed");

		System.out.println("Square root of 4 = " + Stat_Block.sq_rootof4);
		System.out.println("Square root of 9 = " + Stat_Block.sq_rootof9);
	}
}
```

Output:

```
	Static Block Executed
	Constructor Executed
	Square root of 4 = 2
	Square root of 9 = 3
```

/* Thus, you can see that even before any objects are constructed, the *static* block gets executed first!.
*/

2.6 Varargs: VARIABLE LENGTH ARGUMENTS

JDK5 has introduced a new feature which has simplified the creation of methods with a variable number of arguments. This feature is known as *varargs* and the corresponding method is known as a *varargs method*. Before JDK5, two approaches were in vogue for handling such a situation. First, if the maximum number of arguments was small/known, you could use overloaded methods. Second, if the maximum number of arguments was large/unknown, the arguments were put into an array and the array was then passed to the method. This approach is illustrated by means of the following example (Example 46).

Example 46

```
// Traditional_Varargs..java
/* Using an array to pass a variable number of arguments;
Author: Arunesh; Date: 04/07/2011  */
class Traditional_Varargs
{
        static void vTraditional(int vargs[ ])
        {
                System.out.print("Number of arguments = " + vargs.Length +
                                                                        " Contents: ");
                for (int z : vargs)
                        System.out.print(z + " ");
        System.out.println();
        }
        public static void main(String args[])
        {
                int i1[ ] = {5, 10};
                int i2[ ] = {5};
                int i3[ ] = {};
                vTraditional(i1);           // 2 args
                vTraditional(i2);           // 1 arg
                vTraditional(i3);           // No args
        }
}
```

Output:

```
        Number of arguments = 2 Contents: 5 10
        Number of arguments = 1 Contents: 5
        Number of arguments = 0 Contents:
```

In the above example (Example 46), the method *vTraditional()* is passed its arguments through the array *vargs*. It requires for the manual packaging of these arguments into the array before calling the method. This approach is rather tedious and error prone as well.

The *varargs* approach introduced by JDK5 offers a simpler and better way. Here, a variable length argument is specified by three periods *(...)*, e.g., *vTraditional()* using this approach can be written as:

static void vTraditional(int ... vargs)

which tells the compiler that *vTraditional()* can be called with zero ao more arguments. As a consequence, *vargs* is implicitly declared as an array of type *int*. Thus, inside *vTraditional()*, *vargs* is accessed using the normal array syntax. Example 46 is rewritten as Example 47 using the new *vargs* approach.

Example 47

```
// New_Varargs..java
/* Demonstrate the new vargs approach;
Author: Arunesh; Date: 04/07/2011  */
class New_Varargs
{
        static void vNew(int ... vargs)
        {
                System.out.print("Number of arguments = " + vargs.Length +
                                                                        " Contents: ");
                for (int z : vargs)
                        System.out.print(z + " ");
        System.out.println();
        }
        public static void main(String args[])
        {
                vNew(5, 10);    // 2 args
                vNew(5);        // 1 arg
                vNew();         // No args
        }
}
```

Output:

```
        Number of arguments = 2 Contents: 5 10
        Number of arguments = 1 Contents: 5
        Number of arguments = 0 Contents:
```

/* You can see that the output remains the same as in the preceding case (Example 46).
*/

A method can have normal parameters along with a variable-length parameter. But, the variable-length parameter must be the last one in the method declaration. Also, you cannot have a method with more than one variable-length parameters. Again, a method with a variable-length parameter/argument can be overloaded as illustrated in Example 48.

Example 48

```
// Overload_Varargs_Method..java
/* Demonstrate the overloading of a varargs method;
Author: Arunesh; Date: 04/07/2011 */
class Overload_Varargs_Method
{
        static void vA(int z)
        {
                System.out.println("vA(int): " + "No. of arguments = 1"
                                                + " Contents: " + z);
        }

        static void vA(int ... vargs)
        {
                System.out.print("vA(int ...): " + "No. of arguments = "
                                                + vargs.Length + " Contents: ");
                for (int z : vargs)
                        System.out.print(z + " ");
        System.out.println();
        }

        static void vA(String message, int ... vargs)
        {
                System.out.print("vA(String, int ...): " + "No. of arguments = "
                                + (vargs.Length + 1) + " Contents: " + message + " ");
                for (int z : vargs)
                        System.out.print(z + " ");
        System.out.println();
        }

        static void vA(boolean ... vargs)
        {
                System.out.print("vA(boolean ...): " + "No. of arguments = "
                                        + vargs.Length + " Contents: ");
                for (int z : vargs)
                        System.out.print(z + " ");
        System.out.println();
        }

        public static void main(String args[])
        {
                vA(5);
```

```
            vA();
            vA(5, 10);
            vA("Test", 5, 10, 15);
            vA(false, true, true);
        }
}
```

Output:

```
        vA(int): No. of arguments = 1 Contents: 5
        vA(int ...): No. of arguments = 0 Contents:
        vA(int ...): No. of arguments = 2 Contents: 5 10
        vA(String, int ...): No. of arguments = 4 Contents: Test 5 10 15
        vA(boolean ...):  No. of arguments = 3 Contents: false true true
```

You may also note that overloading a method taking a variable number of arguments can lead to unexpected results involving ambiguity as it is possible to create an ambiguous call to an overloaded *varargs method*, e,g., consider the following code:

```
static void vA(int ... vargs)
{
        ..........................
        ..........................
}
static void vA(boolean ... vargs)
{
        ..........................
        ..........................
}
vA(1);  // Okay, call to vA(int ... vargs)
vA(true, false);           // Okay, call to vA(boolean ... vargs)
vA();   /* Error! Inherently ambiguous as this call can be translated into a call to
        both vA(int ... vargs) and vA(boolean ... vargs) */
```

Before concluding this section, we want to highlight one more example of ambiguity:

```
static void vA(int i, int ... vargs)
{
        ..........................
        ..........................
}
static void vA(int ... vargs)
{
        ..........................
        ..........................
}
```

The preceding two overloaded versions of *vA()* are inherently ambiguous even though the first one takes a normal parameter. Consider the following call:

vA(5);

/ Error! Ambiguous as it could mean both vA(int, int ...) and vA(int ...) and the compiler cannot resolve this problem! */*

Such ambiguity errors could force you to use two different method names and avoid overloading. Also, in some cases, such errors throw open a conceptual flaw in your code, which you need to take care of, and quite urgently too!

2.7 WINDING IT UP!

In this section, we introduce the feature - recursion, and one of the best sorting algorithms - Quicksort, which relies on recursion.

First, try to understand what is meant by recursion? Simply put, recursion is the idea/ process of defining something in its own terms. From the point of view of Java, we can say that a method that calls itself is recursive.

When a method calls itself, new local parameters and variables are allocated space on the stack and the method gets executed with these new variables from scratch. In other words, only the arguments are new and a recursive call does not make a new copy of the method per se.

Recursive version of many methods might get executed slower than their iterative counterparts due to the additional overhead of repeated function/subroutine/method calls. In fact, in case a recursive routine runs out of proportion, it could cause a stack overrun or the stack may even get exhausted, in which case the Java run-time system shall raise an exception (the concept of exceptions is dealt with in a separate chapter).

However, recursive methods have certain advantages as well. First, they sometimes lead to clearer and simpler solutions to problems than their iterative counterparts. To take a case in point, the Quicksort algorithm is well nigh difficult to imlement the iterative way. Again, certain situations, especially those related to AI (Artificial Intelligence) lend themselves more easily to recursive solutions. And, last but not the least, some persons have the knack of thinking recursively rather than iteratively.

Some while ago, in fact, in the preceding paragraph, we mentioned the Quicksort algorithm. Quicksort is built upon the notion of partitions. Suppose, we have to sort an array of integer values. The idea is to select a value, called the comparand, and then to prtition the array into two sections. For optimal results, the partition value or the comparand should be exactly in the middle of the range of the array values. (in the worst case, the value is chosen at one extremity; even in this case, Quicksort works correctly, but obviously, it shall take more time to execute.)

All elements less than or equal to the partition value are placed on one side and all those greater than the comparand are put on the other. This procedure is repeated for each remaining section until the array is completely sorted. For instance, given the array:

9, 5, 4, 1, 3, 2; and, using 4 as the partition value or the comparand, the first pass of Quicksort would return the array as:

2, 3, 1, 4, 5, 9; this procedure is repeated for each of the two sections - 2, 3, 1 and 4, 5, 9. You can easily see that the routine is essentially, recursive i nature. In fact, the cleanest implementation of Quicksort is a recursive method.

Another classic example of a recursive method is computing the factorial of a whole number, say w (the factorial of w is the product of all the whole numbers between 1 and w, e.g., the factorial of 3 is 1 * 2 * 3 = 6).

We shall now show you how to compute the factorial of any whole number by means of a recursive method in a Java program (refer Example 49).

Example 49

```
// Recursion.java
/* Simple Demonstration of a recursive method;
Author: Arunesh; Date: 17/03/2011 */
class Fact
{
        int factorial(int w)        // recursive method
        {
                int n;

                if (w == 1)
                        return 1;

                n = factorial(w - 1) * w;

                return n;
        }
}
class Recursion
{
        public static void main(String args[])
        {
                Fact fact = new Fact();

                System.out.println("3 factorial = " + fact.factorial(3));
                System.out.println("4 factorial = " + fact.factorial(4));
        }
}
```

Output:

```
        3 factorial = 6
        4 factorial = 24
```

/* While writing recursive methods, take care to include an *if* statrement somewhere to force the method to return without executing the recursive call. Otherwise, once the recursive method is invoked, it shall never return, causing an exception, as already explained. This is one of the most common programming mistakes made in writing recursive methods.

You will probably be wondering as to how to get out of such a situation. The catch lies in using liberal *println()* statements in your program so that you can actually get to see what is going on at run-time and abort the program once you realize you have ignorantly made an error.
*/

PRACTICAL SESSION

1. What do you mean by a class, an object, and a method?
   Illustrate giving suitable example(s).

2. (a) Design a class to represent a Student. Include the following memers:
   Data Members
   * Name of the student
   * Marks in Physics
   * Marks in Chemistry
   * Marks in Mathematics

   Methods
   * To assign initial values
   * To compute total, average, and percentage marks
   * To display the data (both given and computed)

   (b) Modify part (a) above to incrporate a constructor for assigning initial values.

3. (a) What is the role of static member variables and methods?
   Explain citing suitable example(s) to support your answer.
   (b) What restrictions are imposed on static methods?
   Give an example where a restriction has been violated.

4. Debug the following code fragments:
   (a)
```
class Assign
{
        public static void main(String args[])
        {
                System.out.println("Assign");
        }
};
```
   (b)
```
class Value
{
```

```
        public double value = 9.25;
        public double getvalue()
        {
                System.out.println("Value = " + value);
        }
        public static void main(String args[])
        {
                Value v = new Value();
                v.getvalue();
        }
}
```

(c)
```
public class Name
{
        public String make(String st)
        {
                return("make Name");
        }
        public void make(int i)
        {
        }
        public void make(double d)
        {
        }
}
```

5. Give the <u>output</u> of the following program code:

```
class Jim
{
        public void write(char c)
        {
                System.out.println(c);
        }
        public void write(double d)
        {
                System.out.println(d);
        }
        public void write(int i)
        {
                System.out.println(i);
        }
```

```
        public void write()
        {
                System.out.println("void");
        }

        public void write(String st)
        {
                System.out.println(st);
        }

        public static void main(String args[])
        {
                Jim baker;
                char chr = 'c';
                int num = 99;
                double pie = 3.142;
                String str = "String";
                baker.write();
                baker.write(chr);
                baker.write(num);
                baker.write(pie);
                baker.write(str);
                baker.write();
        }
}
```

6. Point out the error(s), if any, in the following code fragment:

```
class abc
{
        int y;
        private int z;
        void set_abc(int a)
        {
                y = a;
                z = y;
        }
        int get_abc()
        {
                return z;
        }
}
```

7. Create a class Book having the following members:
   <u>Data Members</u>
   * Title
   * Author
   * Publisher
   * Status

   <u>Methods</u>
   * *read_data()* // to assign initial values
   * *get_status()* // to get the Status of any given book
   * *display_data()* // to display the data in the suggested format as follows:

Status of Books

Title	*Author*	*Publisher*	*Status*
....	....	....	....
....	....	....	....

<u>Note</u>: You may assume convenient Status codes such as *available, issued, damaged* etc.

8. What do you understand by overloading? When and under what conditions is it legal?

9. (a) Distinguish between a constructor and a method.
   (b) Is there any limit on the number of constructors a class may have? Why or why not? Elucidate.
   (c) Can a class have only one default constructor? Give suitable reason(s) in support of your answer.

10. Assume that *timer* is an object of the class *clock*.
    Show how to declare the above mentioned assumption using:
    (a) A single statement; and,
    (b) Two separate statements.

11. What is the keyword used to create named constants? Write a program illustrating the use of named constants.

12. Define recursion. Under what circumstances is it useful?
    Elaborate its relative advantages and disadvantages. Also, write a suitable program to illustrate a recursive mnethod.

13. Write True (T) or False (F) for each of the following statements:

    (a) *class* is a keyword/reserved word.
    (b) *main()* is the first method executed in an application.
    (c) *finalize()* method always gets executed when an object goes out of scope.

14. What do you understand by garbage collection?
Is garbage collection a major adsvantage of the Java language? Elaborate.
When is an object garbage collected?

15. Can we have nested classes? If no, why not? If yes, illustrate with a suitable example.

16. Is the use of the *this* keyword redundant?
If not, give an instance where it shall prove to be effective.

17. Distinguish between 'call by value' and 'call by reference' giving appropriate examples, wherever necessary.

18. Briefly explain the 'access control' mechanism supported by Java.

19. Implement:
(a) a *Url* class for representing Internet Uniform resource Locator addresses;
(b) an *Email* class for representing email addresses;
(c) a *Phone* class for representing telephone numbers; and,
(d) an *Address* class for representing postal mailing addresses.

Tip: You may make suitable *assumptions,* wherever necessary.

20. Implement a class for celestial bodies (Sun, planets, their moons etc.).
Include the fields:

```
private String name;
private double mass;            // in grams
private double diameter;        // in kilometers
private double period;          // in earth days
private CelestialBody orbits;
private CelstialBody next;
private CelestialBody list;
```

/* the list field should maintain a linked list of all the objects created while the next field should contain the next object in the linked list. */

Chapter 3

INHERITANCE

3.0 INTRODUCTION

As already pointed out in chapter 1, inheritance is one of the pillars of object-oriented programming (OOP) as it allows the creation of class hierarchies paving the way for reuse of code. The inherited class is known as the superclass and the inheriting class is known as the subclass. You must have understood by now that each subclass is a specialized form of its corresponding superclass. The subclass, in fact, inherits all the public/protected members of the superclass, inclusive of instance variables and methods, and adds its own unique members. In this way, the subclass can use the code of its superclass without having to rewrite it. This is what is meant by code reusability.

3.1 FUNDAMENTALS OF INHERITANCE

The most general form of a subclass declaration that inherits a superclass is as follows:

```
class subclass_name extends superclass_name
{
        // body of subclass
}
```

Note the use of the extends keyword. To inherit a superclass, we incoporate its definition into the subclass by means of this keyword (i.e., “extends”).

Also, note that being a superclass for a subclass does not imply that the superclass cannot be used by itself. Moreover, a sublass can be a superclass for another subclass leading to an hierarchy of inhertance. But, note that no class can be a superclass of itself. Also, unlike C++ but like C#, Java does not support multiple inheritance, i.e., the inheritance of multiple superclasses into one (single) subclass. Let us now consider a simple example (Example 50) demonstrative of the concept of inheritance.

Example 50

```
// Inheritance.java
/* Simple Demonstration of inheritance;
Author: Arunesh; Date: 21/03/2011  */
class X            // superclass
{
        int a, b;
        void disp_ab()
        {
                System.out.println("a = " + a);
                System.out.println("b = " + b);
        }
}
class Y extends X          // subclass
{
        int c;
        void disp_c()
        {
                System.out.println("c = " + c);
        }

        void add_abc()
        {
                System.out.println(a + b + c);
        }
}
class Inheritance
{
        public static void main (String args[ ])
        {
                X super_x = new X();
                Y sub_y = new Y();

                /* the superclass X can be used on its own, that is, by itself */
                super_x.a = 5;
                super_x.b = 10;
                System.out.println("super_x contains:");
                super_x.disp_ab();

                /* the subclass Y can access all the public instance variables of its superclass
                X */
                sub_y.a = 2;
                sub_y.b = 3;
```

```
            sub_y.c = 5;
            System.out.println("sub_y contains:");
            sub_y.disp_ab();          // subclass Y can access all public methods of its
                                      // superclass X
            sub_y.disp_c();
            System.out.println("Sum of a, b, c in sub_y:");
            sub_y.add(abc();
        }
}
```

Output:

```
        super_x contains:
        a = 5
        b = 10
        sub_y contains:
        a = 2
        b = 3
        c = 5
        Sum of a,b, c in sub_y:
        10
```

/* You can easily see that the subclass Y includes all members of its sduperclass - X. It is only for this reason that *sub_y* can access *a, b,* and call *disp_ab()*. Moreover, inside *add_abc()*, *a* & *b* can be used directly as though they were part and parcel of Y. You can also see that X, even though it acts as the superclass for Y, is a stand-alone, completely independent class and can be used by iteself, as such. */

In Example 50, we saw that the subclass Y has access to all the members of its superclass X. However, a class member declared as private, shall be private to its class and not accessible by any code outside its class, inclusive of any subclasses. Consider Example 51 as a case in point.

Example 51

```
// MemberAccess.java
/* Demonstrates that private members are private to their class;
Author: Arunesh; Date: 21/03/2011  */
class X           // superclass
{
        int a;              // by default, a is public
        private int b;      // b is private to X
        void assign(int m, int n)
        {
                a = m;
```

```
            b = n;
        }
}
class Y extends X           // subclass
{
        int sum;
        void add_ab()
        {
            sum = a + b;    // shall result in compile-time error!
                            // X's b is inaccessible to Y
        }
}
class MemberAccess
{
        public static void main (String args[ ])
        {
            Y sub_y = new Y();

            sub_y.assign(5, 10);
            sub_y.add_ab();

            System.out.println("Sum of a, b = " + sub_y.sum);
        }
}
```

/* Here, reference to *b* inside *add_ab()* method of Y causes an access violation since *b* is private to X. Whence, the program shall not compile! */

To demonstrate the power of inheritance, let us add a fourth element, namely, *colour* to the final version of the *Room* class developed in Example 35 (refer previous chapter). Thus, the new class in Example 52 shall contain the *length, width, height,* and *colour* of a room.

<u>Example 52</u>

```
// RoomColourDemo.java
/* Room is extended to include colour;
Author: Arunesh; Date: 21/03/2011  */
class Room
{
        double length;
        double width;
        double height;
```

```
/* constructor with three parameters; used when all dimensions are given */
Room(double l, double w, double h)
{
        length = l;
        width = w;
        height = h;
}

/* constructor with a single parameter; used to create a cubic room when only one
dimension is specified */
Room(double lwh)
{
        length = lwh;
        width = lwh;
        height = lwh;
}

/* constructor with no parameters; used when no dimension is given */
Room()
{
        // using -1 to indicate an uninitialized room
        length = -1;
        width = -1;
        height = -1;
}

/* construct clone of a Room object */
Room(Room r)  // pass Room object as parameter to constructor
{
        length = r.length;
        width = r.width;
        height = r.height;
}

/* compute and print volume of room */
void Volume()
{
        double v;
        v = length * width * height;
        System.out.println("Volume = " + v);
}
}
```

```
/* Now, room is extended to include the colour attribute */
class RoomColour extends Room
{
        int colour ;        // colour of room
        /* You might wonder why colour is taken to be an integer type. This is done for the sake
        of ease and efficiency, e.g., 1 can be the code for "Blue", 2 for "Green", 3 for "Red",
        4 for "Yellow", and so on. */

        // constructor for RoomColour
        RoomColour(double l, double w, double h, int c);
        {
                length = l;
                width = w;
                height = h;

                colour = c;
        }

        // Display colour of room
        void Disp_Colour()
        {
                System.out.println("Colour = " + colour);
        }
}
class RoomColourDemo
{
        public static void main (String args[ ])
        {
                RoomColour room1, room2;
                room1 = new RoomColour(20, 10, 5, 4);
                room2 = new RoomColour(2, 1, 5, 2);

                /* output volume & colour of the two rooms */
                System.out.println("Volume & Colour of room1:");
                room1.Volume();
                room1.Disp_Colour();
                System.out.println();
                System.out.println("Volume & Colour of room2:");
                room2.Volume();
                room2.Disp_Colour();
        }
}
```

<u>Output</u>:

Volume & Colour of room1:
Volume = 1000.0
Colour = 4

Volume & Colour of room2:
Volume = 10.0
Colour = 2

/* *RoomColour* inherits all the features of *Room* and adds the *colour* element/component. Simply put, *RoomColour* can extend *Room* to meet its own specific requirements, and does not need to re-create all the characteristics found in *Room*. */

The essence of inheritance lies in the fact that once we have a superclass defining the most general aspects of an object, then that superclass can be extended to form specialized subclasses, with each subclass adding its own unique features/attributes. For example, the following class inherits *Room* and adds a '*purpose*' attribute.

```
/* The following class extends Room to add purpose */
class RoomPurpose extends Room
{
	String purpose;		// purpose of room

	// constructor for RoomPurpose
	RoomPurpose(double l, double w, double h, String p)
	{
		length = l;
		width = w;
		height = h;

		purpose = p;
	}

	// Display purpose of room
	void Disp_Purpose()
	{
		System.out.println("Purpose: " + purpose);
	}

}
```

We would like to mention one more point before rounding off this section, that is, a superclass variable can reference a subclass object. This feature of inheritance can come quite handy in a variety of situations some of which we shall take up later on in this chapter.

For now, consider the following simple example (Example 53) in this context.

Example 53

```
// DemoReference.java
/* A reference variable of a superclass can be assigned a reference to any subclass derived
from it;
Author: Arunesh; Date: 21/03/2011 */
/* The following class extends Room to add purpose */
class DemoReference
{
        public static void main(String args[])
        {
                RoomPurpose roompurpose = new RoomPurpose(1, 2, 3, "Dining");

                Room room = new Room();

                /* we are assuming here that the superclass Room and the subclass
                RoomPurpose have already been declared as defined earlier in this section. */

                System.out.println("Volume & purpose of roompurpose:");
                roompurpose.Volume();
                roompurpose.Disp_Purpose();

                room = roompurpose; // assigning RoomPurpose reference to Room
                                // which is valid since RoomPurpose is a subclass of Room

                System.out.println("Volume & purpose of room:");
                room.Volume(); // this is fine since Volume() is defined in Room
                // room.Disp_Purpose(); // this line has been commented out, being invalid,
                                        // since Room has no knowledge of purpose
                                        // or Disp_Purpose()
        }
}
```

/* What is important here is to understand the fact that it is the type of the reference variable and not the type of the object it is referring to, which determines the members that are accessible. When a reference to a subclass object is made to a superclass reference variable, only those parts of the object shall be accessible which are defined by the superclass. This makes sense logically as well since the superclass is not in the know-how of what a subclass has added to it.

This is the simple reason why *room* cannot access *purpose/Disp_Purpose()* even though it refers to a *RoomPurpose* object.

*/

3.2 THE KEYWORD - 'super'

The Java keyword, *super*, can be used in two distinct ways. Its first use is to call/invoke a super class constructor. Its second use lies in accessing a member of the superclass that has been hidden by a member of the subclass having the same name. We shall examine these two uses in the following two subsections.

3.2.1 Invoking Superclass Constructors Using 'super'

In all the examples discussed in the previous section, viz., section 3.1, the subclasses of the superclass Room were not implemented very efficiently, e.g., the constructor for *RoomColour* or *RoomPurpose* initializes the *length, width,* and *height* fields of *Room()* explicitly. This duplication of code in *RoomColour* or *RoomPurpose* is not only inefficient but it means that these subclasses must be granted access to all these fields/members of the superclass *Room*. But, there are occasions when the superclass would like to keep its data members private and not allow its subclasses to have access to them. Fortunately, Java provides a solution to this problem by use of the keyword - 'super'. A subclass can call a constructor defined in its immediate superclass by using super as given below:

super(argument_list);

where, *argument_list* specifies any arguments needed by the constructor in the superclass. Note that *super()* must be the first statement executed in the constructor of the subclass always.Also, note that since constructors can be overloaded, *super()* can be invoked using any form defined by the superclass. The constructor that matches the parameters/arguments shall be the one to get executed. As an example, consider the following complete version of *RoomPurpose* (Example 54). You may carefully note the fact that the fields/members *length, width,* and *height* have been declared private in the superclass *Room*.

Example 54

```
// RoomPurposeSuperDemo.java
/* Room is extended to include purpose;
Author: Arunesh; Date: 21/03/2011  */
class Room
{
        private double length;          // now private
        private double width;           // now private
        private double height;          // now private

        /* constructor with three parameters; used when all dimensions are given */
        Room(double l, double w, double h)
        {
                length = l;
                width = w;
                height = h;
        }
```

```
    /* constructor with a single parameter; used to create a cubic room when only one
    dimension is specified */
    Room(double lwh)
    {
            length = lwh;
            width = lwh;
            height = lwh;
    }

    /* constructor with no parameters; used when no dimension is given */
    Room()
    {
            // using -1 to indicate an unitialized room
            length = -1;
            width = -1;
            height = -1;
    }

    /* construct clone of a Room object */
    Room(Room r)  // pass Room object as parameter to constructor
    {
            length = r.length;
            width = r.width;
            height = r.height;
    }

    /* compute and print volume of room */
    void Volume()
    {
            double v;
            v = length * width * height;
            System.out.println("Volume = " + v);
    }
}
/* The following class extends Room to add purpose */
class RoomPurpose extends Room
{
    String purpose;             // purpose of room

    // constructor when all parameters have been given
    RoomPurpose(double l, double w, double h, String p)
    {
```

```
                super(l, w, h);   // invoke superclass constructor
                purpose = p;
        }

        /* constructor used to create a cubic room */
        Room(double lwh, String p)
        {
                super(lwh);
                purpose = p;
        }

        /* constructor with no parameters; default constructor */
        RoomPurpose()
        {
                super();
                purpose = "null";        // Use null to indicate uninitialized purpose
        }

        /* construct clone of a RoomPurpose object */
        RoomPurpose(RoomPurpose rp)
                                // pass RoomPurpose object as parameter to constructor
        {
                super(rp);
                purpose  = rp.purpose;
        }

        // Display purpose of room
        void Disp_Purpose()
        {
                System.out.println("Purpose: " + purpose);
        }

}
class RoomPurposeSuperDemo
{
        public static void main (String args[ ])
        {
                RoomPurpose rp1, rp2, rp3, rp4, rp5;
                rp1 = new RoomPurpose(20, 10, 5, "Dining");
                rp2 = new RoomPurpose(2, 1, 5, "FOR Rest");
                rp3 = new RoomPurpose();
                rp4 = new RoomPurpose(4, "Painting");
                rp5 = new RoomPurpose(rp2);
```

```
        /* output volume & purpose of the five rooms */

        System.out.println("Volume & Purpose of rp1:");
        rp1.Volume();
        rp1.Disp_Purpose();
        System.out.println();

        System.out.println("Volume & Purpose of rp2:");
        rp2.Volume();
        rp2.Disp_Purpose();
        System.out.println();

        System.out.println("Volume & Purpose of rp3:");
        rp3.Volume();
        rp3.Disp_Purpose();
        System.out.println();

        System.out.println("Volume & Purpose of rp4:");
        rp4.Volume();
        rp4.Disp_Purpose();
        System.out.println();

        System.out.println("Volume & Purpose of rp5:");
        rp5.Volume();
        rp5.Disp_Purpose();
    }
}
```

Output:

```
    Volume & Purpose of rp1:
    Volume = 1000.0
    Purpose: Dining

    Volume & Purpose of rp2:
    Volume = 10.0
    Purpose: FOR Rest

    Volume & Purpose of rp3:
    Volume = -1.0
    Purpose: null

    Volume & Purpose of rp4:
    Volume = 64.0
    Purpose: Painting
```

Volume & Purpose of rp5:
Volume = 10.0
Purpose: FOR Rest

The above output is more or less self-explanatory except for the following code:

```
/* construct clone of a RoomPurpose object */
RoomPurpose(RoomPurpose rp)
                    // pass RoomPurpose object as parameter to constructor
{
        super(rp);
        purpose  = rp.purpose;
}
```

You may carefully note that *super()* is invoked with an object of type *RoomPurpose*, and not of type *Room*. This still works and calls the constructor *Room(Room r)*. We have already explained the fact that a superclass variable can reference any object of its subclasses. That's why we are able to pass a *RoomPurpose* object to the *Room* constructor method. Of course, you are right when you say that *Room* knows only about its own members.

/* Herein, we sum up the key ideas about/behind *super()*.

A subclass using *super()* is invoking the constructor of its immediate superclass. In fact, *super()* always refers to the superclass that is immediately above the invoking/calling class. This holds good in a multilevel hierarchy as well.

Finally, *super()* must always be the first statement to be executed within a subclass constructor.

*/

3.2.2 Accessing a Hidden Name Using 'super'

We have already told you about one use of *super* in the previous section, viz., invoking superclass constructors. Now, we introduce you to a second use of *super* that acts in a manner similar to *this* except for the fact that it always refers to the superclass of the subclass in which it is used. The most general form of this usage is:

super.member

where, *member* can either be an instance variable or a method. This form of *super* applies mostly to cases in which member names of a subclass hide members by the same name in the superclass. For instance, we shall see in Example 56 how to overcome name hiding (as seen in Example 55) by use of the keyword *super*.

Example 55

```
// Inherit_Name_Hiding.java
/* Illustrates Name Hiding as Related to Inheritance;
Author: Arunesh; Date: 21/03/2011 */
```

```
class Sup                        // superclass
{
        int m = 0;
        int n = 0;
}
class Sub extends Sup            // subclass
{
        int m, n;                // these m, n in Sub hide the m, n in Sup

        Sub(int y, int z)        // constructor
        {
                m = y;           // m in Sub
                n = z;           // n in Sub
        }
        void disp()
        {
                System.out.println("m in subclass = " + m);
                System.out.println("n in subclass = " + n);
        }
}
class Inherit_Name_Hiding
{
        public static void main(String args[] )
        {
                Sub obj = new Sub( 13, 16);

                obj.disp();
        }
}
```

Output:

```
        m in subclass = 13
        n in subclass = 16
```

/* Since the subclass *Sub* defines its own instance variables *m & n*, it hides the *m & n* in superclass *sup*. Whence, when *disp()* is invoked on an object of type *Sub*, it is not the values of *m & n* as defined in *Sup* that are displayed, but the ones as defined by *Sub*.
*/

Example 56

// Name_Uncovering.java
/ Illustrates use of super to overcome Name Hiding as Related to Inheritance;*
*Author: Arunesh; Date: 21/03/2011 */*

```
class Sup                       // superclass
{
        int m = 0;
        int n = 0;
}
class Sub extends Sup           // subclass
{
        int m, n;               // these m, n in Sub hide the m, n in Sup

        Sub(int y, int z)       // constructor
        {
                super.m = y;    // use of  super uncovers the m in Sup
                super.n = z;    // use of super uncovers the n in Sup
                m = z;          // m in Sub
                n = y;          // n in Sub

        }
        void disp()
        {
                System.out.println("m in superclass = " + super.m);     // displays m in Sup
                System.out.println("m in subclass = " + m);             // displays m in Sub
                System.out.println();
                System.out.println("n in superclass = " + super.n);     // displays n in Sup
                System.out.println("n in subclass = " + n);             // displays n in Sub
        }
}
class Name_Uncovering
{
        public static void main(String args[] )
        {
                Sub obj = new Sub( 13, 16);

                obj.disp();
        }
}
```

Output:

```
        m in superclass = 13
        m in subclass = 16

        n in superclass = 16
        n in subclass = 13
```

/* As this output verifies and confirms, even though the insatance variables *m & n* in the subclass *Sub* hide the *m & n* in the superclass *Sup,* the use of the *super* keyword has allowed access to the instance variables *m & n* as defined in *Sup.*
*/

We had said while outlining the general form of the usage of *super* that even hidden methods could be uncovered by its use. Consider Example 57 as a case in point. Herein, as before, class *Sub* inherits *Sup,* and both *Sub* and *Sup* declare a method called *disp().* Inside *Sub's disp(),* the version of *disp()* defined by *Sup* is called via the use of *super.*

Example 57

```
// Method_Name_Uncovering.java
/* Illustrates use of super to overcome Name Hiding in methods as Related to Inheritance;
Author: Arunesh; Date: 21/03/2011 */
class Sup                       // superclass
{
        int m = 0;
        void disp()             // disp() in Sub
        {
                System.out.println("m in superclass = " + m);   // displays m in Sup
        }
}
class Sub extends Sup           // subclass
{
        int m;                  // this m in Sub hides the m in Sup
        Sub(int y, int z)       // constructor
        {
                base.m = y;     // use of  super uncovers the m in Sup
                m = z;          // m in Sub
        }
        void disp()             // this disp() in Sub hides the disp() in Sup
        {
                base.disp();    // calling disp() in Sup; use of super uncovers the disp() in Sup
                System.out.println("m in subclass = " + m);      // displays m in Sub
        }
}
class Method_Name_Uncovering
{
        public static void main( String args[])
        {
                Sub obj = new Sub( 13, 16);

                obj.disp();
        }
}
```

Output:

m in superclass = 13
m in subclass = 16

/* As the above output verifies and confirms, even though the method *disp()* in the superclass *Sup* is hidden by the method *disp()* in the subclass *Sub,* the use of the *super* keyword has allowed for its use inside *Sub* without ambiguity. In fact, the following line:

super.disp(); // calling disp() in Sup; use of super uncovers the disp() in Sup

calls and invokes the superclass version of *disp()*.
*/

3.3 MULTILEVEL INHERITANCE

So far, we have been using a simple class hierarchy consisting of only one derived class and one base class. But we can have as many layers of inheritance as we like. Thus, if **X, Y,** and **Z** are three classes, then it is, in general, possible to derive **Y** from **X** and **Z** from **Y**. In such a case, **Z** shall inherit all traits and aspects of **Y** and **X**.

The class *RoomPurpose* can be used as a superclass to encapsulate still more special features such as *rent* (of the room in rupees per month) in its subclass *RoomRent* as seen in Example 58. You may again note carefully that the field/member *purpose* has been made private within *RoomPurpose*.

Example 58

```
// RoomRentDemo.java
/* Room is extended to include purpose;
Author: Arunesh; Date: 21/03/2011 */
class Room
{
        private double length;
        private double width;
        private double height;

        /* constructor with three parameters; used when all dimensions are given */
        Room(double l, double w, double h)
        {
                length = l;
                width = w;
                height = h;
        }

        /* constructor with a single parameter; used to create a cubic room when only one
        dimension is specified */
        Room(double lwh)
        {
```

```
            length = lwh;
            width = lwh;
            height = lwh;
        }

        /* constructor with no parameters; used when no dimension is given */
        Room()
        {
            // using -1 to indicate an unitialized room
            length = -1;
            width = -1;
            height = -1;
        }

        /* construct clone of a Room object */
        Room(Room r)  // pass Room object as parameter to constructor
        {
            length = r.length;
            width = r.width;
            height = r.height;
        }

        /* compute and print volume of room */
        void Volume()
        {
            double v;
            v = length * width * height;
            System.out.println("Volume = " + v);
        }
}

/* The following class extends Room to add purpose */
class RoomPurpose extends Room
{
        private String purpose;             // purpose of room now private

        // constructor when all parameters have been given
        RoomPurpose(double l, double w, double h, String p)
        {
            super(l, w, h);   // invoke superclass constructor
            purpose = p;
        }
```

```
        /* constructor used to create a cubic room */
        Room(double lwh, String p)
        {
                super(lwh);
                purpose = p;
        }

        /* constructor with no parameters; default constructor */
        RoomPurpose()
        {
                super();
                purpose = "null";        // Use null to indicate uninitialized purpose
        }

        /* construct clone of a RoomPurpose object */
        RoomPurpose(RoomPurpose rp)
                                // pass RoomPurpose object as parameter to constructor
        {
                super(rp);
                purpose  = rp.purpose;
        }

        // Display purpose of room
        void Disp_Purpose()
        {
                System.out.println("Purpose: " + purpose);
        }

}

/* The following class extends RoomPurpose to add rent */
class RoomRent extends RoomPurpose
{
        double rent;            // rent of room

        // constructor when all parameters have been given
        RoomRent(double l, double w, double h, String p, double r)
        {
                super(l, w, h, p);          // invoke superclass constructor
                rent = r;
        }
```

```
        /* constructor used to create a cubic room */
        Room(double lwh, String p, double r)
        {
                super(lwh, p);
                rent = r;
        }

        /* constructor with no parameters; default constructor */
        RoomRent()
        {
                super();
                rent = -1;          // Use -1 to indicate uninitialized rent
        }

        /* construct clone of a RoomRent object */
        RoomRent(RoomRent rr)          //pass RoomRent object as parameter to constructor
        {
                super(rr);
                rent  = rr.rent;
        }

        // Display rent of room
        void Disp_Rent()
        {
                System.out.println("Rent = " + rent);
        }

}
class RoomRentDemo
{
        public static void main (String args[ ])
        {
                RoomRent rr1, rr2, rr3, rr4, rr5;
                rr1 = new RoomRent(20, 10, 5, "Dining", 500);
                rr2 = new RoomRent(2, 1, 5, "FOR Rest", 3000);
                rr3 = new RoomRent();
                rr4 = new RoomRent(4, "Painting", 20000);
                rr5 = new RoomRent(rr4);
                /* output volume,  purpose, and rent of the five rooms */
                System.out.println("Volume, Purpose, and Rent of rr1:");
                rr1.Volume();
                rr1.Disp_Purpose();
                rr1.Disp_Rent();
                System.out.println();
```

```
            System.out.println("Volume, Purpose, and Rent of rr2:");
            rr2.Volume();
            rr2.Disp_Purpose();
            rr2.Disp_Rent();
            System.out.println();

            System.out.println("Volume, Purpose, and Rent of rr3:");
            rr3.Volume();
            rr3.Disp_Purpose();
            rr3.Disp_Rent();
            System.out.println();

            System.out.println("Volume, Purpose, and Rent of rr4:");
            rr4.Volume();
            rr4.Disp_Purpose();
            rr4.Disp_Rent();
            System.out.println();

            System.out.println("Volume, Purpose, and Rent of rr5:");
            rr5.Volume();
            rr5.Disp_Purpose();
            rr5.Disp_Rent();
      }
}
```

Output:

```
      Volume, Purpose, and Rent of rr1:
      Volume = 1000.0
      Purpose: Dining
      Rent = 500.0

      Volume, Purpose, and Rent of rr2:
      Volume = 10.0
      Purpose: FOR Rest
      Rent = 3000.0

      Volume, Purpose, and Rent of rr3:
      Volume = -1.0
      Purpose: null
      Rent = -1.0

      Volume, Purpose, and Rent of rr4:
      Volume = 64.0
      Purpose: Painting
      Rent = 20000.0
```

Volume, Purpose, and Rent of rr5:
Volume = 64.0
Purpose: Painting
Rent = 20000.0

/* Because of inheritance, the class *RoomRent* can reuse the code of the previously defined classes, *Room* and *RoomPurpose,* adding only the specific extra information it requires for its own, particular application.

There is one more important point to note: *super()* always refers to the constructor in the nearest and closest superclass. In this particular case/example, *super()* in *RoomRent* calls the relevant constructor in *RoomPurpose*; *super()* in *RoomPurpose* calls the relevant constructor in *Room.* Further, in such a multilevel class hierarchy, if a superclass constructor needs some parameters, then all subclasses must pass all those parameters from the bottom-up, that is to say - up the line. This holds good whether or not a subclass requires parameters of its own.
*/

3.3.1 Order of Constructor Execution

In a multilevel hierarchy, another important question is: when a subclass object is created, whose constructor is executed first? The superclass one or the subclass one? For instance, if **X** is the base class and **Y** is the derived class, then, is **X**'s constructor called before **Y**'s, or **Y**'s constructor called before **X**'s? The answer is quite logical and simple, i.e. constructors are called in the order of derivation from the superclass to the subclass. Again, this order remains unchanged irrespective of the fact whether *super()* is used or not. If it is not used, the default (parameterless) constructor of each superclass shall be executed. Example 59 illustrates the order of constructor execution which is in the order of derivation from the uppermost superclass down to to the subclass at the lowest rung of the class hierarchy.

Example 59

```
// Order_of_Constructors.java
/* Illustrates the order of Constructor execution;
Author: Arunesh; Date: 21/03/2011 */
class Sup                    // superclass
{
        Sup()
        {
                System.out.println("Constructor Sup() called");
        }
}
```

```
class Sub1 extends Sup                    // subclass 1
{
    Sub1()
    {
        System.out.println("Constructor Sub1() called");
    }
}
class Sub2 extends Sub1                   // subclass 2 derived from subclass 1
{
    Sub2()
    {
        System.out.println("Constructor Sub2() called");
    }
}
class Order_of_Constructors
{
    public static void main(String args[] )
    {
        Sub2 obj = new Sub2();
    }
}
```

Output:

```
Constructor Sup() called
Constructor Sub1() called
Constructor Sub2() called
```

/* Thus, it can be seen that the constructors are called in the order of derivation from *Sup()* down to *Sub2()*. And, it makes logical sense as well that the constructors are executed in the order of derivation. Since a superclass has no know-how of any subclass, any initialization it needs to do is distinct, separate and possibly a prelude to any initialization by the subclass; whence, it must be executed first.
*/

3.4 OVERRIDDEN METHODS

An overridden method is one that is declared in a superclass and redefined in one or more subclasses. It is possible for each subclass to have its own version of an overidden method. While overriding a method, the name, return type, and signature of the overriding method has to be the same as that of the method being overridden.If this is not the case, then the two methods are simply overloaded.

When an overridden method is called from within a subclass, it will always refer to the version of that method as defined by the subclass. If you wish to access the superclass version of an overridden method, you can do so using *super*. For a case in point, refer Example 57 elaborated earlier in this chapter.

Overridden methods are important considering the fact what happens when one is called through a superclass reference. Java decides at run-time in such a situation as to which version of the overidden method to call depending upon the type of the object referred to by the reference. This concept is known as *dynamic method dispatch*. This ('dynamic method dispatch') forms the technique by means of which a call to an overridden method is resolved at run-time, rather than at compile-time. Its importance is overwhelming since it is the mechanism by which Java is able to implement *run-time polymorphism*. And, polymorphism is essential to OOP as it allows a general class to specify methods that shall be common to all of its derivatives, while allowing the subclasses to have their own implementation of some or all of those methods. In this way, Java supports the "*one interface, multiple methods*" aspect of polymorphism through overridden methods.

In order to enforce polymorphism successfully, it is of paramount importance to understand that the superclasses and subclasses form a class hierarchy moving from lesser to greater specialization. In fact, the superclass provides all the components and elements which a subclass can make use of directly. It also defines those methods that the subclass can implement by itself, that is to say, on its own. In this manner, the subclass is allowed maximum flexibility without compromising on the consistency of the interface. Whence, a superclass, by a suitable combination of inheritance and overridden methods, can define the broad and general outline of the methods that shall be put to use by all of its subclasses.

Before moving on to a practical case study (Example 61) of *method overriding* in the next subsection, it would be useful to look at a case of *dynamic method dispatch* (Example 60).

Example 60

```
// DynamicMethodDispatch.java
/* Illustrates dynamic method dispatch;
Author: Arunesh; Date: 21/03/2011 */
class Sup                       // superclass
{
        void disp()
        {
                System.out.println("disp() in superclass");
        }
}

class Sub1 extends Sup          // subclass 1
{
        void disp()             // Override disp() in superclass : note the use of override
        {
                System.out.println("disp() in subclass 1");
        }
}
```

```
class Sub2 extends Sup              // subclass 2
{
        void disp()                 // Override disp() in superclass : note the use of override
        {
                System.out.println("disp() in subclass 2");
        }
}
class DynamicMethodDispatch
{
        public static void main(String args[])
        {
                Sup Supobj = new Sup();         // object of type Sup
                Sub1 Sub1obj = new Sub1();      // object of type Sub1
                Sub2 Sub2obj = new Sub2();      // object of type Sub2
                Sup SupReference;               // reference of type superclass Sup

                SupReference = Supobj;          // SupReference refers to Sup object
                SupReference.disp();            // call Sup's version of disp()

                SupReference = Sub1obj;         // SupReference refers to Sub1 object
                SupReference.disp();            // call Sub1's version of disp()

                SupReference = Sub2obj;         // SupReference refers to Sub2 object
                SupReference.disp();            // call Sub2's version of disp()
        }
}
```

Output:

```
        disp() in superclass
        disp() in subclass 1
        disp() in subclass 2
```

/* Example 60 illustrates the concepts of method overriding and 'dynamic method dispatch' in a very simple manner.

It creates a superclass *Sup*, and two subclasses, *Sub1* and *Sub2*; *Sup* specifies a method *disp()*, and, *Sub1* and *Sub2* override it, that is to say, provide their own overridden versions of *disp()*; inside *main()*, objects of type *Sup, Sub1,* and *Sub2* are declared; a reference of type *Sup,* viz., *SupReference*, is declared as well; a reference to each type of the three objects, *Sup, Sub1,* and *Sub2*, is then assigned to *SupReference* and further, that reference, in turn, is used to invoke *disp()*; and, as the output shows and verifies, the form of *disp()* that is activated is related to the type of the object being referred to at the time of invocation, not by *SupReference*'s class type.

*/

Method Overriding - A *CASE STUDY*

We now take up a *case study* (Example 61) for a better understanding of the full potential of overridden methods. In fact, we shall apply them to the *ThreeDshapes* class which includes all three-dimensional shapes and figures. For the sake of convenience and better demonstration, the *case study* also adds a field called *term* to *ThreeDshapes*. besides its three dimensions, viz., *length, width,* and *height,* respectively.

Example 61

```
// PolymorphismForms_Demo.java
/* Method Overriding - A case Study;
Author: Arunesh;  Date: 21/03/2011 */
// A class for 3-dimensional objects
class ThreeDshapes
{
        // the three dimensions of ThreeDshapes
        double length;
        double width;
        double height;

        String term;   // type of object

        // Default constructor for ThreeDshapes
        {
                length = width = height = 0.0;
                term = "null";
        }

        // Explicit constructor for ThreeDshapes
        ThreeDshapes(double l, double w, double h, String t)
        {
                length = l; width = w; height = h;
                term = t;
        }

        // Construct object with equal length, width, and height
        ThreeDshapes(double e, String t)
        {
                length = width = height = e;
                term = t;
        }
```

```
    // Construct a copy/clone of  a ThreeDshapes object
    ThreeDshapes(ThreeDshapes obj)
    {
        length = obj.length; width = obj.width; height = obj.height;
        term = obj.term;
    }

    // display dimensions
    void dispdim()
    {
        System.out.println("Length, width & height are: "
                        + "\t" + length + '\t" + width + "\t" + height);
    }

    // display term
    void dispterm()
    {
        System.out.println("Object is of type:\t" + term);
    }

    // display volume
    void dispvol( )
    {
        System.out.println("Warning: Volume of given shape is
                                                    Undefined!);
        System.out.println("Volume, by default, is: \t 0.0");
    }
}
// Cuboid is derived  from ThreeDshapes
class Cuboid extends ThreeDshapes
{
    String colour;// colour of cuboid

    /*Default constructor for Cuboid; this shall invoke the default
    constructor of ThreeDshapes automatically. */
    Cuboid()
    {
        colour = "null";
    }
```

```
        /* Constructor for Cuboid that takes four arguments: Parameterized
        constructor */
        Cuboid{String c, double l, double w, double h)
        {
                super(l, w, h, "cuboid");
                colour = c;
        }

        // Construct a Cube
        Cuboid(String c, double e)
        {
                super(e, "cube");
                colour = c;
        }

        // Construct a copy/clone of  a Cuboid object
        Cuboid(Cuboid obj)
        {
                super (obj);
                colour = obj.colour;
        }

        // display colour
        void dispclr( )
        {
                System.out.println("Colour is: \t " + colour);
        }

        //  DISPLAY VOLUME: override dispvol( ) for Cuboid
        void dispvol( )
        {
                Console.WriteLine("Volume is: \t" +  (length *  width *  height));
        }
}
class PolymorphismForms_Demo
{
        public static void main(String args[])
        {
                ThreeDshapes forms [ ] = new ThreeDshapes[3];
```

```
        forms[0] = ThreeDshapes(10.0, 20.0, 30.0, "Generic");
        forms[1] = new Cuboid("red", 1.0, 2.0,3.0);
        forms[2] = new Cuboid("green", 5.0);

        for (int k =0; k < forms.length; k++)
        // notice the use of the property length
        {
                forms[k].dispterm();
                forms[k].dispdim( );
                forms[k].dispvol( );
                System.out.println( );
        }
    }
}
```

Output:

```
Object is of type:        Generic
Length, width & height are: 10.0    20.0    30.0
Warning: Volume of given shape is Undefined!
Volume, by default, is:          0.0

Object is of type:        cuboid
Length, width & height are: 1.0     2.0     3.0
Volume is:      6.0

Object is of type:        cube
Length, width & height are: 5.0     5.0     5.0
Volume is:      125.0
```

/* This *case study* reveals some interesting facets, two in particular. First, *dispv*[illegible] is simply a placeholder in *ThreeDshapes* class and is overridden by the subclass *Cuboid*. Furt[illegible] each override of *dispvol()* requires an implementation specifically suitable for the type o[illegible] object encapsulated by the subclass, e.g., if you were to implement a *Sphere* class, then *dispvol()* would need to compute the volume of a sphere.

Second, in *main()*, *forms[]* is said to be an array of *ThreeDshapes* objects; but, the elements of this array are assigned *Cuboid* as well as *ThreeDshapes* references. This works here because a superclass reference can refer to a subclass object. The program then makes its way throgh the array, displaying particulars about each object. This looks and is actually simple; yet, it demonstrates the potential of inheritance as also method overriding.

The key point here is that the type of object stored in a superclass reference variable is found out at run-time and acted upon accordingly. In case of any object derived from *ThreeDshapes*, its volume can be computed and obtained by invoking *dispvol()*. This is the basis of *polymorphism* as well since the *interface* to this operation is consistent, in fact, is the same, irrespective of the type of *shape/form* being used.

You may also note that the method *dispclr()* of *Cuboid* has not been used in *main()* at all simply because of the fact that *forms[0]* is a *ThreeDshapes* object (of type "Generic") which has no knowledge about the *colour* field/member of *Cuboid*.

*/

3.5 ABSTRACT METHODS / ABSTRACT CLASSES

We, at times, need to create a superclass that defines only a generalized form that shall be shared by all its subclasses, leaving it to each subclass to fill in its own details for the type of implementation it wants. Example 61 was a case in point. The definition of *dispvol( )* is just a placeholder as it does not calculate the actual volume and only displays a warning message along with a default value of zero in case none of the subclasses override it. Sometimes, we need to ensure that each subclass does indeed override all the necessary methods. An abstract method is Java's solution to this problem. To declare an abstract method, we use the following general form:

abstract type name(parameter_list); // note that no method body is there

where, *name* refers to the name of the method, *type* specifies its return type, and *parameter_list* includes all its parameters/arguments.

Here, we must sound a caveat, i.e., only instance methods (and not static methods) can be abstract. Also, you cannot have abstract constructors.

Further, a class that contains one or more abstract methods must also be preceded by the abstract keyword before its name and declared to be abstract. Since an abstract class does not provide a complete implementation, no objects of an abstract class can be created and trying to do so by using *new* shall generate a compiler error instead.

Furthermore, when a subclass inherits an abstract superclass, it must implement all the abstract methods in the superclass. In case it does not, then it must also be declared as abstract. This chain continues and the abstract attribute keeps on getting inherited until and unless a full implementation is achieved.

Take Example 62 as an illustration of the concept of abstract classes and methods. It improves upon the previous version of *ThreeDshapes* as in Example 61 by declaring the method *dispvol()* inside *ThreeDshapes* as well as the class *ThreeDshapes* as abstract. This would, of course, make it mandatory for all classes derived from *ThreeDshapes* to override *dispvol()*. "Why is it an improvement?", you might ask. The simple answer is that the concept of volume for an undefined three-dimensional figure/shape has virtually no useful meaning.

Example 62

```
// AbstractForms_Demo.java
/* Demonstrates & Illustrates Abstract Methods & Classes;
Author: Arunesh;  Date: 21/03/2011 */
// A class for three-dimensional objects
abstract class ThreeDshapes     // notice the use of abstract keyword
{
        // the three dimensions of ThreeDshapes
        double length;
        double width;
        double height;

        String term;     // type of object

        // Default constructor for ThreeDshapes
        {
                length = width = height = 0.0;
                term = "null";
        }

        // Explicit constructor for ThreeDshapes
        ThreeDshapes(double l, double w, double h, String t)
        {
                length = l; width = w; height = h;
                term = t;
        }

        // Construct object with equal length, width, and height
        ThreeDshapes(double e, String t)
        {
                length = width = height = e;
                term = t;
        }

        // Construct a copy/clone of  a ThreeDshapes object
        ThreeDshapes(ThreeDshapes obj)
        {
                length = obj.length; width = obj.width; height = obj.height;
                term = obj.term;
        }
```

```
    // display dimensions
    void dispdim()
    {
        System.out.println("Length, width & height are: "
                    + "\t" + length + '\t" + width + "\t" + height);
    }

    // display term
    void dispterm()
    {
        System.out.println("Object is of type:\t" + term);
    }

    // display volume
    // dispvol( ) is now abstract and must necessarily be overrdden by all derived classes
     abstract void dispvol( );

}
// Cuboid is derived  from ThreeDshapes
class Cuboid extends ThreeDshapes
{
    String colour;   // colour of cuboid

    /*Default constructor for Cuboid; this shall invoke the default constructor of
    ThreeDshapes automatically. */
    Cuboid()
    {
        colour = "null";
    }

    // Constructor for Cuboid that takes four arguments: Parameterized constructor
    Cuboid{String c, double l, double w, double h)
    {
        super(l, w, h, "cuboid");
        colour = c;
    }

    // Construct a Cube
    Cuboid(String c, double e)
    {
        super(e, "cube");
        colour = c;
    }
```

```
        // Construct a copy/clone of  a Cuboid object
        Cuboid(Cuboid obj)
        {
                super (obj);
                colour = obj.colour;
        }

        // display colour
        void dispclr( )
        {
                System.out.println("Colour is: \t " + colour);
        }

        //  DISPLAY VOLUME: override dispvol( ) for Cuboid
        void dispvol( )
        {
                Console.WriteLine("Volume is: \t" +  (length *  width *  height));
        }
}
class AbstractForms_Demo
{
        public static void main(String args[])
        {
                ThreeDshapes forms [ ] = new ThreeDshapes[2];

                forms[1] = new Cuboid("red", 1.0, 2.0,3.0);
                forms[2] = new Cuboid("green", 5.0);

                for (int k =0; k < forms.length; k++)
                // notice the use of the property length
                {
                        forms[k].dispterm();
                        forms[k].dispclr();
                        forms[k].dispdim( );
                        forms[k].dispvol( );

                        System.out.println();
                }
        }
}
```

Output:

Object is of type: cuboid
Colour is: red
Length, width & height are: 1.0 2.0 3.0
Volume is: 6.0

Object is of type: cube
Colour is: green
Length, width & height are: 5.0 5.0 5.0
Volume is: 125.0

/* This example program (Example 62) amply illustrates the concept of abstract classes and methods. First, the superclass *ThreeDshapes* is specified to be abstract since it contains an abstract method, viz., *dispvol()*. Second, the subclass, *Cuboid*, has overridden *dispvol()*, as it must (or be declared itself as abstract too). Again, it is still possible to create an object reference of type *ThreeDshapes*, and the program does create this reference. But, it is no longer possible to create objects of type *ThreeDshapes* since *ThreeDshapes* is an abstract class. It is, for this very reason, that the *forms[]* array in *main()* has been cut down to 2; the "Generic" *ThreeDshapes* object is not created as was done in the previous example.

We would like to mention just one more point before rounding off this section. And, that is, an abstract class is free to contain concrete methods (other than abstract ones) which a subclass can make use of without any need for overriding. It is just that only the methods specified to be abstract have to be necessarily overridden by the subclasses. This is once again amply illustrated by the concrete methods *dispdim()* and *dispterm()* besides the abstract method *dispvol()* in the abstract superclass *ThreeDshapes*.
*/

3.6 USING THE KEYWORD 'final' WITH INHERITANCE

In the preceding chapter, we had mentioned three uses of the keyword - 'final', namely, creating named constants, preventing method overriding, and preventing inheritance. The first one of these, viz., creating the equivalent of named constants, we had discussed in detail over there. We discuss the other two in the following two subsections.

3.6.1 Using the Keyword 'final' to Prevent Method Overriding

Method overriding remains one of Java's most potent features. Still, there will be occasions when you would like to disallow it. To prevent it from occurrng, the keyword - 'final' is specified at the beginining of the method declaration. The following code illustrates this use of 'final'.

```
class X
{
        final void M()
        {
                System.out.println("final method; cannot be overridden!");
        }
}

class Y extends X
{
        void M()            // Illegal! M() is final!!
        {
                System.out.println("Error!")
        }
}
```

/* Since *M()* is declared to be 'final' in class X, it cannot be overridden in class Y, which is a subclass of X. Trying to do so results in a compile-time error.
*/

3.6.2 Using the Keyword 'final' to Prevent Inheritance

There will sometimes be occasions when you would like to disallow inheritance. This is achieved by preceding the class declaration with the keyword - 'final'. Such a class cannot be inherited further. All the methods in a class declared to be 'final' are themselves inherently 'final' so that they cannot be overridden.

An 'abstract' class being incomplete by itself cannot be declared 'final' as well. This is due to the fact that such a class depends upon its subclasses to provide complete/full implementations.

The following code illustrates a 'final' class:

```
final class X
{
        System.out.println("final class; cannot be inherited!");
}

class Y extends X           // Illegal! X is final!!
{
        System.out.println("Error!")
}
```

/* The above code and the resulting error are self-explanatory. Suffice it to say that since class X is 'final', it cannot be a superclass of any class including Y.
*/

3.7 THE ACCESS SPECIFIER - 'protected'

We had promised you in the previous chapter that we shall discuss the access specifier - '*protected*' in the next chapter (that is to say, the current chapter). Unfortunately, a detailed discussion of this specifier (along with all other specifiers mentioned in the previous chapter) cannot be taken up until and unless we have described in detail the concept of packages in the next chapter, viz., "PACKAGES AND INTERFACES".

For now, suffice it to say that if you wish to allow an element/member to be seen outside your current package, but only to classes that subclass your class directly, then declare that element '*protected*'.

3.8 WINDING IT UP!

In this section, we shall take up one special class defined by Java called *Object*, which is an implicit superclass of all other classes, that is to say, all other classes are subclasses of *Object*. This, in turn, implies that a reference variable of type *Object* can refer to an object of any other class. Moreover, since arrays are implemented as classes, a variable of type *Object* can also refer to any array.

Object defines all the methods listed in Table 3.1. Thus, these methods are availabe in every object.

Table 3.1 Methods Defined by *Object*

Method	Purpose
Object clone()	*Creates a new object that is the same as the object being cloned.*
boolean equals(Object object)	*Determines whether one object is equal to another.*
void finalize()	*Called before an unused object is recycled.*
Class getClass()	*Obtains the class of an object at run-time.*
int hashCode()	*Returns the hash code associated with the invoking object.*
void notify()	*Resumes execution of a thread waiting on the invoking object.*
void notifyAll()	*Resumes execution of all threads waiting on the invoking object.*
String toString()	*Returns a string that describes the object.*
void wait(), void wait(long milliseconds),	
void wait(long milliseconds, int nanoseconds)	*Waits on another thread of execution.*

All the methods except *getClass(), notify(), notifyAll(),* and *wait(),* which are *final,* can be overridden. The *equals()* method compares the contents of two objects, returning *true* if they are equivalent, and *false* otherwise.

PRACTICAL SESSION

1. (a) Brifly explain the concept of inheritance, citing suitable example(s), wherever necessary.
   (b) Distinguish between overloaded and overridden methods.

2. (a) What happens when we declare a method/class *final*?
   (b) What happens when we declare a method/class *abstract*?

3. State True(T) or False(F) for each of the following statements:

   (a) A class that contains at least one *abstract* method must itself be declared *abstract*.
   (b) The *Object* class is a superclass of every other class.
   (c) A subclass can be prevented from having access to the members of a superclass.
   (d) A superclass has access to the members of a subclass.
   (e) A subclass has access to the members of a superclass.
   (f) The keyword *super* is similar to the keyword *base* in C#.
   (g) A superclass reference can refer to a subclass object.

4. Can a class declaration include both the *abstract* and *final* modifiers? Give reason(s) in support of your answer.

5. Declare an *abstract* class *Vehicle* with an *abstract* method called *Wheels()*. Provide subclasses *Truck* and *Car* each of which implement this method. Create instances of these subclasses and demonstrate the use of this method.

6. What is meant by dynamic method dispatch? And, how does it form the basis for run-time polymorphism?

7. (a) Why is method overriding important?
   (b) When an overridden method is called through a superclass reference, which version of the method is executed?

8. Can an object of an *abstract* class be instantiated? Give reason(s) in support of your answer.

9. (a) Show by means of a suitable example how to initialize the members of a subclass using *super*.
   (b) Given the following hierarchy:
      class Circle { ......
      class Hemishere extends Circle { ......
      class Sphere extends Hemisphere { ......

   In what order are the constructors of these three classes, viz., *Circle, Hemisphere,* and *Sphere* called when an object of class *Sphere* is instantiated?

10. Identify and correct the error(s), if any, in each of the following code fragments:

(a)

```
class NonSup
{
        NonSup(String msg)
        {
                System.out.println("ABC");
        }
}

class NonSub extends NonSup
{
}
```

(b)

```
public class ABC
{
        public String Do(String msg)
        {
                return "ABC";
        }

        public void Do(String msg)
        {
        }

        public void Do(int i)
        {
        }
}
```

(c)

```
abstract class Do
{
        int a, b;

        void Figure(int A, int B)
        {
        }

        abstract void Position();
}
```

```
class Did extends Do
{
        void Position()
        {
                System.out.println("Called Position");
        }
}

class Done extends Do
{
        void Figure(int A, int B)
        {
                System.out.println("Called Figure");
        }
}
```

Chapter 4

PACKAGES AND INTERFACES

4.0 INTRODUCTION

This chapter examines two of Java's most innovative features, namely, packages and interfaces. Packages, simply put, are nothing but groups of related classes. They help in the organization of code and provide another layer of encapsulation. An interface, on the other hand, defines a set of methods that will be implemented by a class. An interface is a purely logical construct and does not, by itself, implement any method. In between them, packages and interfaces provide greater control over the organization of a Java program.

4.1 PACKAGES

A package serves two purposes:

(1) It provides a mechanism by means of which related parts of a Java program can be organized as a unit. Classes defined within a package must be accessed through their package name. In this manner, a package provides a means to name a collection or set of classes. In genral, naming a class means allocating a name from the namespace, which defines a declarative region. Now, no two classes can have the same name from the same namespace. In other words, each class name must be unique within a given namespace. All the examples we have discussed so far have used the default global namespace. This works well for short programs. But, as the size of the programs becomes large, the default namespaces gets crowded. In such programs, it gets difficult to find unique names for each and every class. Moreover, there should be no name collisions with the programming code created by other programmers working on the same project. Furthermore, there shouldn't be any name collisions with the Java library.

The solution to all the aforesaid problems is the use of a package. A package provides a means to partition the namespace. Thus, when a class is defined/declared within a package, the name of that package gets attached to it. This, in turn, avoids name collisions with other classes having the same name, but are attached to other packages.

(2) A package helps in the Java access control mechanism. This is due to the fact that classes defined within a package can be declared private to that package and inaccessible by

code outside that package. In this manner, a package provides a way by means of which classes can be encapsulated. As a package, in general, contains a related set of classes, Java defines code outside that package. In this manner, a package provides a way by means of which classes can be encapsulated. As a package, in general, contains a related set of classes, Java defines special access rights to code within a package. By means of a package, you can define code open to other code within the same package but closed to any code outside that package. This, in turn, helps in creating self-contained groups of related classes that keep their operations private to themselves.

4.1.1 How to Define/Declare and Create a Package?

In Java, alll clases belong to one or the other package. When no package statement is specified, the default global package is used. Moreover, this default global package is bereft of any name, making it virtually transparent. It is due to this fact that you did not have to worry about packages so far. The default global package works okay for short and simple programs but is insufficient for real-world applications. This is the reason behind the fact that most of the time you will be defining one or more packages for your code.

To create a package, the package command is put at the top of the Java source file. Then, all the classes defined within that file will belong to the concerned package. Also, since package defines a namespace, the names of the classes declared in that file become part of the namespace of that package. The most general form of the package statement is:

package package1;

where, *package1* specifies the name of the package, e.g., the following statement creates a package called *pkg1*:

package pkg1;

Java makes use of the file system to manage packages, with each package stored in its own directory, e.g., the *.class* files for any classes you create for *pkg1* must be stored in a directory called *pkg1*. Also, note that package names are case sensitive so that the directory in which a package is stored must exactly be the same as the package name. Moreover, more than one file can include the same package statement. This is due to the fact that the package statement simply specifies to which package the classes in a file belong and does not exclude other classes in other files from being a part of that same package. Thus, in most of the real-world applications, packages are spread across many files.

An hierarchy of packages can also be created by simply separating each package name from the one above it by a period (.). the most general form of a multilevel hierarchical pacakge statement is:

package package1.package2. package3..........packageN;

Remember to create the directories that are supportive of such a package hierarchy, for example:

package P1.P2.P3;

must be stored in *..../P1/P2/P3*,

where .... specifies the path to the above mentioned directories.

4.1.2 Finding Packages and CLASSPATH

In Java, packages are mirrored by directories (refer previous section). So, how does the Java run-time system know where to look for packages created by you? The simple answer is:
(1) By default, the Java run-time system uses the current working directory as its starting point so that if your class files are in the current working directory, or a subdirectory of the current working directory, they will be found.
(2) You can specify a directory path / paths by setting the CLASSPATH environmental variable.

Let us consider a practical case of the following package specification:

package pkg;

In order for a program to find pkg, either the program is executed from a directory immediately above *pkg*, or CLASSPATH must be set to include the path to *pkg*.

The first alternative is the easiest and does not require any achange to be made to CLASSPATH. On the other hand, the second alternative lets your program find *pkg* regardless of the directory the program is in. It's for you to make your own choice.

Before rounding off this subsection, we would like to make an important point. And, that is, it is best to keep all *.java* and *.class* files associated with packages in their own package directories. This will help you in avoiding a lot of confusion.

4.1.3 Package Example/Illustration

In the light of the above discussion, we now take up a short package example (Example 63).

Example 63

```
// LibDemo.java
/* Demonstrates & Illustrates use of Packages;
Author: Arunesh;  Date: 21/03/2011 */
package LibPack;          // This file is part of the LibPack package
class Library             // This, in turn, implies that Library is part of LibPack
{
        private String book;
        private String author;
        Library(String b, String a)
        {
                book = b;
                author = a;
        }
        void display()
        {
                System.out.println(book);
                System.out.println(author);
        }
}
```

```
class LibDemo          // LibDemo is a part of LibPack as well
{
    public static void main(String args[])
    {
        Library lib[] = new Library[2];

        lib[0] = new Library("The Essentials of JAVA", "Arunesh Goyal");
        lib[1] = new Library("The Essentials of C# 4.0", "Arunesh Goyal");

        for (int k = 0; k < lib.length; k++)
        {
            lib[i].display();
            System.out.println();
        }
    }
}
```

The source file *LibDemo.java* is to be put into a directory called *LibPack*. The program is then compiled making sure that the resulting *.class* file is also in the *LibPack* directory.On executing the class using the following command line:

java *LibPack.LibDemo*

(while executing this command, the user has to be in a directory above *LibPack* or have the CLASSPATH variable set appropriately.),

we get the output as outlined below.

Output:

The Essentials of JAVA
Arunesh Goyal

The Essentials of C# 4.0
Arunesh Goyal

/* This example program (Example 63) amply illustrates the concept of packages. As pointed out, both *LibDemo* and the class *Library* are part of the package *LibPack*. This, in turn, implies that *LibDemo* cannot be executed on its own. Thus, the following command line cannot be used:

java *LibDemo*

Instead, *LibDemo* has to be qualified with its package name as illustrated above.

*/

4.2 MEMBER ACCESS AND PACKAGES

In the preceding chapters, we have introduced the fundamentals of access control (including private and public access specifiers), but they do not reveal the entire story. This is due to the role of packages in Java's access control mechanism. The visibility of an element is determined by its access specification, namely, private, public, protected, or default and the package to which it belongs. This means that the visibility of an element is determined by its visibility within a class and its visibility within a package. Table 4.1 summarizes the various access levels.

Table 4.1 Class Member Access

	Private Member	Default Member	Protected Member	Public Member
Visible within same class	*Y*	*Y*	*Y*	*Y*
Visible within same package by subclass	*N*	*Y*	*Y*	*Y*
Visible within same package by non-subclas	*N*	*Y*	*Y*	*Y*
Visible within different package by subclass	*N*	*N*	*Y*	*Y*
Visible within different package by non-subclass	*N*	*N*	*N*	*Y*

Y - Yes; N - No

Let us now examine each access option individually.

A member of a class bereft of any explicit access specifier is visible within its package but not outside. It is for this very reason that default access specification should be used for elements that are to be kept private to a package.

Next, members declared to be public are visible everywhere, inclusive of different classes/packages. Thus, there is no restriction on their use/access.

A private member is accessible only to the other members of its class. It is not affected by its membership in a package.

Finally, a member declared as protected is accessible within its package and to all subclasses, inclusive of subclasses in other packages.

4.2.1 Package Access Example/Illustration

In the pakage example illustrated earlier (Example 63), both *Library* and *LibDemo* were in the same package so that there was no problem with *LibDemo* using *Library* since the default access privelege grants access to all members of the same package. However, if *Library* were in one package and *LibDemo* in another, the scenario would completely change with access to *Library* being denied.

To make *Library* available to other packages, three changes need to be introduced:

(1) *Library* must be declared public.

(2) Its constructor must be declared as public.

(3) Its *display()* method must be declared to be public.

This would make them all visible outside of *LibPack*. Thus, in order that *Library* is usable by other packages, it must be recoded as given in Example 64.

Example 64

```
// UseLibrary.java
/* Library recoded for public access;
Author: Arunesh;  Date: 21/03/2011 */
package LibPack;
public class Library                    // Library now public
{
        private String book;
        private String author;
        public Library(String b, String a)          // Constructor now public
        {
                book = b;
                author = a;
        }
        public void display()               // Method now public
        {
                System.out.println(book);
                System.out.println(author);
        }
}
```

To use *Library* from another package, you must use the *import* statement discussed in the next section or you must fully qualify its name to include its full package specification, for instance, the following class (called *UseLibrary* contained in the *LibPack2* package) fully qualifies *Library* in order to use it.

Example 64 (Continued)

```
/* Class UseLibrary contained in LibPack2 package
uses Library contained in LibPack package
by fully qualifying its name, i.e., LibPack.Library;
Author: Arunesh;  Date: 21/03/2011 */
package LibPack2;
class UseLibrary
{
        public static void main(String args[])
        {
                LibPack.Library lib[] = new LibPack.Library[2];

                lib[0] = new LibPack.Library("The Essentials of JAVA", "Arunesh Goyal");
                lib[1] = new LibPack.Library("The Essentials of C# 4.0", "Arunesh Goyal");

                for (int k = 0; k < lib.length; k++)
                {
                        lib[i].display();
                        System.out.println();
                }
        }
}
```

Output:

```
        The Essentials of JAVA
        Arunesh Goyal

        The Essentials of C# 4.0
        Arunesh Goyal
```

/* Note that the output remains the same as in Example 63. Can you tell us, why? Also carefully note that every use of *Library* is preceded by the *LibPack* qualifier. This is essential as otherwise, *Library* would not be found when trying to compile *UseLibrary*.
*/

4.2.2 Understanding Protected Access

The protected specifier is sometimes not clear to Java programmers, especially newcomers. As we have already explained, the protected access specifier creates a member accessible within its package and to subclasses in other packages. In this manner, a protected member can be used by all subclasses but is still protected from arbitrary access by code outside its package.To better understand the effects of protected, let us now work through an example (Example 65). First of all, we change the *Library* class so that its instance variables are protected.

Example 65

```
// DemoProtect.java
/* Make the instance variables of Library protected;
Author: Arunesh;  Date: 21/03/2011 */
package LibPack;
public class Library
{
        protected String book;          // now, protected
        protected String author;        // now, protected
        public Library(String b, String a)
        {
                book = b;
                author = a;
        }
        public void display()
        {
                System.out.println(book);
                System.out.println(author);
        }
}
```

Next, we create a subclass of *Library* called *ExtLibrary,* and a class called *DemoProtect* that uses *ExtLibrary*. *ExtLibrary* adds a field that stores the status ("New", "Old", "Recent" etc.) and several other methods (referred to as accessor methods, the discussion of which is beyond the scope of this text. But, you can refer to our publication - "*The Essentials of C# 4.0* in this context.). Both of these classes will be in their own package called *LibPack2*.

Example 65 (Continued)

```
/* Demonstrate protected access;
Author: Arunesh;  Date: 21/03/2011 */
package LibPack2;
class ExtLibrary extends LibPack.Library
{
        private String status;
```

```
        public ExtLibrary(String b, String a, String s)
        {
                super(b, a);`
                status = s;
        }

        public void display()
        {
                super.display();
                System.out.println(status);
        }

        public String getStatus()          {return status; }
        public void setStatus(String s)    {status = s;}

        // The following are okay since a subclass can access a protected member
        public String getBook()            {return book;}          // access to
        public void setBook(String b)      {book = b;}             // Library's members
        public String getAuthor()          {return author;}        // is allowed
        public void setAuthor(String a)    {author = a;}           // for subclasses
}
class DemoProtect
{
        public static void main(String args[])
        {
                ExtLibrary lib[] = new ExtLibrary[6];

                lib[0] = new ExtLibrary("The Essentials of JAVA", "Arunesh Goyal",
                                                                        "New");
                lib[1] = new ExtLibrary("The Essentials of C# 4.0", "Arunesh Goyal",
                                                                        "Recent");
                lib[2] = new ExtLibrary("The C Programming Language", "Arunesh Goyal",
                                                                        "Old");
                lib[3] = new ExtLibrary("See Thru C++", "Arunesh Goyal", "Recent");
                lib[4] = new ExtLibrary("Systems Analysis and Design", "Arunesh Goyal",
                                                                        "Recent");
                lib[5] = new ExtLibrary("Java - The Complete Reference", "Herbert Schildt",
                                                                        "Old");

                for (int k = 0; k < lib.length; k++)
                {
                        lib[i].display();
                        System.out.println();
                }
```

```
        // Find titles by author
        System.out.println("Displaying all titles by Arunesh Goyal:");
        for (int k = 0; k < lib.length; k++)
            if (lib[k].getAuthor() == "Arunesh Goyal")
                System.out.println("\t" + lib[k].getBook());

        //  lib[0].book = "Testing IT out!";     // Error! not accessible!!
            // access to protected field not allowed by non-subclass

    }
}
```

Output:

```
The Essentials of JAVA
Arunesh Goyal
New

The Essentials of C# 4.0
Arunesh Goyal
Recent

The C Programming Language
Arunesh Goyal
Old

See Thru C++
Arunesh Goyal
Recent

Systems Analysis and Design
Arunesh Goyal
Recent;

Java - The Complete Reference
Herbert Schildt
Old

Displaying all titles by Arunesh Goyal:
        The Essentials of JAVA
        The Essentials of C# 4.0
        The C Programming Language
        See Thru C++
        Systems Analysis and Design
```

/* Note the code inside *ExtLibrary*. Since *ExtLibrary* extends *Library*, it has access to the protected members of *Library* even though *ExtLibrary* is in a different package so that it can access the *book* and *author* fields directly as it does in the accessor methods it creates for these variables.

However, in *DemoProtect*, access to these variables is denied since *DemoProtect* is not a subclass of *Library* so that if you were to remove the comment symbol from the following line:

// *lib[0].book = "Testing IT out!";* *// Error! not accessible!!*

then, the program will report a compile-time error!

*/

4.3 IMPORTING PACKAGES

While using a class from another package, the name of the class has to be fully qualified with the name of its package as we have been doing in Examples 64 & 65. But, such an approach can prove to be extremely cumbersome, especially if the classes being qualified happen to be deeply nested in a package hierarchy. It is thus, no surprise that the inventors of Java came up with a more convenient way of using the package contents, viz., the *import* statement. Using this statement, one can bring one or more members of a package into view. Thus, those members can be used directly without resorting to explicit package qualification. The most general form of the *import* statements is:

import pkgname.classname;

where, *pkgname* is the name of the package, which can include its full path while *classname* refers to the name of the class being imported. We can also import the entire contents of a package by using an asterisk (*) instead of the *classname*. Here are examples of both the forms:

import myPkg.myClass; /* the class *myClass* is imported from the package *myPkg* */

import myPkg.;* /* all the classes are imported from the package *myPkg* */

Note that in a Java source file, the *import* statements must occur immediately following the package statement (if any) and before any class definitions.

The *import* statement can be used to bring the *LibPack* package into view in order that the *Library* class can be used without any qualification. For this to happen, one might simply add the *import* statement to the top of any file (of course, after the package statement, if any) that uses *Library*:

import LibPack.;*

For instance, we have the *UseLibrary* class (Example 64) reworked and recoded as *UseLibrary2* to use the *import* statement (Example 66).

Example 66

```
// UseLibrary2.java
/* Demonstrate the import statement;
Author: Arunesh; Date: 21/03/2011 */
package LibPack2;
import LibPack.*;       // the import statement
class UseLibrary2
{
        public static void main(String args[])
        {
                Library lib[] = new Library[2];
                        // now, Library can be referred to directly without any qualification

                lib[0] = new Library("The Essentials of JAVA", "Arunesh Goyal");
                lib[1] = new Library("The Essentials of C# 4.0", "Arunesh Goyal");

                for (int k = 0; k < lib.length; k++)
                {
                        lib[i].display();
                        System.out.println();
                }
        }
}
```

Output:

The Essentials of JAVA
Arunesh Goyal

The Essentials of C# 4.0
Arunesh Goyal

/* Note that the output remains the same as in Example 64. Also carefully note that we no longer need to qualify Library with the *LibPack* qualifier.
*/

4.4 JAVA STANDARD PACKAGES

Java defines a large number of standard classes that are available to all programs. This class library is generally called the Java API (Application Programming Interface). The Java API is stored in packages. At the top of the package hierarchy is *java*. Descending from *java* are several subpackages (called Java standard packages) including the ones outlined in Table 4.2.

Remark: For a more detailed discussion of the Java API, refer/consult Appendix 'C'.

Table 4.2 Java Standard Packages

Standard Package	Description
java.lang	*Stores a large number of general purpose classes*
java.io	*Stores the Input/Output classes*
java.net	*Stores the classes which support networking*
java.awt	*Stores classes which support the Abstract Windows Toolkit*

We have been using *java.lang* ever since the beginning of this book. It contains, among several others, the *System* class, which we have been using while performing output using *println()*. The *java.lang* package is distinct and unique since it gets automatically imported into every Java program. It is only for this reason that we did not have to import *java.lang* in any of the preceding example programs. However, other packages need to be explicitly imported into Java programs.

4.5 INTERFACES

An interface definers a set of methods that shall be implemented by a class, and does not, by itself, implement any method. In other words, we can say that an inteface is purely a logical construct describing functionality without specifying implementation.

We have already learnt in the concept of abstract methods/classes what a class must do but not how it will do it. In other words, each derived class must provide its own version of the particular abstract method. We can go a step futher in the concept of an interface and totally separate a class's interface from its implementation. Although an interface is syntactically similar to an abstract class, no method in an interface can have a body. In other words, every method in an interface is an abstract method. With the concept of an interface, C# allows us to fully use the "one interface, multiple methods" aspect of polymorphism. An interface is declared by the use of the keyword <u>interface</u> as follows:

```
access interface name
{
        return_type method_name1(parameter_list);
        return_type method_name2(parameter_list);
        ...............................................................
        ...............................................................
        return_type method_nameN(parameter_list);
        type var1 = value;
        type var2 = value;
        ...............................................................
        ...............................................................
        type varN = value;
}
```

where, *name* specifies the interface name and *access* is either public or not used. If no access specifier is used, then default access results and the interface is available only to other members of its package. When public *access is* used, the interface can be used by any other code (note that an interface declared as public must be in a file of the same name).. All methods are abstract methods with only their return types and signatures. Also, each method is public implicitly and no explicit definition is permissible. In an interface, no method can have an implementation. Whence, each class which includes an interface has to necesssarily implement all of the methods. Variables declared in an interface are not instance variables; rather they are implicitly *public, final*, and *static* and must be initialized (thus, they are essentially *constants*).

Here is an example of an interface definition. It specifies the interface to a class that generates a series of numbers.

```
public interface Iseries
{
        int getnext( );             // return next number
        void reset( );              // restart;
        void setstart(int i).       // set starting value
}
```

This interface is declared public so that it can be implemented by code in any package.

4.5.1 Implementing Interfaces

After an interface has been defined, one or more classes can implement it. When a class implements an interface, it must implement the entire interface; it cannot choose to implement certain paets of it, leaving the others, for instance. The general form of a class that implements an interface is as given below:

```
access class class_name extends superclass_name implements interface_name
{
        // body of class
}
```

where, *access* is either public or not used, extends clause is optional and *interface_name* stands for the name of the interface being implemented while *class_name* is the name of the implementing class. A class must fully implement the interface and no partial implementation is permissible. Also, a class can implement more than one interface separated by commas (in a comma-separated list of interfaces). Moreover, a class can inherit a base class as well as implement an interface (in such a case, the extends clause comes into play).

The methods which implement an interface must be declared as public because within an interface, a method is implicitly public; whence its implementation must also be public. Further, the return type and signature of the implementing method must exactly match the return type and signature defined in the interface specification.

Next, we give an example (Example 67) that implements the *Iseries* interface shown earlier. It creates a class called *ByFives*, which generates a series of numbers (each greater than five than the previous one) and a class called *ByFives_Demo* that demonstrates *ByFives*.

Example 67

```
// ByFives_Demo.java
/* Illustrates an Interface and a Class that implements it*/
/* Author: Arunesh; Date: 27/03/2011 */
public interface Iseries
{
        int getnext( );             // return next number
        void reset( );              // restart;
        void setstart(int i).       // set starting value
}
class ByFives implements Iseries        // ByFives implements the interface Iser
{
        int start;
        int value;

        ByFives( )      // defaut constructor
        {
                start = 0;
                value = 0;
        }

        public int getnext( )
        {
                value += 5;
                return value;
        }

        public void reset( )
        {
                start = 0;
                value = 0;
        }

        public void setstart(int i)
        {
                start = i;
                value = i;
        }

        /* notice that the metods getnext(), reset(), and setstart() are declared using the public
        access specifier. This is necessary. Whenever you implement a method defined by an
        interface, it must be implemented as public since all members of an interface are
        implicitly public. */
}
```

```
// Demonstrate ByFives, which has implemented all the three methods defined by Iseries
class ByFives_Demo
{
        public static void main(String args[] )
        {
                ByFives byfives = new ByFives( );

                for (int x = 0; x < 5; x++)          // first five numbers
                        System.out.println("Next value is: \t" +  byfives.getnext( ));

                System.out.println("\nResetting");
                byfives.reset( );
                for (int x = 0; x < 5; x++)          // first five numbers again
                        System.out.println("Next value is: \t" +  byfives.getnext( ));

                System.out.println("\n Starting at 51");
                byfives.setstart(51);
                                    // first five numbers after51
                for (int x = 0; x < 5; x++)
                        System.out.println("Next value is: \t" +  byfives.getnext( ));
        }
}
```

Output:

```
        Next value is     5
        Next value is     10
        Next value is     15
        Next value is     20
        Next value is     25

        Resetting
        Next vaue is      5
        Next value is     10
        Next value is     15
        Next value is     20
        Next value is     25

        Starting at 51
        Next value is     56
        Next value is     61
        Next value is     66
        Next value is     71
        Next value is     76
```

It is both permissible and common for classes that implement interfaces to specify additional members of their own, e.g., the following version of *ByFives* (Example 68) adds the method *getprevious()*, which returns the previous value.

Example 68

```
/* Illustrates implementation of Iseries and an additional method getprevious()*/
/* Author: Arunesh; Date: 27/03/2011 */
public interface Iseries
{
        int getnext( );               // return next number
        void reset( );                // restart;
        void setstart(int i).         // set starting value
}
class ByFives implements Iseries
        // ByFives implements the interface Iseries and adds getprevious()
{
        int start;
        int value;
        int previous;

        public ByFives( )             // defaut constructor
        {
                start = 0;
                value = 0;
                previous = -2;
        }

        public int getnext( )
        {
                previous = value;
                value += 5;
                return value;
        }

        public void reset( )
        {
                start = 0;
                value = 0;
                previous = - 2;
        }
```

```
        public void setstart(int i)
        {
                start = i;
                value = i;
                previous = i - 2;
        }

        public int getprevious() // a method not defined by Iseries
        {
                return previous;
        }
}
```

/* You can note that the addition of *getprevious()* resulted in changed implementations of the methods specified by *Iseries.* Still, the interface to those method has not changed and has not broken preexisting code. This is one of the major advantages of interfaces.
*/

As you know, any number of classes can implement the same interface. Example 69 is a case in point. Here, we have a class called *Primes*, which generates a series of prime numbers. You may note that its implementation of the interface *Iseries* is fundamentally different from that provided by *ByFives in* Example 67.

Example 69

```
// Primes_Demo.java
/* Illustrates a different class implementing the same interface */
/* Author ; Arunesh; Date: 27/03/2011 */
public interface Iseries
{
        int getnext( );                 // return next number
        void reset( );                  // restart;
        void setstart(int i).           // set starting value
}
class Primes Implements Iseries         // class Primes implements the interface Iseries
{
        int start;
        int value;

        Primes( )                       // defaut constructor
        {
                start = 2;
                value = 2;
        }
```

```
        public int getnext( )
        {
                int a, b;
                bool isPri;

                value++;
                for (a = value; a < 10000; a ++)
                {
                        isPri = true;
                        for (b = 2; b < (a/b + 1); b++)
                        {
                                if (a % b ==0)
                                {
                                        isPri = false;
                                        break;
                                }
                        }
                        if (isPri)
                        {
                                value = a;
                                break;
                        }
                }
                return value;
        }

        public void reset( )
        {
                start = 2;
                value = 2;
        }

        public void setstart(int i)
        {
                start = i;
                value = i;
        }
}
// Demonstrate Primes, which has implemented all the three methods defined by Iseries
class Primes_Demo
{
        public static void main(String args[] )
        {
                Primes primes = new Primes( );
```

```
        for (int x = 0; x < 5; x++)        // first five prime numbers
            System.out.println("Next value is: \t" + primes.getnext( ));

        System.out.println("\nResetting");
        primes.reset( );
        for (int x = 0; x < 5; x++)        // first five prime numbers again
            System.out.println("Next value is: \t" + primes.getnext( ));

        System.out.println("\n Starting at 51");
        primes.setstart(51);
                    // first five prime numbers after51
        for (int x = 0; x < 5; x++)
            System.out.println("Next value is: \t" + primes.getnext( ));
    }
}
```

<u>Output</u>:

```
Next value is    3
Next value is    5
Next value is    7
Next value is    11
Next value is    13

Resetting
Next vaue is     3
Next value is    5
Next value is    7
Next value is    11
Next value is    13

Starting at 51
Next value is    53
Next value is    57
Next value is    59
Next value is    61
Next value is    67
```

/* What is important here to understand is the fact that even though *ByFives* and *Primes* generate completely unrelated series of numbers, yet both implement the same interface, viz., *Iseries.* This is because, an interface is totally silent about its implementation, leaving it to each class to implement the interface in any way it deems fit, suitable, and convenient.

*/

4.5.2 Using Interface References

We can declare a reference variable of an interface type, or, in other words, we can create an interface reference variable; such a reference can refer to any object that implements the interface. When a method is invoked on an object via an interface reference, the version of the method implemented by that object gets executed. This concept is just like the one for using a superclass reference to access a subclass object, as already explained in the previous chapter.

Consider Example 70 as a case in point. It uses the same interface reference variable to invoke methods on objects of both *ByFives* and *Primes*.

<u>Example 70</u>

```
//_InterfaceReference.java
/* Illustrates an Interface Reference */
/* Author ; Arunesh; Date: 27/03/2011 */
// specify the interface
public interface Iseries
{
        int getnext( );                     // return next number
        void reset( );                      // restart;
        void setstart(int i).               // set starting value
}
class ByFives implements Iseries            // ByFives implements the interface Iseries
{
        int start;
        int value;

        ByFives( )                          // defaut constructor
        {
                start = 0;
                value = 0;
        }

        public int getnext( )
        {
                value += 5;
                return value;
        }

        public void reset( )
        {
                start = 0;
                value = 0;
        }
```

```
        public void setstart(int i)
        {
                start = i;
                value = i;
        }
}
class Primes implements Iseries          // class Primes implements the interface Iseries
{
        int start;
        int value;

        Primes( )         // defaut constructor
        {
                start = 2;
                value = 2;
        }

        public int getnext( )
        {
                int a, b;
                bool isPri;

                value++;
                for (a = value; a < 10000; a ++)
                {
                        isPri = true;
                        for (b = 2; b < (a/b + 1); b++)
                        {
                                if (a % b ==0)
                                {
                                        isPri = false;
                                        break;
                                }
                        }
                        if (isPri)
                        {
                                value = a;
                                break;
                        }
                }
                return value;
        }
```

```
        public void reset( )
        {
                start = 2;
                value = 2;
        }
        public void setstart(int i)
        {
                start = i;
                value = i;
        }
}
class InterfaceReference
{
        public static void main(String args[] )
        {
                ByFives byfives = new ByFives( );
                Primes primes = new Primes( );
                Iseries obj;

                for (int x = 0; x < 5; x++)
                {
                        obj = byfives;
                        System.out.println("Next ByFives value is: \t" + obj.getnext( ));
                                                // accssing an object via an inteface reference

                        obj = primes;
                        System.out.println("Next Primes value is: \t" + obj.getnext( ));
                                                // accssing an object via an inteface reference

                }
        }
}
```

Output:

```
Next ByFives value is    5
Next Prime number is     7
Next ByFives value is    10
Next Prime number is     11
Next ByFives value is    15
Next Prime number is     17
Next ByFives value is    20
Next Prime number is     23
Next ByFives value is    25
Next Prime number is     29
```

/* In this example program (Example 70), inside *main(), obj* is specified as a reference to the interface *Iseries* so that it can be employed to refer to any object that implements *Iseries*. Herein, it is employed to refer to *byfives* and *primes*, which happen to be objects of type *ByFives* and *Primes*, respectively, and both of these implement *Iseries*.
*/

4.5.3 Variables in Interfaces

As mentined already, we can have variables in interfaces, but they are implicitly *public, static*, and *final*. It might seem that there would be not much use for such variables but large programs typically make use of several constants that denote such things as array size, various limits, special values, and so on. And, because a large program is typically held in a number of distinct and separate source files, there is a great need to make such constant values available to each of these files. Java offers a solution to this problems by means of interface variables.

To declare/define a set od such shared constants, we simply can create an interface that contains only these constant values, without any methods. Each and every file requring access to these constants can then be made to simply "implement" this created interface so as to make these constant values visible. Consider Example 71 as a case in point.

<u>Example 71</u>

```
//_InterfaceVariables.java
/* Illustrates an Interface containing constants */
/* Author ; Arunesh; Date: 27/03/2011 */
// specify the interface
 interface Iconstants
{
        int LOW = 0;
        int HIGH = 10;
        String ERR_MESSAGE = "Out-of-Bounds";
                // these three are constants
}
class InterfaceVariables
{
        public static void main(String args[] )
        {
                int numeral[] = new int[HIGH];

                for (int x = LOW; x < (HIGH + 1); x++)
                {
                        if (x < HIGH)
                        {
                                numeral[x] = x * HIGH;
                                System.out.println(numeral[x]);
                        }
```

```
                else
                        System.out.println(ERR_MESSAGE);
            }
        }
}
```

Output:

```
        0
        10
        20
        30
        40
        50
        60
        70
        80
        90
        Out-of-Bounds
```

4.6 INTERFACES CAN BE EXTENDED

Interfaces can be inherited just like classes. The syntax is exactly the same as for class inheritance. When a clsss implements an interface that inherits another interface, it must provide complete implementation for all the members defined within the interface inheritance ladder. An example follows (Example 72).

Example 72

```
// Interface_Inheritance.java
/* Illustrates Interface Inheritance*/
/* Author: Arunesh; Date: 27/03/2011 */
public interface I1                 // Inteface 1
{
        void M1( );                 // Method/Member 1
        void M2( );                 // Method/Member 2
}

public interface I2 extends I1      // Inteface 2 inherits Interface 1
{
        void M3( );                 // Method/Member 3
}

class NewClass implements I2        // NewClass implements I2 which inherits I1
                                    // whence, it must implement all members of both I2 and I1
```

```
{
        public void M1()
        {
                System.out.println("Implementation of M1() Done");
        }
        public void M2()
        {
                System.out.println("Implementation of M2() Done");
        }

        public void M3()
        {
                System.out.println("Implementation of M3() Done");
        }
}
class Interface_Inheritance
{
        public static void main(String args[])
        {
                NewClass obj = new NewClass();

                obj.M1();
                obj.M2();
                obj.M3();
        }
}
```

Output:

```
        Implementation of M1() Done
        Implementation of M2() Done
        Implementation of M3() Done
```

/* An attempt to remove any of the implementations for *M1(), M2(),* or *M3()* in *NewClass* shall cause a compiler error. This is because a class implementing an interface must mecessarily implement all methods.members in that interface, inclusive of any inherited from other interfaces. */

4.7 NESTING OF INTERFACES

Interfaces can be nested, that is to say, an interface can be member interface of another class/ interface. Such a nested interface can only be declared public, private, or protected in contrast to the top-level interface, which must necessarily be declared as public or have the default access level. If we want to use a nested interface outside of its enclosing scope, it must be fully qualified by the name of the class/interface of which it is a member.

We now take up Example 73 to illustrate the concept of nested interfaces practically.

Example 73

```
// NestedInterface_Demo.java
/* Demonstrates & Illustrates a Nested Interface;
Author: Arunesh; Date: 22/03/2011 */
// A class that contains a member interface
class C
{
        // the following is a nested interface
        public interface NI( )
        {
                boolean isZero(int n);
        }
}
// the following class implements NI
class I implements C.NI
{
        public boolean isZero(int n)
        {
                return (n == 0) ? true : false;
        }
}
class NestedInterface_Demo
{
        public static void main(String args[])
        {
                // the following is a nested interface reference
                C.NI cni = new I();

                If (cni.isZero(0))
                        System.out.println("True");
                else
                        System.out.println("False");

                if (cni.isZero(5))
                        System.out.println("True");
                else
                        System.out.println("False");
        }
}
```

Output:

```
        True
        False
```

/* This example program (Example) amply illustrates the concept of nested interfaces. First, class *C* defines a nested interface *NI*, which is assigned public access. Next, class *I* implements the nested interface as per the following line of code:

class I implements C.NI

You may note that the nested interface name is fully qualified by the name of its enclosing class.

Finally, inside *main()*, a *C.NI* reference called *cni* is created, and it is assigned a reference to an *I* object. Since *I* implements *C,* this is perfectly valid, okay, and legal.

*/

4.8 WINDING IT UP!

In this section, we are going to take up three important matters and answer three important questions.

First, does importing a package have an impact on the performance of the concerned Java program? The answer to this little query is - "Yes and no! Importing a package does create a small amount of overhead at compile-time, but it has no affect on the performance at run-time."

The other two matters and questions relate to the working of C++ vis-à-vis Java:

(1) This one pertains to the relative similarity between the protected access specifiers of C++ and Java. The fact is that they are similar but not the same. In C++, protected access creates a member that can be accessed by subclasses, but is otherwise private. In Java, protected access creates a member that can be accessed by any code within its package but only to subclasses outside of its package.

If you need to port code between C++ and Java, you must take into account this very subtle but significant difference.

(2) This one pertains to the header files and #define statement of C++ and the interface and interface variables of Java. The real question is of converting a C++ program to Java and handling #define statements found in a C++ style header file. Well, Java's answer to the header files and #define statements of C++ is the interface and inteface variables. To port a header file, what one needs to do is simply performing a one-to-one translation.

PRACTICAL SESSION

1. (a) What do you mean by a package in Java? And, how do you go about designing a package?
   (b) When we want to use a specific package, how do we let Java go about it? Illustrate this situation by means of a suitable example.
   (c) Elucidate and throw light on the various levels of access protection available for packages. Also, elaborate upon their implications. Use suitable example(s) wherever necesary..

2. (a) Explain how CLASSPATH is used.
   (b) What do you mean by importing a package?
   Briefly, elaborate on its usefulness as well.

3. When we want to add a class or an interface to a package, how do we let Java go about this task?

4. Given that the following class has been saved in the folder "Square", will the program run smoothly?

```
package square;
class SQUARE
{
        public void dimensions()
        {
        }
        public void display()
        {
        }
        public static void main(String args[])
        {
                System.out.println("Package square created successfully!");
        }
}
```

5. Given that the following code uses the class "SQUARE" as defined in the preceding problem, and that class "ImportSquare" is not defined in the folder "Square", will the program run smoothly?

```
import Square.SQUARE;
class ImportSquare
{
        public static void main(String args[])
        {
                Square.SQUARE SS = new Square.SQUARE();
                System.out.println("Program Over!");
        }
}
```

6. Given that the method dimensions() in "SQUARE" has been declared to be private and that the class "InTheSamePackage" is in the same package as "SQUARE", will this class "InTheSamePackage" be able to use the method dimensions() as per the following code snippet?

```
package Square;
import Square.SQUARE;
class InTheSamePackage
{
        public static void main(String args[])
        {
                SQUARE SQ = new SQUARE();
                SQ.dimensions();
        }
}
```

7. The following program imports a complee package with all its classes. Will the program compile successfully?

```
import Square;
class ImportSquare
{
        public static void main(String args[])
        {
                Square.SQUARE SS = new Square.SQUARE();
                System.out.println("Program Over!");
        }
}
```

8. (a) What do you mean by an interface in Java? And, what are the main advantages of interfaces?
   (b) List the major similarities between an interface and a class.
   (c) List the major differences between an interface and a class.

9. (a) When we want to create a class for implementing a specific interface, how do we let Java go about it? In other words, how do we let Java know about it? Illustrate this situation by means of a suitable example.
   (b) List the various methods or forms of implementing an interface along with a suitable example (code) for each situation.

10. Find errors, if any, in each of the following code segments:

(i)

```
interface Angle
{
        void displayAngle()
        {
                System.out.println("display Angle");
        }
}
```

(ii)

```
interface Angle
{
        void displayAngle();
}
class C1 implements Angle
{
        public void displayAngle()
        {
                System.out.println("display Angle");
        }
}
class C2 implements Angle
{
        public void Publisher_Author()
        {
                System.out.println("Publisher_Author");
        }
}
public class Using Interface
{
        public static void main(String args[])
        {
                C1 publisher = new C1();
                C2 author = new C2();
                publisher.displayAngle();
                author.Publisher_Author();
        }
}
```

(iii)
```
interface Square
{
        void dimensions();
}
interface Rectangle extends Square
{
        void get_dimensions();
        int length = 20;
        int width = 5;
}
class ImlementRectangle implements Rectangle
{
        public void get_dimensions()

        {
                System.out.println(length);
                System.out.println(width);
        }
}
class ExtendingInterface extends Rectangle
{
        public static void main(String args[])
        {
                Square Sq = new Rectangle();
                Sq.get_dimensions();
        }
}
```

11. Can an interface reference variable refer to an object that implements that interface? Give suitable example(s) in support of your answer.

12. (a) How many classes can implement an interface?
    (b) How many interfaces can a class implement?

13. Can interfaces be extended? If yes, illustrate by means of a suitable example.

14. Variables declared in an interface are implicitly *static* and *final*.
    What good are they? In other words, what useful purpose is served by them?

15. (a) What standard Java package is automatically imported into your program, that is to say, in every source file?
    (b) State True (T) or False (F):
    A package is, in essence, just a container for classes.

Chapter 5

EXCEPTION HANDLING

5.0 INTRODUCTION

It's a fact of life that bad things sometimes happen. Tyres get punctured, batteries run down, screw drivers are never found where you left them, and users of your applications behave in an unpredictable manner. In the world of computers, disks fail, other applications running on the same computer as your program run amok and use up alll the available memory, and networks go awry and disconnect at the most awkward and critical moment. Errors can occur at almost any stage when a program runs; so how do you detect them and try to recover? Over the years, numerous mechanisms have evolved. A typical approach adopted by older systems such as UNIX involved arranging for the operating system to set a special global variable whenever a method failed. Then, after each call to a method, you would check the gobal variable to see if the method succeeded. Java and most other object-oriented programming languages do not handle errors this way. It's just too error-prone, clumsy and painful. Rather, they use exceptions; if you want to write robust Java programs, you need to know about exceptions and exception handling.

In simple terms, an exception is an error that occurs at run-time.Exception handling streamlines the process of error-handling by allowing the program to specify a special code block, known as exception handler, that is invoked and executed automatically when an error occurs. Thus, there is no need to check the success/failure of each method call or a specific operation. In the event of an error occurring, the error shall be processed by the provided exception handler.

The main advantage of Java's exception handling mechanism is that it allows us to handle run-time logical errors in an automated orderly fashion. Using exception handling, we can automatically call the specific error-handling routine in the event of a particular error occurring. Exception handling is especially useful for exiting from a deeply nested set of routines when a catastrophic error occurs. Anyway, the main point to note is that exception handling provides a means to an efficient and orderly way/method of handling errors, particulary the run-time ones. This includes rectifying the situation, if somehow possible. Thus, exception handling is designed to provide a structured means to handle or take care of abnormal outputs/ events/situations. Exception handling is also important since Java defines standard exceptions for common programming errors such as divide-by-zero or index-out-of-bounds. To successfully take care of these errors, the Java program must watch out for and handle these exceptions.

5.1 THE EXCEPTION HIERARCHY

In Java, exceptions are represented by classes. And, all exception classes are derived from the built-in exception class *Throwable*, which is, in turn, is a superclass of the two exception subclases, namely, *Exception* and *Error*. Exceptions of type *Error* are generated in the JVM itself and are beyond the control of the programmer. We will only be dealing with errors of type *Exception* such as divide-by-zero, index out-of-bounds etc. One of the important subclasses of *Exception* is *RuntimeException*, which is used to represent common run-time errors. The *java.lang* standard package specifies several built-in exceptions which are derived from *RuntimeException*. You can also create your own exception subclasses derived from *Exception* as we shall see later in this chapter.

5.2 THE BASICS OF EXCEPTION HANDLING

The five keywords, viz., <u>try</u>, <u>catch</u>, and <u>throw,</u> <u>throws</u>, and <u>finally</u> are the foundation on which the whole exception handling mechanism of Java is built on. All program statements that we wish to check for exceptions are contained within the 'try' block. If an error./exception occurs within that try block, it is "thrown". We can monitor this exception using 'catch'. While system-generated exceptions like divide-by-zero and index-out-of-bounds are "thrown" by the Java run-time system automatically, we can use the keyword 'throw' to manually "throw" an exception. In some cases, an exception that is thrown out of a method must be specified as such by the 'throws' keyword. Finally, if we want to make it absolutely mandatory for any code to be executed upon exiting from a 'try' block, it can be put in a 'finally' block.

The most general forms of *try* and *catch* blocks are:

```
try
{
        // body of try block containing statement(s) to monitor for errors
}
catch(Excptype1 ExcpObj)
{
        // body of catch(Excptype1) block
}
catch(Excptype2 ExcpObj)
{
        // body of catch(Excptype2) block
}
..............................................
..............................................
..............................................
catch(ExcptypeN  ExcpObj)                    // N  is a whole number
{
        // body of catch(Excptype N) block
}
```

where, *Excptype* is the type of exception that has taken place. When an exception is thrown, it is caught by its corresponding *catch* statement, which then goes on to handle the exception. As the most general form shows, there can be more than one *catch* statements corresponding to or associated with a *try*. The type of the exception thrown determines which *catch* statement is executed. Thus, whichever of the exception types specified by the *catch* statements matches the type of exception thrown, that particular *catch* statement is executed and the rest are bypassed. When an exception is actually caught, then only does *ExcpObj* receive its value. In case no exception is thrown, then the *try* block ends normally, and all of its *catch* statements are ignored / bypassed, with the execution resuming with the first statement following the last *catch*. In this way, we come to see that *catch* statements are executed only when an exception is thrown.

Here is our first simple exception handling example for you (Example 74).

Example 74

```
// Demo_Excp1.java
/* Illustrates a simple exception;
Author: Arunesh; Date: 27/03/2011 */
class Demo_Excp1
{
	public static void  main(String args[])
	{
		int j = 10;
		System.out.println("begin");
		try
		{
			System.out.println("try BLOCK");
			for (int i = 5; j = j / i; i -= 5)
				System.out.println(j);
			System.out.println("this line shall never print");
		}
		catch(ArithmeticException excep)
		{
			System.out.println("Attempting to Divide by Zero!");
		}
		System.out.println("end");
	}
}
```

Output:

```
	begin
	try BLOCK
	2
	Attempting to Divide by Zero!
	end
```

/* In the second iteration of the *for* loop, the value of *i* becomes zero, giving rise to the *ArithmeticException: an attempt to divide by zero,* which is caught by the *catch* statement. */

If the type of exception thrown doesn't match the type mentioned in the catch statement, the exception shall not be caught and instead, abnornmal program termination shall take place. Example 75 *is a case in point.*

Example 75

```
// Demo_Excp2.java
/*Illustrates Mismatch in Type of Exception;
Author: Arunesh; Date: 27/03/2011 */
class Demo_Excp2
{
	public static void  main(String args[])
	{
		int j = 10;

		System.out.println("begin");
		try
		{
			System.out.println("try BLOCK");
			for (int i = 5; j = j / i; i -= 5)
				System.out.println(j);
			System.out.println("this line shall never print");
		}

		catch(ArrayIndexOutOfBoundsException excep)
		{
			System.out.println("Attempting to Divide by Zero!");
		}

		System.out.println("end");
	}
}
```

Output:

begin
try BLOCK
2
Abnormal program termination

/* The above example also illustrates a case of an *uncaught exception*. And, since the exception is not caught due to *mismatch* in exception type, it results in abnormal program termination, as confirmed by the output.
*/

As we have already pointed out, the code associated with a catch statement shall be executed only if it catches an exception. *Otherwise. the catch statement is bypassed altogether.* Example 76 *is a case in point.*

Example 76

```
// Demo_Excp3.java
/* Illustrates bypassing of code associated with an Exception;
/* Author: Arunesh; Date: 27/03/2011 */
class Demo_Excp3
{
        public static void  main(String args[])
        {
                System.out.println("begin");

                try
                {
                        System.out.println("try BLOCK");
                }

                catch(ArithmeticException excep)
                {
                        System.out.println("Attempting to Divide by Zero!");
                }

                System.out.println("end");
        }
}
```

Output:

```
        begin
        try BLOCK
        end
```

/* Thus, the catch statement is bypassed and ignored altogether as no exception is caught in this instance.
*/

Also, we can have nested try blocks. In such a case, if we have an exception that is not caught by the inner try block, it is transfered to the outer try block.
Example 77 *is a case in point.*

Example 77

```
// Demo_Excp4.java
/* Illustrates Nested try blocks;
Author: Arunesh; Date: 27/03/2011 */
class Demo_Excp4
{
        public static void  main(String args[])
        {
                int j = 10;
                System.out.println("begin");
                try             // outer try block
                {
                        try     // inner try block
                        {
                                System.out.println("innere try BLOCK");
                                for (int i = 5; j = j / i; i -= 5)
                                        System.out.println(j);
                        }
                        catch(ArrayIndexOutOfBoundsException excep)
                        {
                                System.out.println("No Matching Element FOUND");
                        }
                System.out.println("outer try BLOCK");
                catch(ArithmeticException excep)
                {
                        System.out.println("Attempting to Divide by Zero!");
                }
                System.out.println("end");
                }
        }
}
```

Output:

```
begin
inner try BLOCK
2
outer try BLOCK
Attempting to Divide byZero!
end
```

/* Here, the *ArithmeticException* (an attempt to divide by zero) is not caught by the inner try block but by the outer try block, as confirmed by the output. */

5.3 HOW TO HANDLE ERRORS GRACEFULLY?

(Allowing the program to continue running smoothly in case of run-time errors)

In the introductory section to this chapter, we had remarked that exception handling is a tool to prevent the occurrence of abnormal events during the normal execution flow of a program. This means that the error handler must do something rational to manage such a critical situation.

Take, for example, the following simple program (Example 78) *that manages a divide-by-zero error.* In particular, it divides the elements of one array by the elements of another. If a division-by-zero error occurs, an *ArithmeticException* is generated; in the example, this exception is handled by reporting the error and then continuing with further execution of the program. In this orderly manner, an attempt to divide by zero does not result in a catastrophic abnormal termination of the program but, is handled gracefully, by not hindering program execution.

Example 78

```
// Demo_Excp5.java
/* An Application of Exception Handling:  Managing Divide-by-Zero Situation;
Author: Arunesh; Date: 27/03/2011 */
class Demo_Excp5
{
        public static void main(String args[])
        {
                int numerators []  = {2, 4, 8, 16, 32, 64};
                int denominators [] = {2, 0, 4, 0, 0, 4};

                for (int x = 0; x < numerators.length; x++)
                {
                        try
                        {
                                System.out.println("numerators[x] + " / " +
                                                denominators[x]   " = " +
                                                numerators[x]/denominators[x]);
                        }

                        catch (ArithmeticException excep)
                        {
                                System.out.println("Division by zero not allowed");
                        }
                }
        }
}
```

Output:

2 / 2 = 1
Division by zero not allowed
8 / 4 = 2
Division by zero not allowed
Division by zero not allowed
64 / 4 = 16

/* Example 78 *reveals another remarkable point*. And that is, once an exception has been handled, it is removed from the system. Thus, in the program, each pass through the *for* loop enters the *try* block afresh and anew; any prior exceptions have already been handled; this, in turn, allows the program to handle repeated errors and exceptions.
*/

5.4 MULTIPLE CATCH CLAUSES

We can have *more than one catch statements* associated with one try block. However, each such statement must associate with a *different type of exception*.

Example 79 *is a case in point*. It handles both array boundary and divide-by-zero exceptions.

Example 79

```
// Demo_Excp6.java
/* Multiple Catch statements;
Author: Arunesh; Date: 27/03/2011 */
class Demo_Excp6
{
        public static void main(String args[])
        {
                int numerators[] = {2, 4, 8, 16, 32, 64, 128, 128, 256};

                int denominators [] = {2, 0, 4, 8, 0, 4};
                        // numerators is longer than denominators

                for (int x = 0; x < numerators.length; x++)
                {
                        try
                        {
                                System.out.println("numerators[x] + " / "
                                                + denominators[x] + " = "
                                                + numerators[x]/denominators[x]);
                        }
```

```
                catch (ArithmeticException excep)
                {
                        System.out.println("Division by zero not allowed");
                }

                catch(ArrayIndexOutOfBoundsException excep)
                {
                        System.out.println("No Matching Element FOUND"):
                }
            }
        }
}
```

Output:

```
    2 / 2 = 1
    Division by zero not allowed
    8 / 4 = 2
    16 / 8 = 2
    Division by zero not allowed
    64 / 4 = 16
    No matching element FOUND
    No matching element FOUND
    No matching element FOUND
```

/* Thus, each catch statement associates only with its corresponding type. In general, catch expressions are checked in the order in which they occur in a program. Only the first matching statement is executed; and, all other catch statements are bypassed/ignored. */

5.5 CATCHING SUBCLASS EXCEPTIONS

The order of catch clauses is of extreme importance when trying to catch exception types involving both super and sub classes. This is because a catch clause for a superclass shall also match any of its subclasses, e.g., the superclass of all exceptions is *Throwable* and whence, catching *Throwable* catches all possible exceptions.

If you need to catch exceptions of both a superclass type and a subclass type, you must put the subclass first in the catch sequence. This is because a superclass catch will also catch all subclasses. Moreover, if you put the superclass first, it shall lead to a compile-time error since it results in unreachable code.

For example, The *following program* (Example 80) creates two exception classes named *Excpt1* and *Excpt2*. *Excpt1* is derived from *Exception*. *Excpt2* is derived from *Excpt1*. The program then throws an exception of each type.

Example 80

```
// Demo_Excp7.java
/* Subclass Exceptions must come before Superclass Exceptions;
/* Author: Arunesh; Date: 27/03/2011 */
class Demo_Excp7
{
        public static void main(String args[])
        {
                int numerators[] = {2, 4, 8, 16, 32, 64, 128, 128, 256};
                int denominators [] = {2, 0, 4, 8, 0, 4};
                        // numerators is longer than denominators
                for (int x = 0; x < numerators.length; x++)
                {
                        try
                        {
                                System.out.println("numerators[x] + " / "
                                        + denominators[x] + " = "
                                        + numerators[x]/denominators[x]);
                        }
                        catch(ArrayIndexOutOfBoundsException excep)
                        {
                                System.out.println("No Matching Element FOUND"):
                        }
                        catch (Throwable excep)
                        {
                                System.out.println("Some Exception Occurred!");
                        }
                }
        }
}
```

Output:

```
        2 / 2 = 1
        Some Exception Occurred!
        8 / 4 = 2
        16 / 8 = 2
        Some Exception Occurred!
        64 / 16  = 4
        No matching element FOUND
        No matching element FOUND
        No matching element FOUND
```

/* In Example 80, the superclass *Throwable* catches all exceptions exceptions except the *ArrayIndexOutOfBoundsException* exceptions.
*/

The issue of *catching subclass exceptions* is of extreme importance in situations where you create your own subclass exceptions, that is to say, *customized exceptions*.

5.6 THROWING AN EXCEPTION

So far, we have been catching exceptions generated automatically by the JVM. But, it is also possible to throw an exception manually by the use of *throw* statement, whose general form is:

throw exceptionObj;

where throw generates the exception specified by *exceptionObj (*which must be an object of an exception class derived from *Throwable)*. Example 81 illustrates the *throw* statement by manually throwing an *ArithmeticException*.

Example 81

```
// Demo_Excp8.java
/* Illustrates throwing an  exception manually;
Author: Arunesh; Date: 27/03/2011 */
class Demo_Excp8
{
        public static void  main(String args[])
        {
                System.out.println("begin");
                try
                {
                        System.out.println("try BLOCK");
                        throw new ArithmeticException();
                                        // Manually throwing an exception
                        System.out.println("this line shall never print");
                }
                catch(ArithmeticException excep)
                {
                        System.out.println("Caught Exception");
                }
                System.out.println("end");
        }
}
```

Output:

```
begin
try BLOCK
Caught Exception
end
```

/* Carefully note how the *ArithmeticException* was generated/*thrown* using *new* in the *throw* statement. */

5.6.1 Rethrowing an Exception

An exception caught by one *catch* can be *rethrown* allowing it to be caught by an outer *catch*. Rethrowing an exception allows multiple handlers access to the exception. One handler can take care of one aspect of an exception while a second handler takes care of another. To *rethrow* an exception *exc*, simply specify throw as follows:

throw exc;

Example 82 *is a case in point.*

It rethrows an *ArrayIndexOutOfBoundsException*.

Example 82

```
// Demo_Excp9.java
/* Rethrowing an Exception;
Author: Arunesh; Date: 27/03/2011 */
class RethrowHandle
{
	public static void Exception_Generate()
	{
		int numerators = {2, 4, 8, 16, 32, 64, 128};
		int denominators = {2, 0, 4, 8, 0, 4}; // numerators is longer than denominators
		for (int x = 0; x < numerators.length; x++)
		{
			try
			{
				System.out.println("numerators[x] + " / " +
							denominastos[x] + " = "
							+ numerators[x]/denominators[x]);
			}
			catch (ArithmeticException excep)
			{
				System.out.println("Division by zero not allowed");
			}
			catch(ArrayIndexOutOfBoundsException excep)
			{
				System.out.println("No Matching Element FOUND"):
				throw excep;		// retrowing the exception
			}
		}
	}

}
```

```
class Demo_Excp9
{
        public static void  main(String args[])
        {
                try
                {
                        RethrowHandle.Exception_Generate();
                }
                catch(ArrayIndexOutOfBoundsException excep)
                {
                        System.out.println("Fatal ERROR -- Abnormal Program
                                                        Termination");
                }
        }
}
```

Output:

```
2 / 2 = 1
Division by zero not allowed
8 / 4 = 2
16 / 8 = 2
Division by zero not allowed
64 / 4 = 16
No matching element FOUND
Fatal ERROR -- Abnormal Program Termination
```

/* In Example 82, divide-by-zero errors are handled locally by *Exception_Generate()*, but an array boundary error is rethrown. Herein, the *ArrayIndexOutOfBoundsException* is handled by *main()*.
*/

5.7 USING "finally"

If we want certain code to be executed when a try/catch block is exited, we can include a finally block at the end of this try/catch block. The most general form of such a block is:

```
try
{
        // monitoring errors code
}
catch(Excptype1 ExcpObj)
{
        // handling Excptype1 Excp
}
```

```
catch(Excptype2 ExcpObj)
{
        // handling Excptype2Excp
}
..................
..................
catch(ExcptypeN ExcpObj)
{
        // handling ExcptypeN Excp; N is a whole number
}
finally
{
        // code for finally
}
```

The finally block shall necessarily be executed whenever execution leaves a *try/catch* block, irrespective of the conditions responsible for it. The finally block will also get executed if any code within the *try* block or any of its *catch* blocks returns from the method. For instance, the *following program* (Example 83) uses finally.

Example 83

```
// Demo_Excp10.java
/*  Using "finally" */
Author: Arunesh; Date: 27/03/2011;
class Demo_Excp10
{
        public static void  main(String args[])
        {
                int j = 4;
                int [ ] i = {1, 0, 2};
                System.out.println("begin");
                for (k = 0; k < 3; k++)
                        try
                        {
                                System.out.println("try BLOCK");
                                if (k == 2)
                                        i[-1] = k;
                                else
                                        {
                                                j = j / i[k];
                                                System.out.println(j);
                                                return; // back from try
                                        }
                        }
```

```
            catch(ArrayIndexOutOfBoundsException excep)
            {
                    System.out.println("Index is Out of Bounds!");
                    return;  // back from catch
            }
            catch(ArithmeticException excep)
            {
                    System.out.println("Attempting to Divide by Zero!");
            }
            finally
            {
                    System.out.println("finally);
            }
    }
}
```

Output:

```
    begin
    try BLOCK
    4
    finally
    try  BLOCK
    Attempting to Divide byZero!
    finally
    try BLOCK
    Index is Out of Bounds!
    finally
```

/* Thus, in every case, the finally code is executed irrespective of the fact how the try block is exited.
*/

There is one more point we would like to make about using "finally".

And, that is, when a finally block follows a *try* block, no *catch* statements are technically required. In such cases, the finally block is executed after exiting *try*, but exceptions are not handled.

5.8 Throwable REVISITED

So far, we have caught exceptions but have not done with the exception object itself. As you know, a catch statement allows one to specify a exception type and a parameter. This parameter receives a subclass of the exception object. As already explained, since all exceptions are subclassers of *Throwable*, all exceptions support the mthods defined by *Throwable*.

Of all the methods defined by *Throwable*, the three of utmost significance are *printStackTrace(), GetMessage(),* and *toString()*. The standard error messages and a record of all the method calls leading up to the exception can be had by means of *printStackTrace()*. To get Java's standard error message for an exception, use *getMessage()*. As a possible alternative, you can call *toString()* in order to obtain the standard error message. As a point of interest, the *toString()* method also comes into play when an exception is used as an argument to *println()*.

5.9 USING throws

In case a method generates an exception which it does not handle on its own, it must declare that exception in a *throws* clause. The most general form of a method which includes *throws* is as follows:

```
return_type method_name(parameter_list) throws excep_list
{
        // method_body
}
```

where, *excep_list* is a comma-separated list of exceptions which the method might *throw* outside of itself.

Now, you would ask me as to why we did not specify the *throws* clause for some of the previous examples which threw exceptions outside of a method. The simple answer is that exceptions which are subclasses of *Error* or *RuntimeException* need not be mentioned in a *throws* clause. All other exceptions are required to be specified as such else it will lead to a comile-time error.

Let's now take an example (Example 84) which handles *IOException* (we shall be dealing with I/O in detail in the next chapter) using the *throws* statement.

Example 84

```
// Demo_Excp11.java
/* Demonstrates the throws clause;
Author: Arunesh; Date: 22/03/2011 */
import java.io;
class Demo_Excp11
{
        public static char request(String str) throws IOException
        {
```

```
            System.out.print(str + ": ");
            return (char) System.in.read();
        }
        public static void main(String args[])
        {
            char c;
            try
            {
                    c = request("Please Enter a letter");
            }
            catch(IOException excep)
            {
                    System.out.println("An I/O Exception Occurred!");
                    c = 'x';
            }

            System.out.println("Letter Entered by You is " + c);
        }
}
```

/* Example 84 creates a method named *request()* which requests for and needs a character from the keyboard. Since input is being performed, an *IOException* might occur, which the *request()* method does not handle by itself; whence, it specifies a *throws* clause, which, in turn, implies that the calling method, *main()*, in this case, must handle it and deal with the errors, if any.
*/

5.10 BUILT-IN EXCEPTIONS OF JAVA

Java specifies and defines several exception classes (most of these classes are derived from the standard *RuntimeException*) inside its standard package *java.lang*, which being implicitly imported into all Java programs, implies that most of the exceptions derived from *RuntimeException* **are directly available and need not be specified in the throws list of any method.** Theseare known as unchecked exceptions such as *ArithmeticException, ArrayIndexOutOfBoundsException, IndexOutOfBoundsException* etc. Then, there are the checked exceptions such as *IllegalAccessException* defined by *java.lang*, which must be specified in the *throws* statement in case a method generates them and does not handle them by itself. Besides the checked and unchecked exceptions, Java defines several other types of exceptions relating to its various class libraries such as *IOException*.

Note: We have already given an instance of *IOException* in Example 84.

5.11 CREATING CUSTOM EXCEPTION SUBCLASSES

Java's built-in exceptions are able to handle most of the errors. Yet, its exception handling mechanism is not limited to merely these errors. You can create customized exceptions of your own as well. To create an exception, simply define a subclass of *Exception*, which, in turn, is a subclass of *Throwable*. The exception classes you create will have all the methods specified by *Exception* available to them. You may like to override one or more of these methods, though.

Example 85 creates a custom exception called *FractionalResultException*, which is generated when the result of dividing the integer values results in a fractional part. *FractionalResultException* has two fields to hold the integer values, a constructor, and an override of the *toString()* method, which gives the description of the exception to be output using *println()*.

Example 85

```
// Demo_Excp12.java
/* Creates and uses a custom exception;
Author: Arunesh; Date: 22/03/2011 */

class FractionalResultException extends Exception
{
        int numer;      // the numerator
        int denom;      // the denominator

        FractionalResultException(int a,. int b)
        {
                numer = a;
                denom = b;
        }

        public String tostring()
        {
                return "Result of " + numer + " / " + denom + " is Fractional");
        }
}

class Demo_Excp12
{
        public static void main(string args[])
        {
                int n [] = {4, 8, 15, 32, 61, 128, 256, 512};
                int d [] = {2, 0, 4, 0, 4, 2};
```

```
        for (int k = 0; k < n.length; k++)
        {
            try
            {
                if (n[k] % 2 != 0)
                    throw new FractionalResultException(n[k], d[k]);

                System.out.println(n[k] + " / " + d[k]
                                   + " = "+ n[k]/d[k]);
            }

            catch(ArithmeticException excep)
            {
                System.out.println("Division by zero not allowed");
            }

            catch(ArrayIndexOutOfBoundsException excep)
            {
                System.out.println("No matching element FOUND");
            }

            catch(FractionalResultException excep)
            {
                System.out.println(excep);
            }

        }
    }
}
```

Output:

```
4 / 2 = 2
Division by zero not allowed
Result of 15 / 4 is Fractional
Division by zero not allowed
Result of 61 / 4 is Fractional
128 / 2 = 64
No matching element FOUND
No matching element FOUND
```

5.12 WINDING IT UP!

First of all, let's review the conditions that cause an exception to be generated. Exceptions are geneated in three different ways. First, the JVM can generate an exception in response to some internal error beyond your control. Normally, your program won't handle such exceptions. Second, standard exceptions, such as those corresponding to divide-by-zero or index-out-of-bounds, are generated by errors in the prgram code. You do need to handle such eceptions. Third, you can manually generate an exceptions by means of the *throw* statement. **But, the point to be noted is that that no matter how an exception is generated, it is handled in the same way.**

Now, let;s try to see why would you want to catch superclass exceptions. There are two important reasons. First, if you add a catch clause that catches exceptions of type Exception, then, in effect, you have added a 'catch all' clause to your exception handler that deals with all possible program exceptions. **Such a 'catch all' clause would come in extremely handy in a situation where abnormal program termination must be avoided no matter what occurs.** Second, in some cases, an entire category of exceptions can be handled by the same clause. Catching the superclass of these exceptions allows you to handle all without any duplicate code.

Finally, let's try to see **when you would use exception handling in your program and when you would create your own custom exception subclasses.** Since the Java API makes extensive use of exceptions to report errors, nearly all real-world programs will make use of excption handling. his is the part of exception handling that most new Java programmers find easy. It is much harder to decide when and how to use your own custom-made exception subclasses.

In general, errors can be reported in two ways, namely, returning values and exceptions. Which approach is better than the other? Simply put, in Java, exception handling should be the norm. Certainly, in some cases, returning an error code is a valid alternative. But, exception handling is a much more powerful, structured, and streamlined approach to handle errors. And, it is the means by which professional Java programmers handle errors in program code.

PRACTICAL SESSION

1. What do you mean by an 'exception'?
   How is it "handled" in Java?

2. When should a program 'throw' an exception?
   What are the advantages of using the exception handling mechanism in a Java program?

3. What is placed inside the 'try' block? What in the 'catch' block?
   When do we need to use multiple catch handlers?

4. (a) What are the two direct subclasses of Throwable?
   (b) What class is at the top of the exception hierarchy?
   (c) Explain the circumstances/situations under which the following statements would be needed:
      (i) *catch*
      (ii) *throw;*
      (iii) *throws;*

5. State what shall happen *when/if*:
   (i) An exception is rethrown within a catch block.
   (ii) *throw()* is placed in a method header line.
   (iii) *catch* is the first of a cluster of catch handlers.
   (iv) A method throws an unspecified exception.
   (v) A catch handler throws an exception.
   (vi) Several handlers match the type of exception thrown.
   (vii) No catch handler matches the type of exception thrown.
   (viii) An exception is thrown outside a try block.

6. Point out the error(s), if any, in the following Java statements/code:
   (i)
```
.................................
num [8] = 8;
catch(ArrayIndexOutOfBoundsException Excep)
{
        ....................
}
```
   (ii)
```
throw;
```
   (iii)
```
class NewClass
{
        ....................
}
................................
throw new NewClass();.
```

(iv)
```
class J extends Exception
{
        ...................
}
class K extends J
{
        ...................
}
...............................
try
{
        ...................
}
catch(J Excep)
(
        ...................
}
catch (K Excep)
{
        ...................
}
```

(v)
```
try
{
        if (!i) throw ArithmeticException();
}
catch(ArithmeticException excep)
(
        System.out.println(excep);
}
```

7. (a) Where is *throw* used? Give structure of its usage.
   (b) Where is *throws* used? Give structure of its usage along with a suitable example.

8. Write a program that generates a custom exception if any of its command-line arguments is negative.

9. What happens on floating-point division-by-zero? On integer division-by-zero?

10. Is it essential to catch all types of exceptions?

11. How many 'catch' clauses can we use with one 'try' block?

12. What is a 'finally' block? When and how is it used? Give an appropriate example.

13. Identify the error(s), if any, in the following Java program:

```
void compute(int i)
{
        if (i)
                throw new ArithmeticException();
        else
                throw new IndexOutOfBoundsException();
}
void compute(string str)
{
        try
        {
                if (str)
                        throw new ArithmeticException();
                else
                        throw new IndexOutOfBoundsException();
        }
        catch(ArithmeticException excep)
        {
                System.out.println(excep);
        }
}
class Generate_Excp
{
        public static void main(String args[])
        {
                try
                {
                        compute("everybody");
                        compute(1);
                        compute(0);
                }
                catch(ArithmeticException excep)
                {
                        System.out.println(excep);
                }
                catch(IndexOutOfBoundsException excep)
                {
                        System.out.println(excep);
                }
        }
}
```

14. Define an exception called "NoMatchExcep" that is thrown when a string is not equal to "ARUNESH". Write a program that uses this exception.

15. The following code throws an exception in case the desired input is not received. Debug the code:

```
class DEMO_EXCP
{
        public static void main(String args[])
        {
                if (args[0] == "Goyal")
                        System.out.println("Given string is Correct!");
                else
                        throw new Exception("INVALID string!!");
        }
}
```

Chapter 6

INPUT/OUTPUT

6.0 INTRODUCTION

We have already used I/O (Input/Output) earlier such as *System.out.println()* but without formal explanation. It was important first to discuss classes, inheritance, and exceptions in detail. Now, we seek to describe Java's approach to I/O. We shall study both console I/O and file I/O in this chapter.

A relatively new addition to Java is called NIO (New I/O), and it is one of the more interesting packages since it supports a channel-buffer based approach to I/O operations. It must be made clear at the outset that this new approach is meant to supplement, and not supplant the traditional stream-based approach of Java to I/O mechanisms.

Now, a word about the *Formatter* class of Java. With the release of JDK 5 (Java Development Kit 5), Java added a new capability, viz. the ability to easily create formatted output akin to the *printf()* style of functions in C/C++. You might wonder why Java was not able to earlier provide such a facility. The simple reason was that the *printf()* style formatting requires the use of variable-length arguments (*varargs*), which Java did not support before JDK 5. Once *varargs* became available with the release of JDK 5, it was easy pickings to add a general-purpose formatter. At the roots of Java's formatted output is the *Formatter* class, which provides format conversions that let you display numbers, strings, date and time in almost every format as per your requirements very much similar in fashion to the *printf()* function of C/C++.

6.1 STREAMS & STREAM CLASSES

Java performs I/O through streams (NIO is a relatively new addition. We shall discuss it later on in a separate section). Now, what exactly is a stream? A stream is an abstraction that produces/consumes information. A stream is linked to a physical device by the Java I/O system. The original version of Java defined only byte streams but character streams were added rather quickly. While byte streams are especially useful for handling I/O operations on bytes, the character streams are more convenient for handling I/O operations on characters. While byte streams can be conveniently used for reading/writing binary data and working with files, character streams use Unicode representation and hence, can be internationalized, and are, in some cases, more efficient than byte streams. But, we need to sound a caveat at this juncture. And, that is, at the lowest level, all Input/Output is still byte-oriented, with the character streams simply providing an effective means to handle character operations.

Byte streams are defined by using two class hierarchies, at the to of which are two abstract classes, viz. *InputStream* & *OutputStream*. While *InputStream* describes the behaviour of byte input streams, *OutputStream* relates to the behaviour of byte output streams. Similarly, character streams are defined by using two class hierarchies, at the top of which are two abstract classes, viz. *Reader* & *Writer*. While *Reader* is used for input of characters, *Writer* is used for output of characters.

There are also the three predefined standard streams in Java, viz. *System.in, System.out* & *System.err*. *System.in* refer to the standard input stream, the keyboard, by default. *System.out* refers to the standard output stream, the console, by default. *System.err* refers to the standard error stream, the console once again, by default. But, these three streams can be redirected to any compatible I/O device. *System.in* is an object of type *InputStream* while *System.out* & *System.err* are objects of type *PrintStream*. These are all byte streams, even though they are typically used to read/write characters from/to the console.

6.2 I/O USING BYTE STREAMS

As already explained, at the top of the byte stream hierarchy are the *InputStream* & *OutputStream* classes. The methods defined by these two classes are available to all their subclasses, and, in general, throw an *IOException* on error. *InputStream* defines only one input method, *read()*, which reads bytes and its general version is as under:

int read() throws IOException

When reading from *System.in* (which, as already explained, is the keyboard, by default), pressing the <*Enter*> key generates an end-of-stream condition. Example 86 demonstrates reading an array of bytes from *System.in*.

Console output is most easily done with *print()* & *println()*, with which you are already familiar. These methods are defined by *PrintStream*, which is the type of the object referenced by *System.out*, the console, by default, as already explained. Since *PrintStream* is an output stream derived from *OutputStream*, it also implements the low-level *write()* method so that it is possible to write to the console using *write()*, whose simplest form defined by *PrintStream* is as under:

void write(int bytevalue) throws IOException

This method writes the byte specified by *bytevalue* and it is important to note that although *bytevalue* is an integer, only the lower-order 8 bits are written.

Example 87 uses *write()* to output the character 'Z' followed by a newline, a tab and the character 'z'.

Example 86

```
// ReadConsole.java
/* Illustrates reading of bytes from console;
Author: Arunesh; Date: 23/03/2011 */
import java.io.*;
class ReadConsole
{
        public static void  main(String args[]) throws IOException
        {
                byte bytedata [ ]= new byte[25];
                System.out.println("Please enter some characters");
                System.in.read(bytedata);
                        // read an array of bytes from the console (keyboard)
                System.out.println(("The characters entered by you are as follows:-");
                for (int k = 0; k < bytedata.length; k++)
                        System.out.print(char) bytedata[k]);
        }
}
```

Output (A sample Run):

```
        Please enter some characters
        A SAMPLE RUN
        The characters entered by you are as follows:-
        A SAMPLE RUN
```

Example 87

```
// WriteConsole.java
/* Illustrates writing of bytes to console;
Author: Arunesh; Date: 23/03/2011 */
class WriteConsole
{
        public static void  main(String args[])
        {
                int bite;

                bite = 'Z';
                System.out.write(bite); // write a byte to the console
                System.out.write('\n');
                System.out.write('\t');
                bite = 'z';
                System.out.write(bite);
        }
}
```

Output:

```
        Z
                z
```

To create a byte stream linked to a file, we use *FileInputStream* or *FileOutputStream.* To open a file, we simply create an object of one of these classes, specifying the name of the file to the constructor and once the file is open, we can read/write from/to it. A file is opened for input by creating a *FileInputStream* object. The most commonly used constructor for this is as given under:-

FileInputStream(String file) throws FileNotFoundException

where, *file* specifies the name of the file to be opened and in case, the *file* does not exist, a *FileNotFoundException* is thrown.

To read from a file, we use the same version of *read()* as used for reading from the console. Each time it is called, *read()* reads a single byte from the file and returns it as an integer value. It returns -1 when the end-of-file (EOF) is encountered and throws an *IOException* when an error occurs. When you are done with a file, you must close it by using the *close()* method whose general form is given as under:-

void close() throws IOException

Closing a file releases the system resources allocated to it, which then can be used by another file.

Example 88 uses *read()* to intput and display the contents of a text file whose name is specified as a command-line argument.

Example 88

```
// ReadFile.java
/* Illustrates reading and displaying a text file;
Author: Arunesh; Date: 23/03/2011 */
/* To read and display a text file called file.txt, you can use the following command line:
        java ReadFile file.txt   */
import java.io.*;
class ReadFile
{
        public static void  main(String args[]) throws IOException
        {
                int bite;
                FileInputStream fis;

                try
                {
                        fis = new FileInputStream(args[0]);
                }
                catch(FileNotFoundException excp)
                {
                        System.out.println("File NOT Found");
                        return;
                }
```

```
        catch(ArrayIndexOutOfBoundsException excp)
        {
                System.out.println("Usage: ReadFile filename");
                return;
        }
        //      read bytes until EOF is encountered
        do
        {
                bite = fis.read();          // reading from the file
                if (bite != -1)
                        System.out.print((char) bite);
                                    // displaying the contents of the file
        } while (bite != -1);
                // when EOF is reached, bite equals -1
        fis.close();
    }
}
```

/* Note the *try/catch* blocks which handle the two error situations that might occur when this program (Example 88) is used, viz. the specified file being not found or the user forgetting to mention the name of the file. This approach can be used any time you use command-line arguments. */

To open a file for output, we create a *FileOutputStream* object. The two most commonly used constructors for this are given as under:-

FileOutputStream(String file) throws FileNOtFoundException
FileOutputStream(String file, boolean apnd)
throws FileNotFoundException

If the file cannot be created for any reason, a *FileNotfoundException* is thrown. In the first form, when an output file is opened, any preexisting file by the same name is destroyed while in the second form, if *apnd* is true, the output is appended to the end of the file, and if *apnd* is false, the file is overwritten.

To write to a file, we use the same version of *write()* as used for writing to the console. For your reference, we are repeating this form as under:-

void write(int bytevalue) throws IOException

This method writes the byte specified by *bytevalue* to the file and you may note that although *bytevalue* is declared to be an integer, only the lower-order 8 bits are written and if an error occurs during writing, an *IOException* is thrown.

When you are done with an output file, you must close it by using *close()*, shown as under:-

void close() throws IOException

Closing a file releases any system resources allocated to it, which then can be used by another file. Moreover, it ensures that any output left in a disk buffer is actually written to the disk.

Example 89 copies the contents of a text file, the name of the source and the target files being specified as command-line arguments (it writes the contents of the source file to the target file).

Example 89

```
// WriteFile.java
/* Illustrates writing and copying a text file;
Author: Arunesh; Date: 23/03/2011 */
/* To copy a text file called file1.txt to a text file called file2.txt, you can use the following
command line:
        java WriteFile file1.txt file2.txt
*/
import java.io.*;
class WriteFile
{
        public static void main(String args[]) throws IOException
        {
                int bite;
                FileInputStream fis;
                File OutputStram fos;

                try
                {
                        try     // open input file
                        {
                                fis = new FileInputStream(args[0]);
                        }
                        catch(FileNotFoundException excp)
                        {
                                System.out.println("INPUT File NOT Found");
                                return;
                        }
                        try     // open output file
                        {
                                fos = new FileOutputStream(args[1]);
                        }
                        catch(FileNotFoundException excp)
                        {
                                System.out.println("ERROR Opening OUTPUT File");
                                return;
                        }
                }
```

```
        catch(ArrayIndexOutOfBoundsException excp)
        {
                System.out.println("Usage: WriteFile filename1 filename2");
                return;
        }
        //      copy file
        try
        {
                do
                {
                        bite = fis.read();          // reading from the first file
                        if (bite != -1)
                                fos.write(bite); /* writing the contents of the first
                                                    file to the second file */
                } while (bite != -1);
                // when EOF is reached, bite equals -1
        }
        catch (IOException excp)
        {
                System.out.println("FILE Error");
        }
        fis.close();
        fos.close();
    }
}
```

6.3 BINARY I/O

Uptil now, we have been reading/writing bytes containing ASCII characters, but it is possible (and quite common) to read/write binary values of the Java built-in types such as *int, double, short* etc. For this, we shall use *DataOutputStream* and *DataInputStream*. While using these streams, what is important is to understand the fact that this data is read/written using its internal binary form, and not its human-readable text format.

6.3.1 Binary Output (Using DataOutPutStream)

DataOutputStream implements the *DataOutput* interface. This interface defines methods that can write all of Java's simple types. Several of these commonly used methods are shown in Table 6.1. All of them throw an *IOException* on failure.

The constructor for *DataOutputStream* is as under (note that it is built upon an instance of *OutputStream*):-

DataOutputStream(OutputStream output)

where, *output* is the stream to which data is written. To write output to a file, you can use the object created by *FileOutputStream* for this parameter.

Table 6.1 Comonly used Output Methods Defined by *DataOutputStream*

Method	Description
void writeInt(int value)	*Writes the int specified by value*
void writeByte(int value)	*Writes the low-order byte specified by value*
void writeLong(long value)	*Writes the long specified by value*
void writeShort(int value)	*Writes the value specified as a short*
void writeDouble(double value)	*Writes the double specified by value*
void writeFloat(float value)	*Writes the float specified by value*
vovoid writeChar(int value)	*Writes the value as a character*
void writeBoolean(boolean value)	*Writes the boolean specified by value*

6.3.2 Binary Input (Using DataInPutStream)

DataInputStream implements the *DataInput* interface. This interface defines methods that can read all of Java's simple types. Several of these commonly used methods are shown in Table 6.2. All of them throw an *IOException* on failure.

The constructor for *DataInputStream* is as under (note that it is built upon an instance of *InputStream*):-:

DataInputStream(InputStream input)

where, *input* is the stream from where data is read. To read input from a file, you can use the object created by *FileInputStream* for this parameter.

Table 6.2 Comonly used Input Methods Defined by *DataInputStream*

Method	Description
bool readBoolean()	*Reads a boolean*
byte readByte()	*Reads a byte*
charr readChar()	*Reads a char*
double readDouble()	*Reads a double*
float readFloat()	*Reads a float*
int readInt()	*Reads an int*
long readLong()	*Reads a long*
short readShort()	*Reads a short*

Binary I/O - *A CASE STUDY*

In this *case study*, we take up Example 90, which is demonstrative of both *DataOutputStream* and *DataInputStream*. It writes and then reads back various types of data to and from a file called "myfile".

Example 90

```
/* Write and then Read back Binary data using DataOutputStream and
DataInputStream, respectively */
/* Author: Arunesh; Date: 23/03/2011 */

import java.io.*;

class DataWrtRd
{
	public static void main(String args[])
	{
		DataOutputStream datawrt;
		DataInputStream datard;

		int k = 100;
		double d = 2345.67;
		bool b = false;
		float f;

		try	// open file for writing
		{
			datawrt = new DataOutputStream(new FileOutputStream
									("myfile"));
		}
		catch (IOException excep)
		{
			System.out.println("Error opening file");
			return;
			// stop the program since file cannot be opened
		}
```

```
try     // write data to file: "myfile"
{
        System.out.println("Writing to myfile:\t" + k);
        datawrt.writeInt(k);

        System.out.println("Writing to myfile:\t" + d);
        datawrt.writeDouble(d);

        System.out.println("Writing to myfile:\t" + b);
        datawrt.writeBoolean(b);

        System.out.println("Writing to myfile:\t" + (9.1 * 11.3));
        datawrt.writeFloat(9.1 * 11.3)
}
catch (IOException excep)
{
        System.out.println("Write ERROR");
}
finally
{
        datawrt.close();        // close file: myfile
}

System.out.println();

try     // Now, open file for reading
{
        datard = new DataInputStream(new
                        FileInputStream("myfile"));
}
catch (IOException excep)
{
        System.out.println("Error opening file:");
        return;
        // stop the program since file cannot be opened
}
```

```
            try      // read data from file: "myfile"
            {
                     k = datard.readInt();
                     System.out.println("Reading from myfile:\t" + k);

                     d = datard.readDouble();
                     System.out.println(Reading from myfile:\t" + d);

                     b = datard.readBoolean();
                     System.out.println("Reading from myfile:\t" + b);

                     f = datard.readFloat();
                     Console.WriteLine("Reading from myfile:\t" + f);
            }
            catch (IOException excep)
            {
                     System.out.println("Read ERROR");
            }
            finally
            {
                     datard.Close();        // close file: myfile
            }
        }
}
```

<u>**Output**</u>**:**

Writing to myfile: 100
Writing to myfile: 2345.67
Writing to myfile: False
Writing to myfile: 102.83

Reading from myfile: 100
Reading from myfile: 2345.67;
Reading from myfile: False
Reading from myfile: 102.83

/* Upon examination of the file: "*myfile*", produced by this program, you will find that it contains binary data, and not human-readable text.
***/**

6.4 USING RANDOM ACCESS FILES

Uptil now, we have only used *sequential files* - files accessed in a stricly linear fashion, one byte after another. But, the contents of a file can be accessed in a *random order* also. We shall be using *RandomAccessFile* for this, which encapsulates a random-access file. *RandomAccessFile* is not derived from *InputStream* or *OutputStream*. Rather, it implements the two interfaces, viz. *DataInput* and *DataOutput*, which define the basic Input/Output methods. The constructor for *RandomAccessFile* is shown as under:-

RandomAccessFile(String file, String acs) throws FileNotFoundException

where, *file* indicates the name of the file and *acs* indicates the type of file access allowed: in case it is "r", the file is read-only, but if it is ":rw", the file can be read as well as written.

RandomAccessFile also supports positioning requests, i.e., you can position the file pointer within the file with the help of the *seek()* method having the following form:

void seek(long newPosition) throws IOException

where, *newPosition* specifies the new position (in bytes) of the *file pointer* from the beginninig of the file. After a call to *seek()*, the next read/write operation will occur at the new file position. If an error occurs while seeking, an *IOException* is thrown.

RandomAccessFile implements both the *read()* & *write()* methods. As already explained, it also implements the *DataInput* and *DataOutput* interfaces, which, in turn, implies that the methods to read and write the simple types such as *readDouble()* & *writeInt()*, are also available for use.

Example 91 is illustrative of *random access* I/O. It writes the lowercase alphabet in reverse order to a file and then reads it back in non-sequential order.

Example 91

```
/* Demonstrates Random Access I/O  */
/* Author: Arunesh; Date: 23/03/2011 */

import java.io.*;

class RandomAccess
{
        public static void main(String args[]) throws IOException
        {
                char c;
                RandomAccessFile randacsfil;

                try     // open file
                {
                        randacsfil = new RandomAccessFile("myfile.dat", "rw");
                }
```

```
catch(FileNotFoundException excep)
{
        System.out.println("Unable to OPEN File");
        return;         // stop the program since file cannot be opened
}
// write lowercase alphabet to the file in reverse order
for (int k = 0; k < 26; k++)
        try
        {
                randacsfil.writeByte((byte) ('z' - k));
        }
        catch(IOException excep)
        {
                System.out.println("ERROR Writing to FILE");
                return;
        }
try
{
        // read back particular values now
        randacsfil.seek(0);     // seek to 1st byte
        c = (char) randacsfil.readByte();
        System.out.println("First value is:\t" + c);

        randacsfil.seek(1);     // seek to 2nd byte
        c = (char) randacsfil.readByte();
        System.out.println("Second value is:\t" + c);

        randacsfil.seek(4);     // seek to 5th byte
        c = (char) randacsfil.readByte();
        System.out.println("Fifth value is:\t" + c);

        System.out.println();

        // now, read every third value
        System.out.println("Every third value is as follows:);
        for (int k = 0; k < 26; k +=3;)
        {
                randacsfil.seek(k);     // seek to kth byte
                c = (char) randacsfils.readByte();
                System.out.print(c + "\t");
        }
        System.out.println();
}
```

```
            catch (IOException excep)
            {
                  System.out.println("ERROR Seeking/Reading");
            }
            finally
            {
                  randacsfil.close();     // close file
            }
      }
}
```

Output:

```
      First value is: z
      Second value is:       y
      Fifth value is: v

      Every third value is as follows:
      z     w     t     q     n     k     h     e     b
```

6.5 I/O USING CHARACTER STREAMS

As already explained, at the top of the character stream hierarchy are the *Reader* & *Writer* classes. The methods defined by these two abstract classes are available to all their subclasses, and, in general, throw an *IOException* on error.

For code that will be internationalized, reading from the console using character streams is a better option than using byte streams. But, as you know *System.in* is a byte stream. So, it is imperative to wrap it into some type of *Reader*. For reading console input, the best class is *BufferedReader* but this cannot be constructed directly from *System.in*. We must first convert it into a character stream for which we can use *InputStreamReader* that converts bytes into characters. We use the constructor shown as under to obtain an *InputStreamReader* object which is linked to *System.in*:-

```
InputStreamReader(InputStream inputstream)
```

Note that since *System.in* refers to an object of type *InputStream*, it can be used for *inputstream*. The next step is to construct a *BufferedReader* using the object produced by *InputStreamReader* by means of the constructor shown as under:-

```
BufferedReader(Reader inputreader)
```

where, *inputreader* is the stream that is linked to the instance of *BufferedReader*, which is being created.

Thus, we see that *BufferedReader* that is connected to the console is created by the following line of code, putting it all together:-

```
BufferedReader bufrdr =
      new BufferedReader(new InputStreamReader(System.in));
```

After the execution of this line of code, *bufrdr* will be a charcter stream linked to the console via *System.in*.

Reading from *System.in* can be achieved using the *read()* method defined by the BufferedReader similar to the manner we used for byte streams. BufferedReader defines three versions of read() of which the two most commonly used ones are given as under:-

int read() throws IOException
int read(char data[]) throws IOException

The first method reads a single Unicode character and returns -1 when the end-of-stream is reached. The second version reads characters from the input stream and puts them into *data* until the array is full, the *EOF* is reached or an error occurs. It returns the number of characters read or -1 at end-of-stream. Both throw *IOException* on error. While reading from *System.in*, pressing the <*Enter*> key generates an end-of-stream condition. Example 92 is illustrative of *read()* by reading from the console until the user presses '*q*' or '*Q*'.

Example 92

```
// Read1.java
/* Illustrates reading of characters from console using a BufferedReader;
Author: Arunesh; Date: 23/03/2011 */
import java.io.*;
class Read1
{
        public static void  main(String args[]) throws IOException
        {
                char ch;
                BufferedReader bufrdr =
                        new BufferedReader(new InputStreamReader(System.in));
                                // create BufferedReader linked to System.in
                System.out.println("Please enter some characters; 'q' or 'Q' to Quit");
                // now, read the characters
                do
                {
                        ch = (char) bufrdr.read();
                        System.out.println(ch);
                } while (ch != 'q' && ch!= 'Q');
        }
}
```

Output (A sample Run):

```
        Please enter some characters; 'q' or 'Q' to Quit
        ROM q
        R
        O
        M

        q
```

Reading a string from the keyboard is accomplished by using the following version of *readLine()*, which is a mehod of the *BufferedReader* class:-

String readLine() throws IOException

This member of the *BufferedReader* returns a *String* object containing the characters read and returns null if reading is attempted at end-of-stream condition. Example 93 is illustrative of *readLine()* by reading from the console until the user enters "*QUIT*".

<u>Example 93</u>

```
// Read2.java
/* Illustrates reading of Strings from console using a BufferedReader;
Author: Arunesh; Date: 23/03/2011 */
import java.io.*;
class Read2
{
        public static void  main(String args[]) throws IOException
        {
                String s;
                BufferedReader bufrdr =
                        new BufferedReader(new InputStreamReader(System.in));
                                // create BufferedReader linked to System.in
                System.out.println("Please enter some strings; 'QUIT' to STOP");
                // now, read the lines of text/strings
                do
                {
                        s = bufrdr.readLine();
                        System.out.println(s);
                } while (!s.equals("QUIT"));
        }
}
```

For console output, we can use System.out but the preferred way in real-world programs is via a *PrintWriter* stream which is one of the character-based classes, making it easier to internationalize your code. *PrintWriter* defines many constructors of which we shall use as given under:

PrintWriter(OutputStream outputstream, boolean flushOnNewline)

where, *outputstream* is an object of type *OutputStream* and *flushOnNewline* controls the flushing of output stream every time *println()* is called. If it is *true*, flushing occurs automatically else it is not automatic.

PrintWriter supports the *print()* and *println()* methods for all types including *Object* so that these can be used in a similar fashion as with *System.out*. If an argument is not a simple type, the *PrintWriter* methods call the object's *toString()* method and then output the result. To write to the console using *PrintWriter*, you must specify *System.out* for the output stream and flush the stream as well after every call to *println()*, e.g., the line of code as follows creates a *PrintWriter* connected to console output:-

PrintWriter prnwrt = new PrintWriter(System.out, true);

Example 94 is illustrative of using a *PrintWriter* to handle console output.

<u>Example 94</u>

```
// PrtWrt.java
/* Illustrates PrintWriter to handle console output;
Author: Arunesh; Date: 23/03/2011 */
import java.io.*;
public class PrtWrt
{
        public static void  main(String args[])
        {
                PrintWriter prnwrt = new PrintWriter(System.out, true);
                                // create PrintWriter linked to System.out
                int k = 101;
                double dbl = 111.21;

                pw.println("A SAMPLE PrintWriter");
                pw. println(k);
                pw.println(dbl);
                pw.println();
                pw.println(k + " + " dbl + " + " is " k + dbl);
        }
}
```

<u>Output</u> :

```
A SAMPLE PrintWriter
101
111.21

101 + 111.21 is 101111.21
```

Even though byte-based file I/O is quite common, it is possible to use character-oriented streams for this purpose. The main advantage of character streams is that they operate on Unicode characters directly. Thus, for handling unicode text, character streams are the best option. To perform character-based file handling, we use *FileReader* and *FileWriter* for **file input** and **file output,** respectively.

6.5.1 Character-Based File Output (Using FileWriter)

FileWriter creates a *Writer* which can be used for writing to a file. Its commonly used two constructors are as under:-

FileWriter(String file) throws IOException

FileWriter(String file, boolean apnd) throws IOException

where, *file* is the full path name of the file. In the second version, if *apnd* is *true*, the output is appended to the end of file else it is overwritten. Both throw *IOException* on failure.

FileWriter is derived from *OutputStreamWriter* and *Writer* so that it has access to all the methods defined by these latter two classes.

Example 95 is a simple key-to-disk utility that reads line of text entered at the keyboard and writes them to a text file named "*myfile.txt*". Text is read until the user enters the word "STOP". This example uses a *FileWriter* to output to the file "*myfile.txt*".

Example 95

```
// KeyToDisk.java
/* Demonstrates a simple key-to-disk Utility that uses a FileWriter;
Author: Arunesh; Date: 23/03/2011 */
import java.io.*;
class KeyToDisk
{
        public static void main(String args[]) throws IOException
        {
                String s;
                FileWriter fwrt;
                BufferedReader bufrdr =
                        new BufferedReader(new InputStreamReader(System.in));

                try     // open the file stream first
                {
                        fwrt = new FileWriter("myfile.txt");
                }
                catch (IOException excep)
                {
                        System.out.println("Error opening file:");
                        return; // stop the program since file cannot be opened
                }

                System.out.println("Enter text ('STOP' to quit)");
```

```
        do
        {
                System.out.print(": ");
                s = bufrdr.readLine();

                if (s.compareTo("STOP") == 0)
                        break;

                s = s + "\r\n"; // add carriage return and newline
                fwrt.write(s);  // write string to the file
        } while (s.compareTo("STOP") ! = 0);

        fwrt.close();
    }
}
```

6.5.2 Character-Based File Input (Using FileReader)

FileReader creates a *Reader* which can be used for reading from a file. Its commonly used constructor is as under:-

FileReader(String file) throws FileNotFoundException

where, *file* is the full path name of the file. It throws *FileNotFoundException* in case the file does not exist.

FileReader is derived from *InputStreamWriter* and *Reader* so that it has access to all the methods defined by these latter two classes.

Example 96 is a simple disk-to-screen utility that reads a text file named "*myfile.txt*" and displays its contents on the screen so that it is just the complement of the key-to disk utility as shown in Example 95.

Example 96

```
// DiskToScreen.java
/* Demonstrates a simple disk-to-screen Utility that uses a FileReader;
Author: Arunesh; Date: 23/03/2011 */
import java.io.*;
class DiskToScreen
{
    public static void main(String args[]) throws Exception
    {
        String s;

        FileReader frdr = new FileReader("myfile.txt");
        BufferedReader bufrdr = new BufferedReader(frdr);
```

```
        while ((s = bufrdr.readLine()) ! = null)
                System.out.println(s);
                                        // READ LINES OF TEXT FROM THE FILE &
                                        // DISPLAY THEM ON THE SCREEN

        frdr.close();
    }
}
```

/* Notice, how the *FileReader,* frdr, has been wrapped in a *BufferedReader,* bufrdr, in this program, to give iot access to *readLine()* */

6.6 NEW I/O (NIO)

Java 2, version 1.4 added a new way to handle I/O operations. Called the *new I/O APIs*, it is one of the most interesting additions as it supports a channel-based approach to I/O operations. The new I/O classes are contained in *java.nio* and its subordinate packages such as *java.nio.channels* and *java.nio.charset*.

The new I/O system (*NIO*) is built upon two foundational items, namely, *buffers* and *channels*. A buffer holds data. A channel represents an open connection to an I/O device such as a file or a socket. In general, to use NIO, you have to obtain a channel to an I/O device and a buffer to hold data. You then operate on the buffer, inputting/outputting data as per the requirements.

Two other entities used by the new I/O system are *charsets* and *selectors*. A charset defines the way that bytes are mapped on to characters. You can encode a sequence of characters into bytes using an *encoder*. You can decode a sequence of bytes into corresponding characters using a *decoder*. A selector supports key-based, non-blocking, multiplexed I/O, that is to say, selectors enable you to perform I/O through multiple channels. Such selectors are most suitable for socket-based channels.

We might as well point out before finishing off this section that the new I/O subsystem is not meant to replace the existing I/O classes found in *java.io*, which have been discussed in the preceding text of this chapter. Rather, the NIO classes are designed and intended to supplement the standard I/O system, offering an alternative approach, which can prove to be occasionally beneficial.

6.7 THE Formatter CLASS

We have already talked about the *Formatter* class in the introductory section to this chapter. This class works by converting the binary form of data used by a program into formatted text. It stores this text in a buffer from where it can be obtained any time you need. The buffer may be supplied explicitly or you can let the *Formatter* supply it on its own. *Formatter* may be constructed in a variety of ways including the following:-

Formatter()
Formatter(Appendable buf)
Formatter(String file) throws FileNotFoundException
Formatter(File outF) throws FileNotFoundException
Formatter(OutputStream outStrm)

where, *buf* specifies a buffer for the formatted output, *file* specifies the name of the file which shall receive the formatted output, *outF* specifies a reference to an output file which shall receive the output, and *outStrm* specifies a reference to an output stream which shall receive the output.

After creating the *Formatter*, you can use the following *format()* method to create a formatted string:-

Formatter format(String fmtString, Object ... args)

where, *fmtString* contains either characters which are copied as such to the output buffer or *format specifiers* such as *%d* for integers, *%f* for floating-point data and *%s* for strings. An integer placed between the % sign and format conversion code acts as the minimum field-width specifier. The default padding is done with spaces. If you want to pad with 0's, place a 0 before the field-width specifier, e.g., *%05d* will pad a number of less than five digits with 0's so that its length is five. By default, all output is right-justified. You can force output to be left-justified by placing a minus sign directly after the % sign, e.g., *%-10.2f* left-justifies a floating-point number with two decimal places in a *10*-character field. When displaying large numbers, it is often useful to add a comma separator/flag, e.g.,

4337788990.23 is more easily read as *4,337, 788,990.23*. *Formatter* lets you achieve this very easily. *Formatter* also includes a very useful feature that lets you specify the argument to which a *format specifier* applies. In other words, it allows you to use an *argument index*.

6.8 WINDING IT UP!

You might have noticed that *read()* returns *-1* when the end-of-file (*EOF*) has been reached, but that it does not have a special return value for a file error. Let us try to understand why is it like this?

Now, in Java, errors are handled by means of exceptions so that if *read()* or any other Input/Output method returns a value, it implies that no error has occurred. This is a much cleaner way than handling I/O errors by means of using special error codes. That's just the point! Got it? We hope so.

PRACTICAL SESSION

1. (a) What is a file? Why do we require files to store data?
   (b) What is a stream? How is the concept of streams used in Java?

2. (a) What is a random access file? How is it different from a sequential file?
   (b) Why do we need random access files?

3. (a) Create a *DataInputStream* for the file named "inventory.dat".
   (b) Create a *RandomAccessFile* stream for the file "inventory.dat" for updating the inventory information in the file.

4. Write a Java program to concatenate two text files.

5. Which of the following is correct?
   (a) The *InputStream* and *OutputStream* classes are byte-oriented.
   (b) The *Reader* and *Writer* classes are byte-oriented.
   (c) The *Reader* and *Writer* classes provide serialized object output.
   (d) All of the above
   (e) None of the above

6. *Writer* classes can be used to:
   (a) Write characters to output streams using different character encodings.
   (b) Write Unicode characters to output streams.
   (c) Write values of any Java primitive type to output streams.
   (d) Both (a) and (b)
   (e) All of (a), (b) and (c)
   (f) None of the above

7. (a) Write a Java program to find out if a given file is available on your system or not.
   (b) While reading a file, how would you check whether you have reached the end of the file?

8. List two byte-oriented I/O classes and two character-oriented I/O classes respectively.

9. State True (T) or False (F):
   (a) The *readLine()* method returns *null* when it has reached the end of a file.
   (b) The *File* class provides access to the files and sub-directories of the current working directory.

10. (a) Write a Java program that will count the number of characters in a file.
    (b) Modify the above program so that it will also count the number of words and lines in the file.

Chapter 7

STRING HANDLING

7.0 INTRODUCTION

We had discussed strings briefly in Chapter 1. In this chapter, we shall present string handling in detail. Like most other languages, a *string* in Java is a sequence of characters but unlike some languages that implement strings as character arrays, Java implements strings as objects of type *String*. This helps Java to construct strings in myriad ways as well as provide a wide array of features ranging from comparing two strings to changing the case of letters within a string. As already explained in Chapter 1, strings in Java are immutable but if you wish to create a modifiable string, there is a way out by means of the *StringBuffer* class whose objects contain strings that can be changed after their creation. Both the *String* and *StringBuffer* classes are defined in *java.lang* and are thus, available to all Java programs automatically. We shall also briefly discuss the *StringBuilder* class introduced recently by JDK5 in the final "*Winding it Up!*" section of this chapter.

7.1 STRING CONSTRUCTORS

There are several constructors supported by the *String* class. The default constructor constructs an emty string, e.g.,

String str = new String();

creates an instance of *String* without any characters.

To create a *String* initialized by an array of characters, use:

String(char chrs[ ]), e.g.,

char chrs[ ] = {'x', 'y', 'z'};

String str = new String(chrs);

which initializes *str* with the string *"xyz"*.

A subrange of a character array can be specified as an initializer using:

String(char chrs[ ], int startIndx, int numChrs)

where, *startIndx* specifies the index at which the subrange starts while *numChrs* specifies the number of characters to be used, e.g.,

char chrs[ ] = { 'a', 'b', 'c', 'x', y', 'z' };
String str = new String(chrs, 3, 2);

which initializes *str* with the string *"xy"*.

You may note that indexing begins at *0* in all arrays.

A *String* object that contains the same character sequence as another *String* object can be created using the constructor:

String(String sObj)

where, *sObj* is a *String* object, e.g., consider Example 97 as a case in point.

Example 97

```
// ConstructStringObject.java

/* Illustrates construction of one String from another;
Author: Arunesh; Date: 23/03/2011 */

class ConstructStringObject
{
        public static void  main(String args[])
        {

                char chrs[ ] = { 'a', 'b', 'c', 'd', 'e', 'f', 'g', 'h'};

                String s_one = new String(chrs);

                String s_two = new String(s_one);

                System.out.println("s_one = " + s_one);

                System.out.println();

                System.out.println("s_two = " + s_two);

        }
}
```

Output:

```
        s_one  =  abcdefgh

        s_two = abcdefgh
```

/* As is clear from the above output, *s_one* and *s_two* contain identical strings. */

7.2 STRING LENGTH

The length of a string is determined by the number of characters in it. To get this value, use:

int length(), e.g.,

```
char chrs[ ] = { 'a', 'b', 'c', 'd', 'e', 'f', 'g', 'h'};
String str = new String(chrs);
System.out.println(str.length());
```

outputsand prints the value *"8'* since there are *eight* characters in the string *str.*

7.3 STRING LITERALS

In this chapter, we have used string constructors so far to construct a string. However, there is an easier means to achieve the same, viz. by means of string literals, e.g.,

```
char chrs[ ] = { 'a', 'b', 'c', 'd', 'e', 'f', 'g', 'h'};
String str1 = new String(chrs); // use string constructor
String str2 = "abcdefgh"; // use string literal
System.out.println("abcdefgh".length()); // outputs & prints 8
```

7.4 STRING CONCATENATION

Java does not allow operators to be applied to *String* objects with one significant exception, viz. the '+' operator, which concatenates two strings, producing a *String* object as the output. Thus, you can use a chain of '+' operations, e.g.,

```
String yrs = "10";
String str = "He is " + yrs + " years older to his sister."
System.out.println(str);
```

outputs the string:

He is 10 years older to his sister.

One practical use of string concatenation is found in breaking long lines of source code into manageable smaller lines, using the '+' operator to concatenate them.

Strings can be concatenated with other types of data as well, e.g.,

```
int yrs = 10;
String str = "He is " + yrs + " years older to his sister."
System.out.println(str);
```

outputs the string as before:

He is 10 years older to his sister.

In this case, *yrs* is an *int* rather than a *String* but the output remains the same. This is because the Java compiler automatically converts an operand to its string equivalent whenever the other operand of the '+' operator is an instance of *String*.

We must sound a caveat here. You must be very careful while mixing other types of expressions with string concatenation expressions lest you get some surprising results, e.g.,

String str = "eight: " + 4 + 4;
System.out.println(str);

outputs the string:

eight: 44

rather than the expected result:

eight: 8

This has happened because operator precedence has caused the concatenation of the string *"eight: "* with the string equivalent of *4* to occur first. This output then gets concatenated with the string equivalent of *4* again a second time.

In order to complete the integer addition first, you must use parentheses in the following manner:

String str = "eight: " + (4 + 4);
System.out.println(str);

which now outputs the expected string/result:

eight: 8

7.5 STRING CONVERSION AND toString()

To convert data into its string equivalent during concatenation, Java calls one of the overloaded versions of the string conversion method *valueOf()* defined by *String*. For the simple types, *valueOf()* returns a string that is a human-readable form of the value for which it is invoked while for objects, *valueOf()* calls the *toString()* method on the object. Every class implements *toString()* since it is defined by *Object*. But, the default implementation is generally insufficient. For most important classes that you create, you would like to override *toString()* and provide your own string representations. This is easily achievable. The *toString()* method has the general form:

String toString()

and, to implement *toString(),* you have to simply return a *String* object containing the human-readable equibvalent string that describes an object of your class most appropriately. By overriding *toString()* for the classes created by you, you allow them to be seamlessly integrated with the Java programming environment, e.,g., they can be used in concatenation expressions and in the *print()* & *println()* statements.

7.6 CHARACTER EXTRACTION

The *String* class provides several ways to extract the characters from a *String* object. Although the characters within a *String* object cannot be indexed like a character array, many of the *String* methods use an index/offset into the string for their operation, with the string indexes starting at zero just like arrays.

To extract a single character from a *String*, you can use the *charAt()* method whose general form is:

char charAt(int offset)

where, *offset* is the index of the character you want to refer to and extract. Note that the *offset* must be non-negative and specify a location within the string boundaries and *charAt()* returns the character at the specified location, e.g.,

```
char c;
c = "XYZ".charAt(2);
```

assigns the value 'Z' to *c*.

In case you need to extract more than one character at a time, you can make use of the *getChars()* method whose general form is:

```
void getChars(int sourceBegin, int sourceEnd, char target[ ], int targetBegin)
```

where, *sourceBegin* indicates the index of the beginning of the substring while *sourceEnd* indicates an index that is one more than the end of the substring so that the desired substring contains the characters from *sourceBegin* through *sourceEnd -1*. The array receiving the substring is indicated by *target* and the index within the target at which the substring will be copied is indicated by *targetBegin*. You may note that that the target array must be large enough to hold all the characters in the indicated substring.

Consider Example 98 as a case in point.

Example 98

```
// Demo_getChars.java

/* Illustrates the getChars() method;
Author: Arunesh; Date: 23/03/2011 */

class Demo_getChars
{
	public static void  main(String args[])
	{
		String str = "abcdefgh";

		int sourceBegin = 3;

		int sourceEnd = 6;

		char chrs[] = new char[sourceEnd - sourceStart];

		str.getChars(sourceBegin, sourceEnd, chrs, 0);

		System.out.println("chrs []  = " + chrs);
	}
}
```

Output:

```
	chrs[]  = defg
```

7.7 STRING COMPARISON METHODS

The string class contains several important methods which compare strings or substrings within strings. Some of these are *equals()* and *equalsIgnoreCase(), sartsWith()* and *endsWith()*, and *compareTo()*. We shall now take up each one of these as well as compare *equals()* vis-à-vis = =.

To compare two strings for equality, make use of *equals()* with the general form:

boolean equals(Object s)

where, *s* is the *String* object being compared with the invoking *String*. It returns *true* if the two strings contain the same characters in the same order, and *false* otherwise. This comparison is case-sensitive.

To perform a comparison that ignores case differences, make use of *equalsIgnoreCase()* which considers *a-z* to be the same as *A-Z*. Its most general form is:

boolean equalsIgnoreCase(String s)

This method works similar to *equals()* except that it ignores case differences, if any.

We shall now take up Example 99 to illustrate these two methods.

Example 99

```
// Demo_Equals.java

/* Illustrates the equals() & equalsIgnoreCase() methods;
Author: Arunesh; Date: 23/03/2011 */

class Demo_Equals
{
        public static void  main(String args[])
        {
                String str 1= "abc";
                String str2 = "abc";
                String str3 = "xyz";
                String str4 = "XYZ";

                System.out.println(str1 + " equals " + str2 + " : " + str1.equals(str2));
                System.out.println(str1 + " equals " + str3 + " : " + str1.equals(str3));
                System.out.println(str3 + " equals " + str4 + " : " + str3.equals(str4));
                System.out.println(str3 + " equalsIgnoreCase " + str2 + " : "
                                                + str3.equalsIgnore Case(str4));
        }
}
```

Output:

```
abc equals abc : true
abc equals xyz : false
xyz equals XYZ : false
xyz equalsIgnoreCase XYZ : true
```

The *startsWith()* method determines whether a given *String* starts with a specified string while the *endsWith()* method determines whether a given *String* ends with a specified string. Their general form is:

boolean startsWith(String s)
boolean endsWith(String s)

where, *s* is the *String* under test. If the string matches, *true* is returned and *false* is returned otherwise, e.g.,

"abcxyz".startsWith("abc")
&
"abcxyz".endsWith("xyz")

are both *true*.

Now, we shall compare *equals()* vs. = =. They perform two different operations although at a cursory glance, they might seem to be alike. As already explained, *equals()* compares the character contents inside a *String* object. In contrast, the = = operator compares two object references to check if they refer to the same instance. Example 100 verifies this fact by illustrating how two different string objects can contain the same characters, but references to these objects are not equal.

Example 100

```
// EqualsVersusNotEqualTo.java

/* Illustrates the fact that equals() & == are not alike;
Author: Arunesh; Date: 23/03/2011 */

class EqualsVersusNotEqualTo
{
        public static void main(String args[])
        {
                String str 1= "XYZ";
                String str2 = new String(str1);
                String str3 = "xyz";
                String str4 = "XYZ";

                System.out.println(str1 + " equals " + str2 + " : " + str1.equals(str2));
                System.out.println(str1 + " == " + str2 + " : " + (str1 == str2));
        }
}
```

Output:

```
XYZ equals XYZ : true
XYZ == XYZ : false
```

/* The reason for this output is not far to seek. The variable *str1* refers to the *String* instance created by "*XYZ*". The object referred to by *str2* is created with *str1* as an initializer. Thus, the contents of the two string objects, *str1* & *str2*, are identical, but they are distinct objects, that is to say, they do not refer to the same object, and are therefore not ==.
*/

For sorting purposes, it is not enough to know whether two given strings are identical. We must also know, which is less than, equal to, or greater than the other. The idea of greater than and less than is implied by their dictionary order. Whichever of the two comes first in dictionary order is less than the latter while the other is greater than the former. The *String* method *compareTo()* is often used for this purpoe. Its general form is:

int compareTo(String s)

where, *s* is the *String* being compared to the invoking *String*. The result of the comparison is an integer returned and interpreted as: if less than 0, the invoking strig is less than *s*; if greater than 0, the invoking string is greater than *s*; and, if equal to 0, the invoking string is equal to *s*.

compareTo() is case-sensitive and takes into account the values in the ASCII character set. If you want to ignore the case differences, make use of *compareToIgnoreCase()* with the general form:

int compareToIgnoreCase(String s)

This method works identical to *compareTo()* except for the fact that it ignores case differences, if any.

As a case in point, Example 101 illustrates both these methods.

Example 101

```
// Comparison.java
/* Illustrates the comareTo() & compareToIgnoreCase() methods;
Author: Arunesh; Date: 23/03/2011 */
class Comparison
{
	public static void  main(String args[])
	{
		String str 1= "XYZ";
		String str2 = "xyz";
		if (str1.compareTo(str2) < 0 )
			System.out.println(str1 + " is less than " + str2);
		if (str1.compareToIgnoreCase(str2) == 0 )
			System.out.println("Ignoring case differences, " + str1
					+ " is equal to " + str2);
}
```

Output:

```
XYZ is less than xyz
Ignoring case differences, XYZ is equal to xyz
```

7.8 STRING SEARCH METHODS

String includes two methods, namely, *indexOf()* & *lastIndexOf()* which allow you to search for the first occurrence of a character/substring and the last occurence of a character/substring respectively, in a specified string.

To search for the first/last occurrence of a character, use:

int indexOf(int c) & int lastIndexOf(int c)

where, *c* is is the character being searched for.

Similarly, to search for the first/last occurrence of a substring, use:

int indexOf(String s) & int lastIndexOf(String s)

where, *s* is is the substring being searched for.

Example 102 is a case in point.

Example 102

```
// Search_Demo.java
/* Illustrates indexOf() & lastIndexOf() methods;
Author: Arunesh; Date: 24/12/2011 */
class Search_Demo
{
        public static void main(String args[])
        {
                String str = new String("Arunesh is Arunesh !");
                int k;

                k = str.indexOf("run");
                System.out.println("First Index of run: " + k);
                k = str.lastIndexOf("run");
                System.out.println("Last Index of run: " + k);

                System.out.println();

                k = str.indexOf('e');
                System.out.println("First Index of e: " + k);
                k = str.lastIndexOf('e');
                System.out.println("Last Index of e: " + k);
        }
}
```

Output:

```
First Index of run: 1
Last Index of run: 12

First Index of e: 4
Last Index of e: 15
```

7.9 STRING MODIFICATION METHODS

String objects being immutable must either be copied into a StringBuffer or use one of the substring(), concat(), replace() or trim() String methods, which will construct a new copy of the string with the desired modifications.

Part or portion of a string can be obtained using the *substring()* method, which has two forms:

String substring(int startIndx)
String substring(int startIndx, int endIndx)

where, the substring starts at *startIndx* and runs to the end of the invoking string in the first form, while in the second form, it starts at *startIndx* and runs up to endIndx -1. In both the forms, the new substring is returned.

Take Example 103 as a case in point.

Example 103

```
// Substr.java
/* Illustrates substring();
Author: Arunesh; Date: 23/03/2011 */
class Substr
{
        public static void  main(String args[])
        {
                String s = "abcdefgh";

                System.out.println("s:\t" + s);
                System.out.println();

                System.out.print("s.substring(3):\t");
                String subs = s.substring(3);
                System.out.println(subs);

                System.out.println("s.substring(0, 3):\t");
                string subs = s.substring(0, 3);
                System.out.println(subs);
        }
}
```

Output:

```
        s:        abcdefgh

        s.substring(3):  defgh
        s.substring(0, 3):        abc
```

There are two ways of concatenating two or more strings. Either you can make use of the + operator, as we have been doing so far or you can make use of the concatenation meethod as defined by *String*. The method that carries out concatenation is called *concat()*, whose general form is:

String concat(String s)

This method returns a new String that has *s* concatenated to the end of *the* invoking *String.*

Take Example 104 as a case in point.

Example 104

```
// Conct.java
/* Illustrates concat() method;
Author: Arunesh; Date: 23/03/2011 */
class Conct
{
	public static void  main(String args[])
	{
		String str1 = "abc";

		String str2  = str1.concat("xyz");
		System.out.println(str2);

		String str3 = str1 + "xyz";
		System.out.println(str3);
	}
}
```

Output:

```
abcxyz
abcxyz
```

/* As is clear from te above output, *concat()* works on two *Strings* just like the '+' operator.

*/

A portion of a string can be replaced using the *replace()* method, shown as follows:

String replace(char oldChar, char newChar)

where, all occurrences of *oldChar* in the invoking *String* are replaced with *newChar* and the resulting new *String* is returned.

Take Example 105 as a case in point.

Example 105

```
// Replc.java
/* Illustrates replace();
Author: Arunesh; Date: 23/03/2011 */
class Replc
{
	public static void main(String args[])
	{
		String s = "Testing it OUT!";
		System.out.println("Original String:\t" + s);

		s = s.replace('T', 'z');
		System.out.println(String after replacement:\t" + s);
	}
}
```

Output:

```
	Original String:	.	Testing it OUT!
	String after replacement:	zesting it OUz!
```

At times, there is a need to remove trailing and leading spaces from a String. This type of operation, referred to as *trimming*, is quite often required by command processors. For *trimming*, use the following *trim()* method:

String trim()

where, leading and trailing whitespace are removed from the invoking *String*, and the new resulting *String* is returned..

Take Example 106 as a case in point.

Example 106

```
// Trm.java
/* Illustrates Trimming by means of the trim() method;
Author: Arunesh; Date: 23/03/2011 */
class Trm
{
	public static void main(String args[])
	{
		String s = "      OVER      ";
		System.out.println("Original string:\t" + s);

		s = s.Trim();	// trim leading & trailing spaces
		System.out.println("String after trimming: " + s);
	}
}
```

Output:

Original String: OVER
String after trimming: OVER

7.10 CHANGING THE CASE OF CHARACTERS WITHIN A STRING

To convert all characters in a string to lowercase, use *toLowerCase()* while to convert all charactersin a string to uppercase, use to*UpperCase()*. Note that non-alphabetical characters, such as digits, hyphen, underscore, period etc. are unaffected by these two operations whose general form is:

String toLowerCase()
String toUpperCase()

These two methods return a *String* object containing the lowercase and uppercase equivalents of the invoking *String*, respectively.

Example 107 is a case in point.

Example 107

```
// CaseChange_Demo.java
/* Illustrates toLowerCase() & toupperCase() methods;
Author: Arunesh; Date: 24/12/2011 */
class CaseChange_Demo
{
        public static void main(String args[])
        {

                String str = new String("Arunesh is Arunesh !");

                System.out.println("Original Version: " + str);

                String lwr = str.toLowerCase(0;
                String upr = str.toUpperCase();

                System.out.println("Lowercase Version: " + lwr);
                System.out.println("Uppercase Version: " + upr);

        }
}
```

Output:

Original Version: Arunesh is Arunesh !
Lowercase Version: arunesh is arunesh !
Uppercase version: ARUNESH IS ARUNESH !

7.11 THE StringBuffer CLASS

StringBuffer is a peer class of *String* that provides much of the functionality of strings. As already explained, *String* represents fixed-length immutable character sequences. In stark contrast to this, *StringBuffer* allows for growable and writeable character sequences. It may have characters or substrings appended to the end or inserted anywhere in the middle. It will automatcally grw to make room for such additions and often has more space (characters) preallocated than are needed actually, to allow for such growth. The two most commonly used *StringBuffer* constructors are:

1. *StringBuffer()*
2. *StringBuffer(String s)*

You can get a portion of *StringBuffer* by calling the *substring()* method with the following two forms:

1. *String substring(int startIndx)*
2. *String substring(int startIndx, int endIndx)*

The first version returns the substring beginning at *startIndx* up to the end of the invoking *StringBuffer* object while the second version returns a substring beginning at *startIndx* and runs through *endIndx - 1.*

StringBuffer includes some commonly used additional methods such as *indexOf()* & *lastIndexOf()* which are illustrated by the following example (Example 108).

Example 108

```
// Index_Demo.java
/* Illustrates indexOf() & lastIndexOf() methods for StringBuffer;
Author: Arunesh; Date: 24/12/2011 */
class Index_Demo
{
	public static void main(String args[])
	{

		StringBuffer strbuf = new StringBuffer("Arunesh is Arunesh !");
		int k;

		k = strbuf.indexOf("Arunesh");
		System.out.println("First Index of Arunesh: " + k);

		k = strbuf.lastIndexOf("Arunesh");
		System.out.println("Last Index of Arunesh: " + k);

	}
}
```

Output:

First Index of Arunesh: 0
Last Index of Arunesh: 11

7.12 WINDING IT UP!

In this section, we will introduce you to *StringBuilder*, a recent addition to Java's string handling capabilities by JDK5. In short, *StringBuilder* is identical to *StringBuffer* with one important exception, viz. it's not synchronized, which, in turn, implies that it's not thread-safe.

The main advantage and benefit of *StringBuilder* is faster performance. But, there is a caveat. In cases where you are using multithreading, you must make use of *StringBuffer* instead of *StringBuilder*.

PRACTICAL SESSION

1. (a) How is a string implemented in Java?
   (b) What is the difference between the *String* and *StringBuffer* classes?
   (c) Write a short note on the *StringBuilder* class.

2. Explain any three of the methods defined in the *StringBuffer* class citing an appropriate example of each one.

3. State True (T) or False (F):
   (a) In Java, strings are implemented as an array of characters.
   (b) *StringBuffer* objects are constant.
   (c) In Java, it is possible to convert a *String* into an *int* type data.

4. (a) Suppose you write a long line and store it in a *String* named *message*. Now, you have a nagging feeling that you misspelled *Friday* as *Frday* somewhere in the string. Write down the statement(s) that would be able to find and correct the misspelling.
   (b) Write a program which counts the number of occurrences of a given word in a text document.

5. (a) Write a program with the help of a *for* loop and the *length()* method to display the contents of a *String* object.
   (b) Give two methods for concatenating strings.

Chapter 8

TYPE WRAPPERS, AUTOBOXING, ENUMERATIONS AND ANNOTATIONS

8.0 INTRODUCTION

In this final chapter, we shall be discussing three relatively new additions to the Java language, namely, enumerations, autoboxing and annotations (referred to as metadata as well). We shall also discuss type wrappers briefly. Each expands the power of the Java language by providing a means to streamlined handling of the common programming tasks.

8.1 TYPE WRAPPERS

In this section, we shall examine a technique which is very useful when reading numeric strings. As you already know, the *println()* method of Java provides a convenient and efficient means to output various types of data to the console, including numeric values of the built-in types such as *int* or *double*. Thus, we see that *println()* automatically convets numeric data into its human-readable form. But, Java doesn't provide an input method that reads and converts strings containing numeric data into their internal, binary form, e.g., there is no input method that lets you enter at the keyboard a string like "*999*" and have it automatically converted into its corresponding binary value which is able to be stored in an *int* variable. In order to accomplish this, you need to use one of the type wrappers of Java.

The type wrappers of Java are classes which encapsulate/wrap the simple types. They are required since the simple types are not objects limiting their use to some extent, e,g., a simple type cannot be passed by reference. To solve this problem, Java provides classes which correspond to each of the simple types.

The type wrappers are *Double, Float, Long, Integer, Short, Byte, Character,* and *Boolean*. These classes offer a wide range of methods which allow you to to fully integrate the simple types into the object hierarchy of Java. As an extra benefit, the numeric wrappers also define methods which convert a numeric string into its corresponding binary equivalent. These conversion methods are shown in Table 8.1. Each returns a binar value corresponding to the string. The integer wrappers also offer a second parsing method which allows you to specify the radix. The parsing methods provide an easy means to convert a numeric value, read a string from the keyboard or a text file, into its proper internal binary format.

Table 8.1 Type Wrappers & Conversion Methods

Type Wrapper	Conversion Method
Double	*static double parseDouble(String str) throws NumberFormatException*
Float	*static float parseFloat(String str) throws NumberFormatException*
Long	*static long parseLong(String str) throws NumberFormatException*
Integer	*static int parseInte(String str) throws NumberFormatException*
Short	*static short parseShort(String str) throws NumberFormatException*
Byte	*static byte parseByte(String str) throws NumberFormatException*

8.2 AUTOBOXING

Java added two new features, namely, autoboxing & auto-unboxing, beginning with JDK 5. Autoboxing is the means by which a primitive type is automatically encapsulated or "boxed" into its equivalent type wrapper whenever an object of that type is required. Thus, there is no need to explicitly construct an object. Auto-unboxing is the reverse process by means of which the value of a "boxed" object is automatically extracted or "unboxed" from a type wrapper when its value is required. There is no need to explicitly call a method such as *intValue()* or *doubleValue()*. Autoboxing and auto-unboxing streamlines the coding of several algorithms as also helps to prevent errors. It is extremely important to generics, which operates only on objects, and makes working with the Java Collections Framework much more smooth and easier.

With autoboxing, it is no longer required to manually construct an object in order to wrap a primitive type; it is only required to assign that value to a type-wrapper reference; and, Java automatically constructs the desired object, e.g., to construct an *Integer* object with the vlue *999*, we can declare:

Integer intObj = 999; // autobox an int

Take note that no object is explicitly created through new. Java handles this by itself.

Similarly, to unbox an object, simply assign that object reference to a primitive-type variable, e.g., to unbox *intObj*, use:

int val = intObj; // auto-unbox

Once again, Java handles the details on your behalf on its own.

In addition to the simple case of assignments, autoboxing occurs automatically whenever a primitive type has to be converted into an object while auto-unboxing occurs whenever an object has to be converted into a primitive type so that autoboxing/unboxing can take place when an argument is passed to a method, or when a value is returned by a method.

In general, autoboxing and unboxing occur whenever a conversion into an object or from an object is needed. This applies to expressions as well. Within an expression, a numeric object is automatically unboxed. The result of the expression is reboxed, if necessary.

As explained earlier, Java also supplies wrappers for *boolean* and *char* which are called *Boolean* and *Charcter*, respectively. Autoboxing/unboxing applies to these wrappers as well.

In addition to convenience of use, autoboxing/unboxing can also help to prevent errors such as those produced by manual boxing/unboxing.

However, there is a word of caution that needs to be sounded at this juncture. Now that Java includes autoboxing/unboxing, many might be tempted to use objects such as *Integer* or *Double* exclusively, eliminating primitives altogether. You must note that each autobox and auto-unbox adds overhead which is absent if the primitive type is used.

8.3 ENUMERATIONS

Enumerations were added to Java with the release of JDK 5. An enumeration is a way of assigning names to integer constants. To give you a practical example of the need for enumerations, imagine a scenario where you wanted to represent the seasons of the year in a program. You could very well use the integers *0, 1, 2,* and *3* to represent *spring, summer, autumn,* and *winter* respectively. This solution would work but it is not very innovative, e.g., if you used the integer value *0* in the program code, it would not be very obvious that a particular *0* represented *spring*. Futhermore, it would also not be a very robust solution to the problem, e.g., if you declare an integer variable called *season* , there is nothing to prevent you from assigining the variable *season* any legal integer value other than *0, 1, 2,* or *3*. Enumerations offer a much better solution. You can create an enumeration (sometimes called an *enum* type), whose values would be limited to a set of symbolic names, e,g., in this particular case, it could be: *enum season{spring, summer, autumn, winter}*

The most general form of an enumeration is:

enum enum_name {enum_list } // notice the keyword '*enum*'!

where, *enum_name* is the name of the said enumeration and *enum_list* is a comma-separated list of identifiers. Take for instance the following enumeration, which enumerates various types of fruits.:

enum Fruit {Apple, Banana, Orange, Mango }

What is important to understand about an enumeration is that each of the symbols/ identifiers stands for a constant. Further, because an enumeration represents constant values, it can be used to control a for loop or a switch construct, for instance.

The members of an enumeration can be acccessed via their type name through the dot (.) operator, e.g.,

System.out.println("Fruit.Mango has the value " + Fruit.Mango);

displays the following output:

Fruit.Mango has the value Mango

The above output confirms the fact that when an enumerated value is displayed, its name is used. The following example (Example 109) is illustrative of the above enumeration, namely, *Fruit*.

Example 109

```
// EnumIllustrative.java
/* Illustrates the ENUMERATION: Fruit;
Author: Arunesh; Date:27 /03/2011 */
class EnumIllustrative
{
	enum Fruit {Apple, Banana, Orange, Mango }

	public static void main(String args[])
	{
		String val [ ] = { "zero", "one", "two", "three" };

		Fruit F;		// enum variable

		F = Fruit.Mango;
		System.out.println("Value of F: " + F);

		if (F == Fruit.Mango)
			System.out.println("F contains Mango.");

		switch(F)
		{
			case Apple:
				System.out.println(val[0]);
				break;
			case Banana:
				System.out.println(val[1]);
				break;
			case Orange:
				System.out.println(val[2]);
				break;
```

```
                case Mango:
                        System.out.println(val[3]);
                        break;
            }
    }
}
```

Output:

```
    Value of F: Mango
    F contains Mango.
    three
```

8.3.1 values() & valueOf() Methods

All enumerations contain two pre-defined methods, namely, *values()* & *ValueOf()*, automatically. Their general forms are:

public static enum_type[ ] values()
public static enum_type valueOf(String s)

The *values()* method returns an array containing a list of the enumeration constants while the *valueOf()* method returns the enumeration constant whose value corresponds to the string passed in *s*. In both cases, *enum_type* is the type of the enumeration. The following example (Example 110) is illustrative of the above *two methods*.

Example 110

```
// EnumMethods.java
/* Illustrates the values() & valueOf() methods ;
Author: Arunesh; Date:27 /03/2011 */
class EnumMethods
{
    enum Fruit {Apple, Banana, Orange, Mango }

    public static void main(String args[])
    {
        Fruit frt;        // enum variable

        System.out.println("Here are all the Fruit constants:-");

        Fruit allfruits [] = Fruit.values(); // use values()

        for (Fruit f : allfruits)
            System.out.println(f);

        System.out.println();
```

```
            frt = Fruit.valueOf("Mango");          // use valueOf()
            System.out.println("frt contains " + frt);
      }
}
```

Output:

```
      Here are all the Fruit constants:-
      Apple
      Banana
      Orange
      Mango

      frt contains Mango.
```

/* Notice how the *for-each* style loop was used to cycle through the array of constants obtained by calling *values()*.
*/

8.3.2 Java Enumerations are Class Types

Java enumeratins are class types. Although an *enum* is not instantiated using new, it has more or less the same capabilities as other classes. This feature adds to the power of Java enumerations in a big way, e.g., you can give them constructors, add instance variables/methods, and even implement interfaces. It is important to realize that each *enum* constant is an object of its enumeration type so that when you define a constructor for an *enum*, the constructor is invoked when each enum constant is created. Moreover, each *enum* constant has its own copy of any instance variables defined by the enumeration, e.g., consider the following version of *Fruit* as a case in point (Example 111).

Example 111

```
// EnumClassType_Demo.java
/* Illustrates the use of an enum constructor, instance variable, and a method;
Author: Arunesh; Date:27 /03/2011 */
class EnumClassType_Demo
{
      enum Fruit
      {     Apple (5), Banana (10), Orange (15), Mango (20);
            private int cost;          // cost of each fruit: instance variable
            // constructor
            Fruit(int c)
            { cost = c; }
            int getCost()   // method
            { return cost; }
      }
```

```
    public static void main(String args[])
    {
        Fruit f;

        // print cost of Mango
        System.out.println("Mango costs " + Fruit.Mango.getCost() + " rupees");

        System.out.println();

        // Display all fruits along with their costs
        System.out.println("Here are all Fruit prices:-");
        for (Fruit frt  : Fruit.values())
            System.out.println(frt + " costs " + frt.getCost() + " rupees");
    }
}
```

Output:

```
    Mango costs 20 rupees

    Here are all Fruit prices:-
    Apple costs 5 rupees
    Banana costs 10 rupees
    Orange costs 15 rupees
    Mango costs 20 rupees
```

Although Example 111 contains only one constructor, an *enum* can offer two or more overloaded constructors, just like any other class. this is illustrated by the following lines of code:

```
    // use two constructors
    enum Fruit
    {   Apple (5), Banana, Orange (15), Mango (20);

        private int cost;       // cost of each fruit: instance variable

        // constructor
        Fruit(int c)
        { cost = c; }

        // overloaded constructor
        Fruit()
        { cost = -1; }

        int getCost()   // method
        { return cost; }
    }
```

/* Take note that in this form of *Fruit, Banana* is not given an argument so that the default constructor is invoked, and *Banana*'s cost variable is assigned the value -1.
*/

8.3.3 Enumeration Restrictions

There are two important restrictions which apply to enumerations:

(1) An enumeration cannot inherit another class.

(2) An enumeration cannot be a superclass.

Thus, an enumeration cannnot be extended. Otherwise, enumerations act jut like any other class type.

What is important is to understand the fact that each *enum* constant is an object of the class in which it is defined/declared.

8.4 ANNOTATIONS (METADATA)

JDK 5 introduced a new feature into the Java language, viz. annotations (metadata) by means of which you could embed supplemental information into a source file. in fact, this information is itself called an annotation, which leaves the semantics/actions of a program unchanged but can be used by various tools both during deployment and development, e.g., an annotation can be processed by a source-code generator.

An annotation is created by means of a mechanism based on the *interface*. To declare an annotation, say, *MyAnnotation*, we proceed as follows:

```
// A simple annotation ype
@interface MyAnnotation
{
        String s();
        int value();
}
```

Take note of the @ preceding the keyword inteface. This indicates t the compiler that an annotation is being created. Now, take note of the two members, *s()* and *value()*. All annotations solely consist of method declarations. But, you don't provide bodies for these methods; Java implements these methods instead. Also, the methods act much like fileds as we shall see shortly.

Once an annotation is declared, it can be used to annotate any declaration, which means that any type of declaration can have an annotation associated with it, e.g., classes, methods, fields, parameters, and *enum* constants may be annotated. In fact, even an annotation may be annotated. In all cases, the annotation comes before the rest of the declaration. When applying an annotation, its members are given values, e.g., here is an example of *MyAnnotation* being applied to a method:

```
// Annotate a method
@MyAnnotation(s = "string", value = 999)
public static void myMethod()
{
        // ..................
}
```

Thus, *MyAnnotation* is linked with the method *myMethod()*. Take note of the annotation syntax. The name of the annotation, preced by a *@,* is followed by a parenthized list of member initializations. Also, take note of the fact that no parentheses follow *s* or *value* in this assignment of initial values so that annotation members act like fields in this regard.

8.4.1 Specifying a Retention Policy

A retention policy determines at what point an annotation is discarded. Java defines three retention policies which are encapsulated within the *java.lang.annotation.RetentionPolicy* enumeration. These three are respectively, SOURCE, CLASS, and RUNTIME. An annotation with a retention policy of SOURCE is retained only in the source file and is discarded during compilation. An Annotation with a retention policy of CLASS is stored in the *.class* file during compilation but is not available throgh the JVM during run-time. Finally, an annotation with a retention policy of RUNTIME is stored in the *.class* file during compilation and is available through the JVM during run-time. Thus, we come to see that an annotation with a retention policy of RUNTIME has the greatest persistence.

A retention policy is specified for an annotation by means of one of Java's built-in annotations, viz. *@Retention*. Its general form is:

```
@Retention(retention_policy)
```

where, *retention_policy* must be one of the three: SOURCE, CLASS and RUNTIME. In case no retention policy is specified, the default retention policy of CLASS is used.

The following version of *MyAnnotation* uses the *@Retention* to indicate the RUNTIME policy so that *MyAnnotation* shall be availabe to the JVM during program execution at run-time:

```
@Retention(RetentionPolicy.RUNTIME)
@interface MyAnnotation
{
        String s();
        int value();
}
```

8.4.2 Marker Annotations & Java's Built-In Annotations

A marker annotation is a specialized annotation with no members. Its lone purpose is to mark a declaration, that is to say, its presence as an annotation is enough. The best way to find out whether a marker annotation is present is by using the is*AnnotationPresent()* method, which is defined by the *AnnotatedElement* interface.

Java defines several built-in annotations. Most of these are specialized but seven of them are general purpse, with four of them being imported from *java.lang.annotation*, namely, *@Retention, @Documented, @Target,* and *@Inherited*, and the rest three are included in *java.lang*, namely, *@Override, @Deprecated,* and *@SuppressWarnings*.

8.5 WINDING IT UP!

In this section, we will first take up the additional benefits of type wrappers. The simple type wrappers provide a number of methods which help in integrating the simple types int Java's object hierarchy, e.g., the various storage mechanisms provided by the Java library inclusive of maps, lists, and sets work only with objects. Thus, we see that to store an *int*, for instance, in a list (say), it must be wrapped in an object. Also, all type wrappers have a method called *compareTo(),* which compares the value contained within the wrapper; a method called *equals(),* which tests two values for equality; and, methods which return the simple-type value of the object in different forms.

But, there is a caveat. In general, use of type wrappers should be restricted to those cases only where an object representation of a primitive type is needed. Autoboxing/unboxing should not be used as a "round about" way of eliminating or getting around the primitive types.

Now, we shall discuss a bit about enumerations. Although you can't inherit a superclass when declaring an *enum*, all enumerations automatically inherit *java.lang.Enum*. This class defines several methods such as *ordinal()*, *compareTo()*, and *equals()*, which are available for use by all enumerations. Herein, we shall discuss only one of these methods, namely, *ordinal()* whose general form is:

final int ordinal()

By means of this method, you can obtain a value that indicates an *enum* constant's position in the list of constants, which is called its *ordinal value*. The method returns the *ordinal value* of the invoking constant. Note that ordinal values begin at zero.

We shall round off this section with a brief overview of the restrictions that apply to annotation declarations. These restrictions can be elaborated as follows:

(1) No anotation can inherit another.

(2) Annotations must not be generic, i.e., they can't take type parameters.

(3) Annontation methods cannot have a *throws* clause.

(4) All methods declared by annotations must be parameterless. Moreover, they must return one of the following:-

   (i) A primitive type such as an *int* or *double*
   (ii) An object of type *String* or *Class*
   (iii) An *enum* type
   (iv) Another annotation type
   (v) An array of one of the preceding types

PRACTICAL SESSION

1. State True(T) or False(F):
   The *Object* class is the superclass of all classes in Java.

2. What do you mean by type wrappers in Java?
   Elucidate citing suitable example(s), wherever necessary.

3 (a) What role do enumerations play in Java programming?
   Elucidate giving suitable example(s), wherever necessary.

   (b) Find errors, if any, in the following code segments:
      (i) *enum abc {a, b, c(-78) }*
      (ii) *enum paint {p, a, i, n, t }*

4. What do you understand by autoboxing in Java? How is it useful?
   Explain giving appropriate example(s).

5. (a) Why are attributes also referred to as 'metadata'? What is their role in Java?
   (b) What are marker annotations?
   (c) List the four built-in Java annotations.

JAVA INTERVIEW QUESTIONS (solved)

Q.1 Discuss the significance of the Java language.

ANSWER: Java is the preeminent language of the Internet. Apart from this, many of its features are influencing upcoming languages such as C#.

Q.2 Compare in brief C/C++, C#, and Java.

ANSWER: Java derives its syntax from C. Many of the object-oriented features of Java were strongly influenced by C++. But, it would be improper to consider Java as the "Internet version of C++". C# and Java are similar in the sense that they both share the same C++ syntax, support distributed programming, and both make use of the same object model. But, in spite of this, there are stark differences between the two.

Q.3 Why is Java important to the Internet?

ANSWER: Java's ability to create and run applets and its portability because of its ability to create bytecodes to be run by the Java Virtual Machine (JVM) render it extremely suitable for the internet.

Q.4 Elaborate on the main features of Java.

ANSWER: Some of the main features of Java include the following:-

(i) Simple and secure
(ii) Portable and architecture-neutral
(iii) Object-oriented
(iv) Robust and multithreaded
(v) Interpreted and high performance
(vi) Distributed and dynamic

Q.5 Name the three Object-Oriented Programming (OOP) principles.

ANSWER: The three object-oriented programming (OOP) principles are:-

(i) Encapsulation
(ii) Inheritance
(iii) Polymorphism

These three principles work together in unision.

Q.6 Distinguish between "call-by-value" and "call-by-reference".

ANSWER: There are, in general, two ways that a computer language can pass an argument to a subroutine. The first way is referred to as "call-by-value" while the second is known as "call-by-reference". In "call-by-value", the method copies the value of an argument into the formal parameter of the subroutine, and whence, changes made to the parameter of the subroutine have no effect on the argument. In contrast to this, a reference to an argument, and, not the value of the argument is passed to the parameter in the "call-by-reference" approach. Inside the subroutine, this reference is then used to access the actual argument specified in the call so that changes made to the parameter will affect the argument used to call the subroutine. In Java, when a simple type is passed to a method, it is done through "call-by-value" whereas objects are passed through "call-by-reference".

Q.7 What is recursion? Does Java support recursion?

ANSWER: Recursion is the process of defining something in terms of itself. Java does support recursion as it allows a method to call itself. Such a method is said to be recursive. A classic case of recursion is computing the factorial of a number.

Q.8 How can you determine the size of an array?

ANSWER: The size of an array, that is to say, the number of elements it can hold, is found in its length instance variable.

Q.9 How are command-line arguments passed in Java?

ANSWER: In Java, all command-line arguments are passed as strings only. If you wish to pass numeric values, they must be converted to their internal forms manually.

Q.10 What is the difference between the prefix increment ++x and the postfix increment x++?

ANSWER: The statement:

```
y = y + x++;
```

adds the current values of x and y and assigns this result back to y. The value of x is only incremented after the value of y has been thus obtained.

On the other hand, the statement:

```
y = y + ++x;
```

obtains the value of x, increments x, then adds that value to the current value of y, and this result is assigned to y.

You can see for yourself (by assigning some initial values to x and y) that simply changing ++x to x++ changes the results quite substantially when both of the above statements are run over a loop.

Q.11 What is the use of short-circuit logical operators | | OR and && AND?

ANSWER: Contrary to the normal counterparts | and &, the short circuit operators | | and && evaluate the second operand only when necessary. That is to say, the result of the OR operation will always be true if the first operand is true irrespective of the second operand. Similarly, the result of the AND operation will always be false if the first operand is false irrespective of the second operand. In both these cases, || and && do not evaluate the second operand unlike their normal counterparts | and &, which evaluate both the operands in all situations.

Q.12 Can you name an operator in Java that takes three operands?

ANSWER: The ternary operator with the most general form:

exp1 ? exp2 : exp3;

(if exp1 is true, exp2 becomes the value of the whole expression else exp3 becomes the value of the whole expression)

Q.13 Can you create a 'for' loop without any conditional expressions? What does it amount to?

ANSWER: Leaving the conditional expressions in a 'for' loop makes it an infinite loop that will run forever:

```
for ( ; ; )          // intentional infinite loop
{
        ..............................
        ..............................
}
```

Q.14 What does the "for-each" style loop do?

ANSWER: The "foreach" style loop is meant for cycling through the elements of a collection, from first to last.

Q.15 What do the break and continue statements do? Bring out the main point of difference between them.

ANSWER: The break statement causes an early termination of the loop whereas the continue statement causes an early iteration of the loop.

Q.16 Explain the use of the keyword new.

ANSWER: The keyword new is used to create objects, e.g.

House building = new House ();

Here, building by itself does not contain the object (House). Rather, it contains a reference to it.

On the other hand, consider:

int i = 100;

Here, i contains the value 100 since i is a variable of type int, which, in turn, is a value type.

Again, consider:

House building1 = new House ();

House building2 = new House ();

building2 = building1;

House building3 = new House ();

building2 = building3;

After the execution of this sequence, building2 refers to the same object (House) as building3. The object (House) referred to by building1 is unchanged.

Q.17 What are the two uses of the keyword super?

ANSWER: (i) A subclass can call a constructor defined in its superclass by using the keyword super.

(ii) The second use of super relates to situations in which member names of a subclass hide members by the same name in the superclass. In such a case, you can refer to the superclass member by using super.member.

Q.18 Point out the difference between C++ and Java as regards release of previously allocated memory.

ANSWER: In C++, the delete operator is used to free memory that was previously allocated. But, Java uses a different, more trouble-free approach, viz. garbage collection.

Q.19 What is the purpose of the finalize() method in Java?

ANSWER: We can define a method in Java that shall be called just prior to the object's final destruction by the garbage collector. This method is known as the finalize() method, which can be used in some highly specialized situations to ensure that the object is destroyed / terminated cleanly.

Q.20 What do you understand by 'this'?

ANSWER: When a method is called, it is, by itself, passed a reference to the invoking object, i.e. the object on which the method is called. This reference is referred to as 'this'.

Q.21 Can you elaborate on the concept of jagged arrays?

ANSWER: In general, when we create a two-dimensional array, we are creating what is a rectangular array with the length of each row being the same for the entire array, e.g. a 2 x 3 array implies an array of two rows with three elements in each row. But, Java allows you to create a special two-dimensional array called a jagged array, which is an array of arrays, where the length of each array can differ. In this way, we can have a table where the lengths of the rows differ, e.g.

```
int jag [ ] [ ] = new int [4] [ ];
```

```
jag [0] = new int [10]; // length of first array is ten
jag [1] = new int [2];  // length of second array is two
jag [2] = new int [5];  // length of third array is five
jag [3] = new int [8];  // length of fourth array is eight
```

Q.22 Can you point out the main difference between C/C++ strings and Java strings?

ANSWER: In C/C++, strings are simply arrays of characters terminated by the '\0' null character whereas in Java, string is a built-in data type. In fact, in Java, strings are objects and thus, reference types.

Q.23 Can the contents of strings in Java be changed?

ANSWER: No, strings in Java are immutable. This might seem to be a drawback but since unused string objects are automatically garbage-collected, you can simply create a new string with the desired changes.

Q.24 What are Java's access modifiers?

ANSWER: In Java, member access control is achieved through three access modifiers, namely, public, private, and protected. The protected modifier applies only in case of inheritance. When a member of a class is modified by the public specifier, then that member can be accessed by any code in your program. If a member of a class is specified to be private, it can then only be accessed by other members of its class so that methods in other classes will not be able to access a private member of another class.

Q.25 Which feature of C/C++ is similar to overridden methods in Java?

ANSWER: Overridden methods in Java are similar to virtual functions in C/C++.

Q.26 Is it possible to have a variable number of arguments in Java?

ANSWER: Yes, this is a recently added new feature to Java. It was added by JDK 5. The addition of this feature has enabled formatted output in Java akin to the printf() family of functions in C.

Q.27 Can you declare a class as both abstract and final?

ANSWER: An abstract class is incomplete by itself and relies upon its subclasses to provide complete implementation. Whence, it is illegal to declare a class as both abstract and final.

Q.28 When do you declare an element as protected?

ANSWER: In Java, if you want to allow an element to be visible outside your current package, but only to classes that subclass your class directly, then you declare that element as protected.

Q.29 Where does the package statement occur in a Java source file?

ANSWER: The package statement must be the first statement in a Java source file.

Q.30 Where does the import statement occur in a Java source file?

ANSWER: The import statement in a Java source file must occur immediately after the package statement, if any, and before any class definitions.

Q.31 Specify the forms of the Main () method available in Java.

ANSWER: The following four versions of Main () are currently available in Java:-

(i) public static void main ()
(ii) public static int main ()
(iii) public static void main (String args[ ])
(iv) public static int main (String args[ ])

Q.32 Elucidate the role of the keyword static.

ANSWER: In general, a class member has to be accessed through an object of its instance. But, it is possible in Java to create a member that can be used by itself, without any reference to a specific instance. To create such a member, you have to precede its declaration with the keyword static.

Q.33 Point out any four restrictions on static methods?

ANSWER: First, a static method cannot have a 'this' reference. Second, a static method cannot refer to super in any way. Third, a static method can directly call only other static methods. Finally, a static method can have access only to static data.

Q.34 Which feature of Java is akin to multiple inheritance in C++?

ANSWER: Interfaces in Java provide most of the functionality associated with multiple inheritance in C++.

Q.35 Can Java interfaces be inherited?

ANSWER: The answer to this query is indeed in the affirmative.

Q.36 Give a one line definition of an exception.

ANSWER: An exception is a run-time error.

Q.37 Which class is at the top of the exception hierarchy?

ANSWER: Throwable.

Q.38 Which are the two important subclasses of Throwable?

ANSWER: Exception and Error.

Q.39 Can you name the all important subclass of Exception?

ANSWER: RuntimeException.

Q.40 What is RuntimeException?

ANSWER: RuntimeException is a subclass of Exception and includes such run-time programming error conditions such as divide-by-zero and invalid array index.

Q.41 What does the throws clause do?

ANSWER: A throws clause lists all the types of exceptions that a method might throw but does not handle them by itself.

Q.42 How is java.lang related to exceptions?

ANSWER: Inside its standard package java.lang, Java defines several exception classes. The most general of these exceptions are subclasses of the standard type RuntimeException. Since java.lang is implicitly imported into all Java programs, most of the exceptions derived from RuntimeException are automatically available and need not be included in the throws list of any method. In terms of Java, these are known as unchecked exceptions since the Java compiler does not check to see if a method handles or throws these exceptions.

Q.43 Can you create your own custom exceptions in Java?

ANSWER: Although Java's built-in exceptions are capable of handling the most common errors, there will still be occasions when you would like to create your own exception types specific to your applications. This is quite simply done by defining a subclass of Exception, which, in turn, is in fact a subclass of Throwable.

Q.44 What do you understand by chained exceptions?

ANSWER: Java 2, version 1.4 added the feature of chained exceptions to the exception subsystem of Java. This feature allows you to associate one exception with another where the second exception describes the cause of the first exception. For instance, take the case when an ArithmeticException occurred because of an attempt to divide-by-zero. But, the actual cause of the problem was that an I/O error occurred, which caused the divisor to be set to zero. In such a scenario, the method must certainly throw an ArithmeticException but you also might want to let the calling code know that the underlying cause was an I/O error: chained exception allow you to do this and any similar situation where layers of exceptions exist, thus forming a chain.

Q.45 Both the subclass and the superclass can have their own constructors. So, what constructor is responsible for building an object of the subclass – the one in the superclass, or the one in the subclass, or both?

ANSWER: The constructor for the superclass constructs the superclass part of the object and the constructor for the subclass builds the subclass portion of the object.

Q.46 How does a subclass call a constructor defined in its superclass?

ANSWER: A subclass can call a constructor defined in its superclass by using the super keyword in the following manner:-

super (param_list);

where, param_list specifies any parameters required by the constructor in the superclass. Note that super must always be the first statement executed inside a subclass' constructor.

Q.47 In what order are constructors called in a class hierarchy?

ANSWER: In a class hierarchy, constructors are called in their order of derivation, that is, from superclass to subclass.

Q.48 What do you mean by method overriding?

ANSWER: When a method in a subclass has the same name, return type, and signature as that in the superclass, it is said to override the method in the superclass and this phenomenon is referred to as method overriding in Java.

Q.49 What do you understand by dynamic method dispatch?

ANSWER: Dynamic method dispatch is the means by which a call to an overridden method is resolved at run-time rather than at compile time. It is important since Java implements run-time polymorphism this way.

Q.50 Can you give one good reason for using overridden methods?

ANSWER: Overridden methods are another way that Java implements the 'one interface, multiple methods' aspect of polymorphism.

Q.51 Can an abstract method have a body?

ANSWER: No, not at all!

Q.52 Can you create an object of an abstract class using new?

ANSWER: An abstract class does not specify a complete implementation and whence, there can be no objects of an abstract class. Therefore, attempting to create an object of an abstract class using new will lead to a consequent compile time error.

Q.53 What are the three uses of the keyword final?

ANSWER:

(i) You can use final to prevent a class from being inherited by preceding the class declaration with the keyword final.

(ii) You can use final to prevent further overriding of a method by preceding its declaration with the keyword final.

(iii) The keyword final can be used to create what are known as final named constants.

Q.54 What do you mean or understand by type wrappers?

ANSWER: In Java, simple types such as int or char are not part of the object hierarchy. They are passed by value to methods and cannot be directly passed by reference. Moreover, there is no way for two methods to refer to the same instance of an int. There will be occasions when you need to create an object representation for one of these simple types, e.g., there are the enumeration classes, which deal only with objects, and thus, to store a simple type in one of these classes, you must wrap the simple type in a class. To take care of this need, Java provides for classes that correspond to each of these simple types. These classes essentially encapsulate or wrap the simple types within a class and whence, they are commonly referred to as type wrappers.

Q.55 What do you mean by autoboxing and auto-unboxing?

ANSWER: Beginning with JDK 5, Java added two important features, namely, autoboxing and auto-unboxing. Auto-boxing is the process by which a primitive type is automatically encapsulated ("boxed") into its equivalent type wrapper whenever an object of that type is required. There is thus, no need to construct an object explicitly as such.

Auto-unboxing is the process by means of which the valued of a "boxed" object is automatically extracted ("unboxed") from a type wrapper when its value is required. There is thus, no need to explicitly invoke a method such as intValue() or doubleValue() etc.

Q.56 What is the Object class in Java?

ANSWER: There is one special class, Object, defined by Java, which is a superclass of all other classes. This means that a reference variable of type Object can refer to object of any other class. Moreover, since arrays are implemented as classes in Java, a variable of type Object can also refer to any array.

Q.57 Define an interface in Java.

ANSWER: An interface defines a set of methods that will be implemented by a class. An interface, by itself, does not implement any method. In this way, we see that an interface is a purely logical construct that describes functionality without defining any implementation whatsoever.

Q.58 What is the similarity and difference between interfaces and abstract classes?

ANSWER: Interfaces are syntactically similar to abstract classes. But, in an interface, no method can have a body. Thus, an interface does not provide any implementation at all. It tells what is to be done but is completely silent about how it is to be done. Once an interface is specified, any number of classes can implement it. Moreover, one class may implement any number of interfaces.

Q.59 How will you choose between an interface and an abstract class?

ANSWER: When you can fully describe the concept in terms of 'what it does' without any need to specify 'how it does it', you should use an interface. However, if you need to include at least some implementation details, you should use an abstract class to represent your concept.

Q.60 What do you understand by multithreading?

ANSWER: Java has built-in support for multithreaded programming. A multithreaded program contains two or more parts that can run concurrently. Each such part is called a thread, and each thread defines a separate path of execution. A text editor formatting its text and printing at the same time is a good example of multithreading. In this way, we see that multithreading is a specialized version of multitasking.

Q.61 Can multithreading lead to problems at times?

ANSWER: Multithreading can lead to problems at times especially when you create too many threads. In such a case, you actually degrade the performance of your program rather than enhance it as multithreading is supposed to do. This is because some overhead is always associated with context switching. If you create too many threads, more CPU time will be spent changing contexts rather than executing your program! You must always remember and be aware of this vital fact.

Q.62 What is the use of the isAlive() method?

ANSWER: How can one thread know when another thread has ended? You can call isAlive() on the thread. This method is defined by Thread, and its most general form is as follows:

```
final boolean isAlive()
```

The isAlive() method returns true if the thread upon which it is called is still running and false otherwise.

Q.63 What is the use of the join() method?

ANSWER: There is a second way to know when a thread has ended apart from the IsAlive() method described above in Q.62. While isAlive() is occasionally useful, the method, which you will more often use to wait for a thread to finish is called join(), whose most general form is as follows:

```
final void join() throws InterruptedException
```

This method waits until the thread on which it is called terminates/finishes. Its name comes from the concept of the calling thread waiting until the specified thread joins it. Apart from the form of join() elaborated above, there are additional forms, which allow you to specify the maximum amount of time that you want to wait for the specified thread to terminate/finish.

Q.64 What do you mean by a deadlock?

ANSWER: There is a special type of error relating specifically to multitasking that you need to avoid. It is known as a deadlock, which occurs when two threads have a circular dependency on a pair of synchronized objects.

Q.65 What is an exception handler?

ANSWER: As we have already stated in the answer to Q.36, an exception is an error which occurs at run-time. Exception handling streamlines error handling by allowing the program to specify a block of code, called an exception handler, which is executed automatically in case of an error. Exception handler eliminates the need to manually check the success / failure of each specific operation or method call. In case an error occurs, it is processed / handled by the exception handler gracefully.

Q.66 Can you elaborate on the consequences of an uncaught exception?

ANSWER: In general, if your program does not catch an exception, it will be caught by the run-time system, which, in turn, will report an error and terminate the program abnormally / ungracefully.

Q.67 What is the major benefit of exception handling?

ANSWER: One of the major benefits of exception handling is that it enables your program to respond to an error and then continue running, that is, handle the error gracefully, and then continue further.

Q.68 Can you have a try block followed by a finally block with no catch clauses?

ANSWER: Syntactically, when a finally block follows a try block, no catch clauses are technically required. In such a case, the finally block gets executed after exit from the try block, but no exceptions are handled in such a case / event.

Q.69 What is a stream in Java?

ANSWER: Java programs perform Input / Output through streams. A stream is an abstraction that produces / consumes information. A stream is liked to a physical device by the I/O system. It is useful to note that all streams behave in the same manner irrespective of the physical device they might be linked to.

Q.70 Elucidate the benefits of the streams.

ANSWER: The streaming interface to I/O in Java provides a clean abstraction for a complex and often cumbersome task. The composition of the filtered stream classes allows you to dynamically build the custom streaming interface to suit your data transfer requirements. Java programs written to adhere to the abstract, high-level InputStream, OutputStream, Reader, and Writer classes will function properly even in the future when new and improved concrete stream classes are invented. This model works very well even when we switch from a file system-based set of streams to the network and socket streams. Moreover, serialization of objects is expected to play an increasingly important role in the future Java programming. In fact, Java's serialization I/O classes provide a portable solution to this sometimes tricky task/proposition.

Q.71 Name the predefined I/O streams in Java.

ANSWER: System.in, System.out, and System.err are the three predefined I/O streams in Java. By default, System.in refers to the keyboard while System.out and System.err refer to the console.

Q.72 Name the two byte streams and the two character streams related to File I/O in Java, respectively.

ANSWER: FileInputStream & FileOutputStream are the two byte streams and FIleReader & FileWriter are the two character streams, respectively, related to File I/O in Java.

Q.73 How is binary data read and written?

ANSWER: Binary data is read and written using the DataInputStream and DataOutputStreams streams, respectively.

Q.74 Name the two classes at the top of the byte stream classes.

ANSWER: InputStream and OutputStream.

Q.75 Name the two classes at the top of the character stream classes.

ANSWER: Reader and Writer.

Q.76 Does Java have a generalized console input formatter akin to the standard C function scanf() or the C++ input operators?

ANSWER: Yes, added by JDK 5 recently, Java has the Scanner class which reads formatted input and converts it into its binary form. The Scanner class is the complement of the Formatter class of Java which has made formatted output in Java very easy akin to the printf() style of functions in C/C++.

Q.77 Elucidate the New I/O system.

ANSWER: Java 2, version 1.4 added a new way to handle I/O operations. Called the new I/O APIs, it supports a channel-based approach to I/O operations. The new I/O (NIO) system is built on two foundational items, viz. buffers and channels. A buffer holds data. A channel represents an open connection to an I/O device, such as a file or a socket. In general, to use the

NIO system, you obtain a channel to an I/O device and a buffer to hold data. You then operate on the buffer, inputting / outputting data as needed. We must, at this stage, sound a caveat as to whether NIO is the future of I/O handling? The channel/buffer based NIO approach is currently designed to supplement, and not supplant the traditional and standard stream-based I/O mechanisms.

Q.78 What types of comments are supported by Java? Does it support documentation comments?

ANSWER: Java supports three types of comments – the first two are // and /* */. The third type is called a documentation comment. A documentation comment begins with /** and ends with */. Using such documentation comments, you can embed information about your program into the program itself; and, later on, you can use the javadoc utility program to extract this information and put it into an HTML file.

Q.79 Define a package.

ANSWER: A package is a container for classes that is used to keep the class name space compartmentalized.

Q.80 Can you create a hierarchy of packages?

ANSWER: You can indeed create a hierarchy of packages. To do so, simply separate each package name from the one above it by using a period. The most general form of a multileveled package statement is as follows:

```
package pkg1[.pkg2[.pkg3.[pkg4]]];
```

Note that a package hierarchy must be reflected in the file system of your Java development system.

Q.81 What does the Math class contain?

ANSWER: The Math class contains all the floating-point functions that are used for geometry and trigonometry such as sin(), as well as several general-purpose methods such as sqrt().

Q.82 What do you mean by generics?

ANSWER: Generics imply parameterized types. They provide a streamlined and type-safe approach to deal with different data types as also promote reusability of code. Generics were introduced by JDK 5 and are somewhat similar to templates in C++.

Q.83 How is java.util useful?

ANSWER: The java.util package contains one of Java's most powerful subsystems, viz. collections. In addition to collections, java.util contains a wide assortment of classes and interfaces, which support a broad range of functionality such as generating pseudorandom numbers, manipulating date and time, observing events, manipulating sets of bits, and tokenizing strings. These classes and interfaces are used throughout the core Java packages and are, of course, available for use in the programs you write.

Q.84 Elucidate the utility of collections.

ANSWER: Collections simplify many programs by providing off-the-shelf solutions to several common but at times difficult to develop data structures. For instance, there are built-in collections that support dynamic arrays, linked lists, stacks, queues, and hash tables.

Q.85 On what principle does a Stack operate?

ANSWER: Stack is a First-in, Last-out list. To visualize a stack, imagine a stack of plates on a table. The first plate put down is the last one to be retrieved.

Q.86 What is the principle behind the Queue?

ANSWER: Queue is a First-in, First-out list, i.e. the first item put in a queue is the first item retrieved from it. Queues are common in real life, e.g. lines at a bank or railway reservation center are queues.

Q.87 What is a Hashtable?

ANSWER: Hashtable creates a collection which uses a hash table for storage (the hash table, in turn, stores information using a mechanism known as hashing).

Q.88 What is the ArrayList class?

ANSWER: The ArrayList class supports dynamic arrays, which can grow or shrink as per the user requirements.

Q.89 Should collections be limited to "large jobs" such as corporate databases, inventory systems, or mailing lists?

ANSWER: Collections need not be reserved for only the "large jobs" such as corporate databases, inventory systems, or mailing lists. They are equally effective when applied to smaller jobs, e.g., a TreeMap would be ideal to hold the directory structure of a set of files and a TreeSet would be an excellent choice for storing project-management information.

Q.90 How can you obtain an Array from an ArrayList?

ANSWER: When working with ArrayList, you might want to obtain an actual array, which contains the contents of the list. You can easily accomplish this by calling the toArray() method.

Q.91 Are the == and the equals() method the same? If not, point out the difference between the two.

ANSWER: It is important to understand that the equals() method and the == operator perform two different operations. While the equals() method compares the characters inside a String object, the == operator compares two object references to see whether they refer to the same instance.

Q.92 How can you create a string in Java that is mutable?

ANSWER: A mutable string in Java can be created by means of the StringBuffer class. In the StringBuffer class, characters can be inserted in the middle or appended to the end of a string.

Q.93 Can an enumeration be used to control a switch statement?

ANSWER: Yes, enumerations can easily be used to control a switch statement. Of course, all of the case statements must use constants from the same enum as that used by the switch expression.

Q.94 What is the client/server model in the context of networking?

ANSWER: The term client/server is often heard in the context of networking. A server is anything that has some resource which can be shared. Thus, there are compute servers which provide computing power; print servers which manage a collection of printers; disk servers which provide networked disk space; and web servers which store web pages. And, a client is simply any other entity that wants to gain access to a particular server.

Q.95 What are proxy servers?

ANSWER: A proxy server speaks the client side of a protocol to another server. This is often required when clients have certain restrictions on which servers they can connect to. Thus, a client would connect to a proxy server, which did not have such restrictions, and the proxy server would, in turn, communicate for the client.

Q.96 What is the use of the URLs?

ANSWER: The Uniform Resource Locators (URLs) provide a reasonably intelligible form to uniquely identify/address information on the Internet.

Q.97 Define an applet in Java.

ANSWER: There are two classes of programs in Java, namely, the applications and the applets. Applications are the normal programs while applets are small applications that are accessed on an Internet server, transported over the Internet, automatically installed, and run as part of a Web document.

Q.98 What are the two packages that all applets must import?

ANSWER: (i) java.applet; and,

(ii) java.awt.

Q.99 What do you understand by double buffering?

ANSWER: Images are not only useful for storing pictures, but you can also use them as offscreen drawing surfaces. This allows you to render any image, including text and graphics, to an offscreen buffer which you can display later on. The main advantage of doing this is that the image is seen only when it is complete. Drawing a complicated image could take several milliseconds or more, which can be seen by the user as flashing/flickering. This flickering/flashing is distracting and causes the user to perceive your rendering as slower than it actually is. Use of an offscreen image to reduce flicker is known as double buffering, since the screen is considered as a buffer for pixels, and the offscreen image is the second buffer, where you can prepare pixels for display.

Q.100 What are the methods called in order when an applet begins and ends, respectively?

ANSWER: When an applet begins, the AWT calls the following methods in order:-

(i) init()
(ii) start()
(iii) paint()

When an applet terminates/ends, the following order of methods comes into play:-

(i) stop()
(ii) destroy()

MISCELLANEOUS PROBLEMS (A Full Practical Session)

1. Select the correct option in each of the following multiple choice problems:
   (i) A good reason to use an object-oriented language is that:
      (a) You can define various data types.
      (b) Program statements are simpler than those in procedural languages.
      (c) It is easier to conceptualize an object-oriented program and reuse the code.
      (d) An object-oriented program can correct its own mistakes.
      (e) All of the above.
      (f) None of the above.

   (ii) The characteristic that data can be manipulated only through the member functions which are part of a specified class is called:
      (a) Data dependency
      (b) Encapsulation
      (c) Inheritance
      (d) Polymorphism
      (e) All of the above
      (f) None of the above

   (iii) Which of the following is a valid main() method:
      (a) public static void main()
      (b) public static void main(String str[])
      (c) void main(String args[])
      (d) main(String str[])
      (e) All of the above
      (f) None of the above

(iv) Classes are useful because they::
- (a) Permit data to be hidden from other classes.
- (b) Can closely model objects in the real world.
- (c) Bring together all aspects of an entity in one place.
- (d) Help in reusability of code via inheritance.
- (e) All of the above
- (f) None of the above

(v) Which one out of the following must be true of the object thrown by a *throw* statement:
- (a) It must be assignable to the *Throwable* type.
- (b) It must be assignable to the *Error* type.
- (c) It must be assignable to the *Exception* type.
- (d) It must be assignable to the *String* type.
- (e) All of the above
- (f) None of the above

(vi) Which one of the following is the main use of a package:
- (a) Categorizes data.
- (b) Makes compiling faster.
- (c) Resolves name conflicts.
- (d) Makes programming easier.
- (e) All of the above
- (f) None of the above

(vii) A base class is inherited by a:
- (a) super class
- (b) derived class
- (c) constructor
- (d) main() method
- (e) All of the above
- (f) None of te above

(viii) The first statement in a Java source file should be the:
- (a) import statement
- (b) package statement
- (c) main() method
- (d) exception handling statement
- (e) Any of the above
- (f) None of the above

(ix) Sharing of coomon information is achieved by the concept of::
- (a) Polymorphism
- (b) Encapsulation
- (c) Inheritance
- (d) Instantiation.
- (e) All of the above
- (f) None of the above

(x) Which of the following is a valid Java comment:
- (a) * A Comment *\
- (b) \\ A Comment
- (c) /** A Comment
- (d) /* A Comment */
- (e) All of the above
- (f) None of the above

(xi) Which one of the following is the most appropriate statement:
- (a) All variables must be declared before they are used in Java.
- (b) All variables can be declared at the end of the Java program.
- (c) The data types of variables is assigned dynamically in Java.
- (d) All variables are implicitly declared in Java.
- (e) All of the above
- (f) None of the above

(xii) A member method of a class can always access the data in:
- (a) The object of which it is a member.
- (b) The class of which it is a member.
- (c) Any object of the class of which it is a member.
- (d) Public methods.
- (e) All of the above
- (f) None of the above

(xiii) The advantage of a *switch* statement over an *else-if* construction is that:
- (a) A default condition can be used in the *switch* statement.
- (b) The *switch* statement is easier to understand.
- (c) Several different statements can be executed for each case in a *switch*.
- (d) Several different conditions can cause one set of statements to be executed in a *switch*.
- (e) All of the above
- (f) None of the above

(xiiv) The class used to perform basic console I/O is:
- (a) System
- (b) Security Manager.
- (c) Math
- d) Run-time
- (e) Any of the above
- (f) None of the above

(xv) The specific location where a Java compiler looks for a class is known as the:
- (a) Euclidean path
- (b) Inheritance path.
- (c) Run-time path
- (d) Classpath.
- (e) Any of the above
- (f) None of the above

2. State True (T) or False (F) against each of the following statements:

(i) It is perfectly all right to use variables of different data types in the same arithmetic expression.

(ii) Keyword 'this' points to the current object.

(iii) After an exception is handled, the program is terminated..

(iv) Organizing data with methods that operate on the data and creates a new data type is called encapsulation.

(v) The "==" operator is used to indicate equality in Java.

(vi) In a 'for' loop, --*i* and *i*--, always give the same result.

(vii) Only one single value can be returned from a method.

(viii) Enumeration class provides the capability to implement a growable array of objects.

(ix) The *Object* class is the highest-level class in the Java class hierarchy.

(x) Java is a 4 GL.

(xi) The public access modifier allowws access to its members even if objects of classes belongi to another package.

(xii) Comments make the program to execute faster.

(xiii) The following syntax is valid: *for (; ;) ;*

(xiv) Declaring a variable is advantageous because it simplifies writing of shorter programs.

(xv) There can be many *finally* statements for one *try* statement.

(xvi) The continue statement is used to skip the rest of the loop and start again from the beginning of the loop.

(xvii) The main difference in operation between an *if* statement and a *while* loop is that the body of the *while* loop may be executed many times but the body of the *if* statement will be executed only once.

(xviii) If a package statement is included in a source code file, it must appear as the first non-blank line.

(xix) Methods define the behaviour of objects instantiated from a class.

(xx) The Java interpreter will interpret and run bytecode while interpreting it.

3. Give the output of each of the following codes:

(i)
```
class TestingItOut
{
        public static void main (String args[])
        {
                System.out.println(s[0]);
        }
}
```
(assume that the program is invoked usiing the following command line:

java TestingItOut Is this Testing it out?)

(ii)
```
public class Test
{
        public static void main(String args[])
        {
                TestClass tc = new TestClass();
                tc.meth();
        }
}
class TestClass
{
        private void meth()
        {
                System.out.println("Welcome to the world of Java");
        }
}
```

(iii)
```
class TestingItOut
{
        public static void main (String args[])
        {
                int i  = 7; int j = 8;
                int n = (i | j) % (i & j);
                System.out.println(n);
        }
}
```

(iv)
```
try
{
        int i;
        return;
}
catch (Exception e)
{
        System.out.println("Here");
        return;
}
finally
{
        System.out.println("Welcome");
}
```

(v)
```
class TestingItOut
{
        public static void main (String args[])
        {
                byte [] b  = new byte [2];
                b[1] = 3;
                b[2] = b[1] * 10;
                System.out.println(b[1]);
                System.out.print("\n // Is it a Comment?");
        }
}
```

4. What are the reasons which led to the popularity of object-oriented programming? Give any three features of OOP citing a suitable example in each case.

5 How does Java implement the portability of code?

6. (a) Write a Java program to convert a given distance in metres to kilometres and display the result in kilometres.
   (b) Write a Java program that reverses a given number declared as a constant and displays the reveresed number.
   (c) Write a Java program to output the fibonacci series:
   1 1 2 3 5 8
   (d) Write a Java program that will accept the first character of the day of the week and guess its full name; e.g., if the user enters "w' or "W', your program should guess that it's "Wednesday", If the user enters "s" or "S', your program should display "It must be Saturday! Press Y (yes) or N (no)!!".; if the user responds with "Y", it's "Saturday", else it's "Sunday".

7. Give the result of each of the following expressions:
   (i) 10*2/3<128/10+3|100/20*3>25
   (ii) 10*2/3<128/10+3^100/20*3>25
   (iii) 10*2/3<128/10+3&100/20*3>25
   (iv) 10*2/3<128/10+3&&100/20*3>25
   (iv) 10*2/3<128/10+3| |00/20*3>25

8. (a) What do you understand by method overloading? What are its advantages?
   (b) How can we disable method overriding, that is, call a method from a superclass which has the same signature as a method in the subclass?

9. What is inheritance? What is its purpose? Bring out the significance of the protected access specifier.

10. Elaborate the procedure to handle exceptions.

11. Give the output of the following program:

```
class TestingBits
{
        public static void main (String args[])
        {
                int i = 5; int j = 6;
                System.out.println("i =  " + i);
                System.out.println("j =  " + j);
                System.out.println("i & j=  " + (i&j));
                System.out.println("i | j=  " + (i|j));
                System.out.println("i ^ j=  " + (i^j));
        }
}
```

12. Give the output of the following program:

```
class TestingShift
{
        public static void main (String args[])
        {
                int i = 7;
                System.out.println("i =  " + i);
                System.out.println("i >>2j=  " + (i>>2));
                System.out.println("i << 1=  " + (i<<1));
                System.out.println("i >>>1j=  " + (i>>>1));
        }
}
```

13. What are packages? What is CLASSPATH?

14. (a) When is the import statement used?
    (b) abc.cbac is a package name. What will the following import statements do:
        (i) import abc.cbac;
        (ii) import abc.cbac.*;
        (iii) import abc.cbac.CaseExample;

15. Consider the following Java program:

```
public class TestingExample
{
        public static void main (String args[])
        {
                TestingClass  tc = new TestingClass(100, 200);
                System.out.println("tc.m);
                System.out.println("tc.n);
                tc.m = 10;
                tc.n = 20;
                System.out.println("tc.m);
                System.out.println("tc.n);
        }
}
class TestingClass
{
        public static void main (String args[])
        {
                public int m;
                private int n;

                public TestingClass(int i, int j)
                {
                        m = i;
                        n = j;
                }
        }
}
```

The above program will compile and run successfully, if certain statements are commented out. What are those statements? And, what will be the result on running the program after commenting out the said statements?

Appendix

THE JAVAAPI PACKAGE

The JAVAAPI (*Java Application Programming Interface*) is made up of fifty-nine libraries called packages. We enumerate below the important ones (for full details, you are advised to consult the *index.html* of the *API* sub-directory of the *docs* directory of the Official Java Documentation):

java.applet	Supplies the intefaces and the class necessary for the creation of of Java applets, enablling you to display images and read audio files.
java.awt	Supplies the interfaces and classes necessary for the creation of GUI, in addition to graphics and drawings.
java.beans	Supplies intefaces and classes in relation to the JavaBean development platform, enabling the creation of software components that are reusable as beans.
java.io	Supplies the interfaces and classes that access the system entrance/ exit flux.
java.lang	Supplies the interfaces and classes that are fundamental to Java Programming. It is the core of the Java language.
java.math	Supplies the interfaces and classes that operate on floating-point values, or very large integers.
java.net	Supplies the interfaces and classes that handle network applications such as the handling of sockets and URLs.
java.rmi	Supplies the interfaces and classes that create Java applications in the form of distributed objects, enabling the calling of the methods of distant objects.

java.security Supplies the interfaces and classes that implement the digital signatures and certification of Java components.

java.sql Supplies the interfaces and classes that connect to databases through SQL.

java.text Supplies the interfaces and classes that create character strings from objects and that convert them into other objects.

java.util Supplies the interfaces and classes that handle random numbers, time, date, or object collections.

javax.accessibility
Supplies the interfaces and classes that extend the functions of GUIs, enabling the implementation of assistance technology such as Braille terminals, or voice-recognition systems.

javax.swing Supplies the interfaces and classes that extend the java.awt package by supplying enriched components for the management of the GUI. The advantage of javax.swing over java.awt is that you can make an application in which the GUI automatically adapts to the system on which it is running, or takes on an aspect defined by the programmer.

org.omg.CORBA
Defines the architecture of the OMG CORBA bus in order to transit distributed objects in a Java client/server application.

org.omg..CosNaming
Supplies the interfaces and classes that offer a file naming service for Java IDL.

org.omg.CosNamingContext-package
Supplies the classes and exceptions used by the *org.omg.CosNaming* package.

ACRONYMS

AI	Artificial Intelligence
API	Application Programming Interface
AWT	Abstract Window (or, Windowing) Toolkit
CAD	Computer Aided Design
CAE	Computer Aided Education
CAI	Computer Aided Instruction
CAM	Computer Aided Manufacturing
CGI	Common Gateway Interface
DBMS	Data Base Management System
DLL	Dynamic Link Library
DOS	Disk Operating System
E-mail	Electronic Mail
FAQs	Frequently Asked Questions
FIFO	First In, First Out
FTP	File Transfer Protocol
GIF	Graphics Interchange Format

GUI	Graphical User Interface
HTML	Hypertext Markup Language
HTTP	Hypertext Transfer Protocol
I/O	Input/Output
IDE	Integrated Development (or, Developer) Environment
ISP	Internet Service Provider
IT	Information Technology
JDK	Java Development (or, Developers') Kit
JIT	Just-In-Time (Java bytecode Compiler)
JPEG	Joint Photography Engineering Group
JVM	Java Virtual Machine
LIFO	Last In, First Out
MIME	Multipurpose Internet Mail Extension
PC	Personal Computer
POP	Post Office Protocol
SMTP	Simple Mail Transfer Protocol
SQL	Structured Query Language
TCP/IP	Transmission Control Protocol/Internet Protocol
URL	Uniform Resource Locator
WWW	World Wide Web
Y2K	Year 2 Thousand

GLOSSARY

3 GL — Third-generation language such as C, COBOL, FORTRAN or Pascal that provides developers with considerable flexibility at the expense of ease of use. Most of 3 GLs can handle such detailed tasks as direct memory manipulation and physical disk access, which most 4 GLs cannot handle. 3GLs are, however, much more complex and require much more development time for applications.

4 GL — A term applied to languages designed for interacting with the programmer, often used to define languages used with relational databases such as SQL. The intent was to imply that such languages are a step up from 3GLs and are generally preferable for creating database applications and for use with popular development tools.

Abstraction — The act of representing the essential features of something without including the unnecessary details.

Algorithm — A sequence of precise and unambiguous instructions for solving a problem in a finite number of operations.

Applet — A small application unable to run by itself.

Application Programs — Software designed for a specific purpose such as payroll, inventory control etc.

Applications — Specific uses for a program. With MS-Word, you can, for example, create letters, mailing lists, resumes, and so on.

Artificial Intelligence — A branch of computer science that deals with computers which possess reasoning, learning, and thinking capabilities resembling those of human beings.

Base Class Also *Super Class*; new classes can be created/derived from it.

Byte Consisting of 8 bits. A bit is either 0 or 1.

Chip A thin wafer of silicon on which integrated electronic components/ circuits are deposited/stored.

Class It unites data and the code/methods acting upon the data; it is the basic language construct in C# for creating user-defined data types.

Coding The process of writing computer instructions in a programming language.

Compiler A system software package that converts a high-level language to the machine language form.

Computer Aided Design Use of computers to automate design operations.

Computer Aided Education Ageneral term that refers to teaching with the help of a computer.

Computer Aided Instruction *See* Computer Aided Education.

Computer Aided Manufacturing Use of computers to automate manufacturing operations.

Constructor It is a method with the same name as its class. It is invoked automatically , by default, when an instance of a class i.e., an object is created. However, the user can define his own constructors as well to instantiate an object of the class.

Cyberspace A synonym for the Internet.

Database A collection of data files integrated and organized into a single comrehensive file system, which is arranged to minimize duplication of data and to provide convenient access to information within that system to satisy a wide range of user needs.

Data Base Management System A general-purpose software package used as a tool for building individual database systems.

Data Hiding It means that the implementation details are hidden from the user by providing a suitable interface.

Data Member A variable declared in its class definition.

Debugging The process of finding and correcting program errors/bugs. There are, in general, two types of bugs in a program, viz. syntax and run-time bugs.

Default Parameter A parameter whose value is already provided for at the time of method declaration and this value is used by default if the corresponding actual parameter is missing at the time of the method call.

Derived Class A class that inherits properties/attributes from a base class.

Documentation Documentation of a software system involves collecting, organizing, storing, and otherwise maintaining a complete historical record of programs and other documents used/prepared during different phases of the system.

Dynamic Allocation In Java, objects are *dynamically allocated* from a pool of free memory using the *new* operator.

Dynamic Binding Also known as *run-time or late binding* as it postpones the binding of the method call till run-time.

Early Binding Also known as *static or compile-time binding* as in this case, the method call is bound at compile-time.

Electronic mail A general term used to describe the transmission of messages by the use of computing systems and telecommunication facilities.

Encapsulation It means binding of the code and the data into a single unit free from external interference. This concept is achieved by means of the *class* mechanism.

End user Any individual who uses the informatiion generated by a computer based system.

Exception An unusual but predictable abnormal condition in a program used to notify the error to the user and avoid disruption of the running program.

Exception Handling It is the means by which the actual notification is done to make the user aware of the *exception* and avoid abnormal program termination.

Fifth Generation Computers Fifth generation computers shall be introduced shortly. These computers will use a large number of processors working concurrently and independently. Simpler programming languages and knowledge based system implementations are expected in this generation of computers.

File A collection of related records.

Fourth Generation Computers Computers built between the period 1975 to date. They use large scale integrated circuits, semiconductor memories and powerful high-level languages and operating systems.

Garbage Collection In Java, memory is dynamically allocated using *new* operator. However, *new* can fail as there might not be sufficient memory to allocate/create the desired object. For this reason, there is a need to recover free memory from unused objects. In lanuages like C++, recovery of previously allocated memory is handled mnually using the d*elete* operator. But, Java uses a more sophisticated approach, viz. *Garbage Collection.*

Generics It is a technique for defining software components that have more than one interpretation depending on the parameters' data type. It allows the declaration of data items without specifying their exact data type. These data types are resolved at the time of their actual usage at run-time.

Inheritance It involves derivation of new classes from existing ones thus, enabling the creation of an hierarchy of classes *simulating* the real world. This phenomenon enables *reuse* of existing code and elimination of tedious repetitive work.

Instance A variable or an object of a class is referred to as an *instance* of that class.

Hard Copy Printed/Filmed output from a computer device in human readable form.

Hardware The physical components of a computer system such as electronic, magnetic and mechanical devices are referred to as hardware.

Header Text/Graphics that appear at the top of every page.

High-level Language A programming language whose structure is application oriented and is independent of the structure of the computer.

Input/Output Pertaining to the techniques, media, and devices used for man-machine interaction.

Information Information is the result of data manipulation or data processing which can be used to help people make decisions.

Information Technology Information Technology (IT) encompasses any combination of equipment (hardware) that facilitates the acquisition, creation, modification, retrieval, storage and transmission of information using electronic media. Thus, IT includes both computing and communication technology. Various aspects of IT are hardware, software, connectivity, telecommunications, science and human-computer interface.

JIT *Just-In-Time*. Java bytecode is translated into executable code by the JIT compiler.

Machine Language A low-level language that is directly understandable by the computer system. Each model of a computer has a unique machine language.

Member Data and methods defined within a class are called its *members*. Also, *see* Private/Protected/Public Members.

Message Passing A *message* is a request sent to an object; *message passing* is the process of invoking an operation on an object.

Method Overloading Methods having the same name but differing in the number of parameters or their data types.

Nibble Half a byte; 4 bits.

new The *new* operator allocates memory at run-time (this is referred to as *dynamic allocation* of memory) for an object and returns a reference to it. This reference is then stored in a variable. Thus, in Java, all *class objects* must be *dynamically allocated* and *new* can be used to create an object of any *class type*.

Object	An *instance* of a class is called an *object* or a variable of that class. This is much nearer the real-world entity than the *abstract* concept of a *class*.
OO	*Object-Oriented.*
OOD	*Object-Oriented Design.*
OOP	*Object-Oriented Programming.*
Operator Overloading	The same *operator* can be used for carrying out different operations.
Pass by Reference	In this case, the *address* of an actual parameter is *implicitly* passed to a method.
Pass by Value	A *copy* of the actual parameter is passed to the method in this case.
Password	A code by means of which an user gains access to a computer system. It is used for security purposes/reasons.
Personal Computer	A small and inexpensive computer (usually a microcomputer) used by individuals for personal applications such as entertainment, home management, and hobbies.
Polymorphism	It allows for one name/*interface*, many operations/*methods*.
Private/Protected/Public Members	A class member accessible only to other members of the class is called a *private member*; a class member with the same access characteristics as the *private* member except that it is inheritable is called a *protected member*; finally, a class member accessible both within and outside its class is called a *public member*.
Real-time Systems	Pertains to on-line computer processing systems which receive and process data quickly enough to produce output so as to be able to control, direct, or affect the outcome of an ongoing activity/process.
Reusability	In Java, *reuse* of code is achieved by the concept of *class* hierarchy/*mechanism*.

Scope The part of code where a variable is visible is called its *scope*.

Simulation Simulation implies representing and analyzing properties/ behaviour of a physical or hypothetical system by the behaviour of a system model.

Soft Copy Computer output which is displayed on the screen of a terminal without a permanent/printed copy.

Software The set of computer programs, procedures, and associated documentation related to the effective operation of a computer system is referred to as software.

Stack A memory in which the information stored last is on top and is retrieved first; also known as *LIFO* storage.

Static Member A *static member* of a class is shared by all the instances of that class.

Stream Programs perform *Input/Output* through streams. A *stream* is an abstraction that either produces or consumes information. For example, there are byte, character, and binary *streams*.

Structured Programming A top-down software development and programming technique that employs *modular* procedural decomposition into *subtasks*. This is the traditional style of *programming* just in contrast to *Object-Oriented Programming.*

Structured Query Language Structurted Query Language is better known as its abbreviated form - *SQL*, a relational data-access language created by IBM. Most database server engines use *SQL* as a standard way of accessing data from client applications.

Subclass *See* Derived Class.

Super Class *See* Base Class.

System *System* is the *class* used by all Java programs.

Throughput The total amount of useful processing carried out by a computer system within a given time period. It is a measure of the effiiciency of the computer system.

this When a method is invoked, it is implicitly passed an argument which is a reference to the calling *object* and this reference is referred to as "*this*".

UNIX A popular operating system for 32 and 16-bit mini and micro computers that was designed by Bell Telephone Laboratories, USA.

Web Camera A simple web camera consists of a digital camera attached to a computer through USB or parallel port. In the digital camera, light strikes an array of photosensitive diodes instead of a film. Software associated with the web cam (camera) grabs a still image from the camera at a regular interval (say, 30 seconds). the software then turns that image into a normal JPEG file and uploads it to the web server.

World Wide Web Also called Web, www, and W3, an interlinked collection of hypertext documents (Web pages) residing on Web servers and other document, menus and databases available via URLs (Uniform Resource Locators) .

INDEX